Distant Suffering examines the moral and political implications for a spectator of the distant suffering of others as
presented through the media. What are the morally
acceptable responses to the sight of suffering on television, for example, when the viewer cannot act directly to
affect the circumstances in which the suffering takes
place? Luc Boltanski argues that spectators can actively
involve themselves and others by talking about what they
have seen and how they were affected by it. Developing
the idea of the spectator in Adam Smith's moral theory,
he examines three rhetorical 'topics' available for the
expression of the spectator's response to suffering and
which have existed since pity became central to politics at
the end of the eighteenth century: the topic of *denunciation*, the topic of *sentiment* and the *aesthetic* topic. The
book concludes with a discussion of a 'crisis of pity' in
relation to modern forms of humanitarianism and suggests a possible way out of this crisis which involves an
emphasis and focus on present suffering.

LUC BOLTANSKI is Director of the Ecole des Hautes
Etudes en Sciences Sociales in Paris. His book publica-
tions include *The Making of a Class* (1997), *L'Amour et la
Justice comme compétences* (1990) and, with Laurent
Thévenot, *De la justification* (1991).

GRAHAM BURCHELL is a freelance researcher and translator, currently living in Italy, who has translated, taught
and promoted the work of leading French scholars in
Britain and Australia.

D1500906

Distant Suffering

Cambridge Cultural Social Studies

Series editors: JEFFREY C. ALEXANDER, *Department of Sociology, University of California, Los Angeles, and* STEVEN SEIDMAN, *Department of Sociology, University at Albany, State University of New York.*

Distant Suffering

Morality, Media and Politics

Luc Boltanski

Translated by Graham Burchell

CAMBRIDGE
UNIVERSITY PRESS

PUBLISHED BY THE PRESS SYNDICATE OF THE UNIVERSITY OF CAMBRIDGE
The Pitt Building, Trumpington Street, Cambridge CB2 1RP, United Kingdom

CAMBRIDGE UNIVERSITY PRESS
The Edinburgh Building, Cambridge CB2 2RU, United Kingdom
  http://www.cup.cam.ac.uk
40 West 20th Street, New York, NY 10011–4211, USA   http://www.cup.org
10 Stamford Road, Oakleigh, Melbourne 3166, Australia

Originally published in French as *La Souffrance à Distance* by
Editions Métailié 1993
© Editions Métailié 1993

First published in English by Cambridge University Press 1999 as
Distant Suffering
English translation © Cambridge University Press 1999

First published 1999

Printed in the United Kingdom at the University Press, Cambridge

Typeset in 10/12.5 pt Times New Roman in QuarkXPress™   [SE]

A catalogue record for this book is available from the British Library

ISBN 0 521 57389 0 hardback
ISBN 0 521 65953 1 paperback

The world in which we Westerners live today has grave faults and dangers, but when compared to former times our world has a tremendous advantage: everyone can know everything about everything. Information today is the 'fourth estate': at least in theory the reporter, the journalist and the news photographer have free access everywhere; nobody has the right to stop them or to send them away. Everything is easy: if you wish you can receive radio or television broadcasts from your own or any other country. You can go to the newsstand and choose the newspaper you prefer; an Italian newspaper of any political tendency, an American or Soviet newspaper, there is an extremely wide choice. You can buy and read the books you want without risk of being incriminated for 'anti-Italian activities' or attracting a search of your house by the political police. Certainly it is not easy to avoid *all* conditioning, but at least you can pick the conditioning you prefer . . .

In Hitler's Germany a particular code was widespread: those who knew did not talk; those who did not know did not ask questions; those who did ask questions received no answers. In this way the typical German citizen won and defended his ignorance, which seemed to him sufficient justification of his adherence to Nazism. Shutting his mouth, his eyes and his ears, he built for himself the illusion of not knowing, hence not being an accomplice to the things taking place in front of his very door.

Primo Levi, Afterword to *If This is a Man*, in *If This is a Man and The Truce*, trans. Stuart Woolf, intro. Paul Bailey, London: Abacus/Sphere, 1987, pp. 382–3 and 386 [translation slightly modified].

Contents

Preface

The subject of this book is the question of humanitarianism which has been revived by the recent debate on humanitarian action but has been on the agenda for at least two centuries. Our aim is first of all to clarify this debate by taking up the discussions and models which accompanied the introduction of the argument of pity into politics in the eighteenth and nineteenth centuries. One of the purposes of this return to the past is to show that the argument between those in favour of humanitarian altruism and those who deny its possibility was fixed when political theory began to be concerned with what Hannah Arendt calls the 'politics of pity'.

We are not attempting to show that there is nothing new under the sun however. To the contrary, it seems to us that over the last twenty years the development of a number of non-governmental organisations involved in humanitarian action throughout the world, and the importance and significance this movement is in the process of acquiring, is something new. What is more, this nascent humanitarian movement lies at the heart of two tensions within today's Western societies.

The first of these tensions is between an abstract universalism and a narrow communitarianism. Moreover, it is often in terms of this opposition that promoters and opponents of humanitarian action confront each other, the first siding with global solidarity against national particularisms and preferences, while the second unmasks the hypocrisy or, at best, naive eirenic idealism which ignores the primacy of interests and ties forged by history. Particularly ominous today, this tension may be reduced however by the development of forms of universalism connected to the historical traditions from which they arose and which are rooted in local groups and actions, that is by what Michael Walzer, whose reflections on the possibility of a third way between universalism and communitarianism are particularly innovative and promising, calls an emergent universalism.[1] We will conclude by suggesting that the consolidation of the humanitarian movement depends, at least in part, on its ability to clarify and make explicit the connection, which is often realised in practice by its members, between distant causes and the traditions, sensibilities and even interests of those who organise support for these causes.

The second tension lies at the heart of what Charles Taylor calls the 'culture of authenticity', an important component of the modern identities whose history he presents in his great book, *Sources of the Self*.[2] Charles Taylor clearly shows that the culture of authenticity cannot be reduced either to a hyper-individualism or to a soft relativism as is frequently claimed by the prophets or denigrators of modernity or post-modernity in order either to celebrate or deplore it. The culture of authenticity requires everyone to be themselves, but by choosing between objectives which are taken for granted and transcend the self.[3] Hence the wavering between the egoistic ideal of self-realisation and an altruistic commitment to causes which enables one to 'realise oneself' through action. The interest aroused by the humanitarian movement is one of the areas in which this tension is most clearly expressed today, as Charles Taylor suggests at the end of *Sources of the Self*.[4] However, with the current decline of the workers' movement, humanitarian action, which is the focus of most altruistic yearnings[5] and is familiar to the vast majority of people only through the media, is also denounced for giving everyone the opportunity to cultivate themselves through absorption in their own pity at the spectacle of someone else's suffering.

Much of the book is taken up with an attempt to analyse this tension without falling into either a smug celebration of the return of kindness or an easy denunciation of the perverse spectator. On the one hand we have tried to show that insofar as State politics must be detached from the here and now in order to embrace a generality, the introduction of the argument of pity into politics led by a kind of logical necessity to a consideration of distant suffering. The spectator's dilemma is not the automatic conse-

---

[1] Cf. M. Walzer, *Spheres of Justice. A Defence of Pluralism and Equality,* New York: Basic Books, 1983, and for a survey of his current view of the tension between universalism and communitarianism, see M. Walzer, 'Les deux universalismes', *Esprit,* no. 187 (1992), pp. 114–33.

[2] C. Taylor, *Sources of the Self. The Making of Modern Identity,* Cambridge MA: Harvard University Press, 1989.

[3] C. Taylor, *The Malaise of Modernity*, Concord, Ontario: Anansi Press, 1991, especially pp. 31–41.   [4] *Ibid.*, pp. 516–21.

[5] In addition to other indications, there is evidence for this in the responses given to opinion polls on the popularity of personalities who have become famous for their humanitarian action and in the record sales of their biographies or the books they write.

quence of modern media even if it has been dramatised by the development of these media over the last thirty years, and especially by the development of television. On the other hand, we have tried to take the moral demands imposed on the spectator seriously. On what conditions is the spectacle of distant suffering brought to us by the media morally acceptable?

Finally, the confluence of these two sets of constraints – politico-technical necessities and moral demands – have led us to re-open discussion of the two somewhat unfashionable themes of commitment and ideologies.

In effect, when confronted with suffering all moral demands converge on the single imperative of action. Commitment is commitment to action, the intention to act and orientation towards a horizon of action. But what form can this commitment take when those called upon to act are thousands of miles away from the person suffering, comfortably installed in front of the television set in the shelter of the family living-room? The answer we propose in part I is that one can commit oneself through speech; by adopting the stance, even when alone in front of the television, of someone who speaks to somebody else about what they have seen.

But to be an acceptable response to the shocking spectacle of distant suffering, must this speech be given a definite form? Our hypothesis is that speech must at the same time report to the other both what was seen and how this personally affected and involved the spectator. There is only a finite number of ways in which this can be done. Part II presents three forms, or topics, which were established through the formation of different literary genres (pamphlets, novels, art criticism) between the middle of the eighteenth century and around the middle of the nineteenth century, in which speech about suffering can be formulated in a way which enables us to join together a description of the person suffering and the concern of someone informed of this suffering. We call these three forms, the *topic of denunciation*, the *topic of sentiment*, and the *aesthetic topic*.

The word topic should be understood in the sense of ancient rhetoric, that is to say as involving inseparably both an argumentative and an affective dimension. Speech here is affected and it is especially by means of *emotions* that we can conceive of the coordination of spectators – each of whom is also a speaker – and consequently the transition from individual speech and concern to collective commitment. To get from these topics, each of which can be formulated in very different ways, to political *ideologies* which can be aligned on a Left–Right axis, precise descriptions must be given of how the system of places which constitutes the general armature of these topics (which we take from Adam Smith's *The Theory of Moral Sentiments*) are filled.

However, to tell others how one was affected by the spectacle of distant suffering is not on its own enough to satisfy the demand for commitment to action. For while commitment, and political commitment in particular, is always mediated by speech, as well as speech that may readily be called *effective* there is also speech that is derisively described as *merely verbal*, as just words, precisely in order to indicate the fact that these words in no way commit the person who utters them.

On what conditions can speech about suffering be considered effective? This, principally, is the question broached in part III which considers the contemporary crisis of pity which is characterised, precisely, by a loss of confidence in the effectiveness of committed speech, by a focus on the media and the 'spectacle' effects they produce, by a temptation to fall back on the community, and finally, and most profoundly, by a scepticism with regard to any form of political action orientated towards a horizon of moral ideals. Here again, clarification of the implicit principles which underlie humanitarian action may help us to redefine political commitment and, as a result, to reaffirm the political dimension of life.

Acknowledgements

Preparation of this book was undertaken while I was at the Institute for Advanced Study at Princeton and it would not have been possible without the resources I found there; not just the calm, the weather, and the excellent libraries, but also the working relationships and seminars which have directly influenced the questions I have raised. My thanks go above all to Albert Hirschman and to his generous erudition, to Clifford Geerz, to Joan Scott and, in particular Michael Walzer, who was the person in charge for the year and whose work and interests, especially on justice and social criticism, have had a direct impact on my own preoccupations.[1] I have also benefited from many discussions with Allan Silver of the University of Columbia and, above all, during this stay and no less since then, with Elisabeth Claverie.

It is almost impossible to name all those who have helped me with their advice or by their reading more or less developed drafts of this book. My thanks go particularly to Bruno Latour for his exacting reading, and to Daniel Arasse, Isabelle Bassanger, Jean-Elie Boltanski, Nicolas Dodier, Jacques Hoarau, Dominique Julia, Steven Kaplan, Michèle Lamont, Arno Meyer, Phillippe Roussin, Abram de Swann and Laurent Thévenot. Bruno Frappat helped me once again through the mazes of the PAF.

Work for this book gave rise to a series of presentations given at the EHESS in 1992–1993 within my seminar which was devoted that year to the 'spectacle of suffering'. I have also benefited greatly from research presented by thesis students or colleagues at this seminar. Among the students who have helped my with their questions, objections and presentations, my thanks go particularly to P. Adam (on films seeking to encourage solidarity with victims of AIDS), D. Cardon (on radio broadcasts which appeal

---

[1] In particular, his *Company of Critics,* New York, Basic Books, 1990.

for listeners' views), C. Lemieux (on the journalistic treatment of scandals), T. Perilleux (on the public expression of psychical suffering), S. Pharabod (on television programmes in which people talk about their misfortunes), J. Siméant (on hunger strikes and their representation in the media). The seminar also brought together researchers whose work bears directly or indirectly on the representation of suffering, particularly K. Scherer on the social psychology of emotions, E. De la Tour on the representation of the very old in short films, S. Chalvon on a corpus of synopses for television, and also Alain Rèmond, television critic for *Télérama,* who gave us the benefit of his expertise with images. I would like to thank all these here for teaching and discussions which have given me a great deal.

I must confess, in conclusion, that while writing I often found myself thinking of my brother Christian, whose own work on the holocaust is reflected, without aesthetic indulgence, in a large part of this work, and of my son, Christophe, an honest and courageous young reporter in parts of the world afflicted with violence. This book is therefore dedicated to them.

The English-language edition of this book is published with the assistance of the Ministère Français Chargé de la Culture: Centre National du Livre and the Maison de Sciences de l'Homme, Paris, and of the French Ministry for Foreign Affairs as part of the Burgess Programme headed for the French Embassy in London by the Institut Français du Royaume-Uni.

institut français

PART I

The question of the spectator

1

The politics of pity

1.1 Pity and justice

In the second chapter of her essay *On Revolution,* 'The Social Question',[1] Hannah Arendt takes up the idea that in contrast with the American Revolution, the French Revolution neglected the question of liberty and of the form of government able to guarantee it. It developed instead a *politics of pity* that, if its typical manifestations became apparent only with Robespierre and Saint-Just, had been in preparation since the mid eighteenth century, notably in the work of Rousseau. Her characterisation of this politics is based on specific features that can be summarised briefly. First of all, it involves a distinction between those who suffer and those who do not. As Max Scheler notes, we do not say that a father and mother who weep over the body of their child experience 'pity' for him or her precisely because they are themselves also suffering misfortune.[2] Secondly, there is a focus on what is seen and on looking, that is, on *the spectacle of suffering.*[3] What is meant by spectacle in this context? To a large extent Hannah Arendt's demonstration consists in drawing out the latent implications of a politics which is distinguished by not being centred directly on *action*, on the power of the *strong* over the *weak*, but on *observation*: observation of the *unfortunate* by those who do not share their suffering, who do not experience it directly[4] and who, as such, may be regarded as fortunate or *lucky* people.

To start with, let us note that a *politics of pity* is clearly distinguished from what could be called, to make the comparison clearer, a *politics of justice.*[5] As a first approximation we could describe action coming from above taken by rulers seeking to promote justice as *meritocratic*, whatever norm is used to define and evaluate the respective merits of citizens. In all likelihood, such a politics will be based upon what we have elsewhere called a *City model.*[6] According to this model, the proper function of the magistrates who administer the city is the resolution of disputes. Their prudence

consists in the successful restoration of harmony by arriving at fair out-
comes to disputes. A politics of justice is therefore more or less explicitly
based upon a theory of justice which takes into account a common understanding of fairness.

This framework is different from that in which a politics of pity functions
in at least three essential respects. First, a city orientated towards justice
does not focus on the opposition between the fortunate and the unfortunate, but on the distinction between the *great* and the *small*. The disputes
it is called upon to settle concern precisely whether the ranking of people
in terms of size and worth is just. A satisfactory answer to this question first
and foremost requires recourse to a convention of equivalence.

A second difference is essential. In the model directed towards justice, the
possession of greatness, the fact of being someone great or someone of less
account, is not a status definitively attached to someone. People are qualified by their greatness or smallness, but whether or not one is great or small
is not a *condition*. The 'great' and the 'small' do not form distinct groups
according to their size. Thus, formally at least, there are no *classes* of the
'great' and 'small'. In the terms of a politics of pity, however, good fortune
and misfortune are conditions that define separate groups. The politics of
pity regards the unfortunate together *en masse*, even if, as we shall see, it is
necessary to single out particular misfortunes from the mass in order to
inspire pity.

Finally, following from the fact that qualities of greatness and smallness
are not attached to persons, a politics of justice must settle disputes by
bringing the convention of equivalence to bear in a *test*. It is only at the
outcome of the test, in the course of which the conflicting parties are
induced to cite the objects and aims of a shared world, that their state of
'greatness' is revealed. It is because their claims are confronted with reality
that the order brought to light by the test (which a different test could challenge) can be qualified as *just*. However, according to this logic what
matters is not whether someone 'small' is fortunate or unfortunate. They
have what they deserve whatever the state of their fortune. Even if fair magistrates evince a concern for mitigating the harshness of the ranking
brought to light by the trial, they are not moved by considerations of misfortune so much as by their taking into account *movements of greatness*
(*transports de grandeur*)[7] which have affected the results of the trial, either
positively or negatively, through the unequal distribution of privileges and
handicaps. In equity it is always the point of view of justice that ultimately
prevails.

What is thought to be important in a politics of pity is the opposite of
this. A politics of pity does not ask whether the misery of the unfortunate

is justified. We will see that in some of its formulations, and specifically when the unfortunate is regarded as a *victim*, this politics may compromise with justice and consequently pose the question of justification – but it always does so in order to give a negative answer; the question remains rhetorical and is not tested. Besides, we know intuitively how indecent and scandalous it would be to raise this question when faced with what are often incredible displays of suffering. Who, for example, would dream of saying that the inhabitants of a country ravaged by famine have what they deserve? For a politics of pity, the urgency of the action needing to be taken to bring an end to the suffering invoked always prevails over considerations of justice. From such a perspective it is only in a world from which suffering has been banished that justice could enforce its rights.

1.2 Compassion and pity

The development of a politics of pity thus assumes two classes which are not unequal by reference to merit, as in the problematic of justice, but solely by reference to luck. However, there must be sufficient contact between these two classes for those who are fortunate to be able to observe, either directly or indirectly, the misery of the unfortunate, while at the same time the classes must be sufficiently distant or separate for their experiences and actions to remain clearly distinct. None the less, Hannah Arendt notes that the spectacle of misery does not necessarily lead to a politics of pity. Two scenarios appear.

The misery of the unfortunate may simply be ignored and thus inspire no pity. Hannah Arendt takes the example of the Founding Fathers of the American Revolution who are upset by slavery insofar as it conflicts with the demands of liberty but in whom one looks in vain for a word of pity for the condition of about one quarter of the American population existing under the yoke of necessity, absolute want and violence. In this, as in many other historical situations, the fortunate and unfortunate can live in the same country without the former seeing the latter, either as the result of a kind of physical blindness arising from a subtle separation of the spaces within which they each move, that is of their social networks, or, and the two phenomena are commonly found mixed together, due to a moral blindness, when the discrepancy between their respective conditions creates a gulf that prevents the class of 'those who do not suffer' from forming an idea of the suffering of the unfortunate.

There is however another possibility that is particularly relevant for our purposes. Those who are more fortunate may show a benevolent concern for the unfortunate without this being describable as a *politics*. We follow

Hannah Arendt again when she claims that until the eighteenth century 'compassion operated outside the political realm and frequently outside the established hierarchy of the Church' (pp. 70–1).

To show how, within the framework of Western traditions and especially in early Christianity, a benevolent concern for the suffering of others may manifest itself outside the political dimension, Hannah Arendt takes up the contrast between *compassion* and *pity* (pp. 85–95). Her description of compassion, which is based on an analysis of two works of fiction, *Billy Budd* by Melville and *The Grand Inquisitor* by Dostoyevsky, emphasises those features which bring out an analysis of the notion of Christian love or Agape, especially in its contrast with justice.[8] For Arendt the principal characteristic of compassion is that it is directed towards particular individuals, particular suffering beings, without seeking to develop any 'capacity for generalisation'. It possesses thereby a *practical* character in the sense that it can only be actualised in particular situations in which those who do not suffer meet and come face to face with those who do. Face to face presence in compassion has two important consequences on which Arendt repeatedly and rightly insists. On the one hand, compared with pity compassion is not loquacious and, on the other, it shows no great interest in *emotion*. Not having to 'generalise', Arendt says, compassion is content with a 'curious muteness' in comparison with the 'eloquence' of pity. To be more precise, compassion is not so much mute as that its language 'consists in gestures and expressions of countenance rather than in words' (p. 86): 'compassion speaks only to the extent that it has to reply directly to the sheer expressionist sound and gestures through which suffering becomes audible and visible in the world' (p. 86). As a direct response to the expression of suffering, compassion is not 'talkative and argumentative' (p. 86), and for this very reason emotion plays no great part in it. Perhaps we should postulate the existence of a compassionate emotion, but to the extent that the person it affects is immediately moved no place is left for its expression as such. Quite the opposite is the case with pity which generalises in order to deal with distance, and in order to generalise becomes eloquent, recognising and discovering itself as emotion and feeling.

However, as Hannah Arendt's analysis again suggests, the opposition between compassion – which is linked to presence and thereby apparently local – and pity – which generalises and integrates the dimension of distance – only works analytically if we keep in mind the position from which this opposition was arrived at. Actually, it is only from a world in which the principal mechanism of generalisation is political that compassion can appear to be something purely local. Now in its theological understanding compassion is supported by a different mechanism of generalisation which is that of the union of the baptised (and, by extension, all human beings) in the mystical body of Christ. The *Communion of Saints* is precisely that form of union which brings the baptised together, beyond the constraints of space and time, in an 'exchange of prayers' ('*commerce de prières*') in such a way that 'everything received in holiness by each belongs somehow to all'[9] and 'what each must do and suffer is not gauged by his needs alone, but on the needs of all'[10] so that we cannot say who receives and who gives (or, in other respects, who is great and who small, what is cause and what effect, etc.) because those who 'thus act on each other' are all equally 'members of each other.'[11]

This is the theological background against which, for example, the confraternities of penitents were founded, those 'organised groups of the laity with a religious character' that Maurice Agulhon tells us 'congregated' in Provence from the sixteenth century up to the second half of the eighteenth century, and which, besides undertaking religious duties, assumed responsibility for the upkeep of the hospital (that is to say, for aid to the poor) and, in particular, for burial services for the indigent and for execution victims, requiring 'almost physical contact with the dead' which was especially dangerous in times of epidemics.[12] To start with these works were occasions for soliciting prayers from those 'privileged intercessors', the poor.[13] Maurice Agulhon suggests that the decline of these fraternities around the 1770s, which were criticised by 'reforming bishops' as well as by 'enlightened opinion', was linked with the secularisation of philanthropy and, in particular, with municipalities taking greater responsibility for public assistance. It is thus tempting to see, if not a causal relationship between the two phenomena, at least the sign of a shift in the forms of generality on which the relationship to suffering rests. The movement which led from a spiritual to a political kind of generality thus takes on an explicit concern with the dimension of *distance*. In fact, distance is a fundamental dimension of a politics which has the specific task of a *unification* which overcomes dispersion by setting up the 'durable institutions' needed to establish equivalence between spatially and temporally *local* situations.

1.3 The Good Samaritan

We can attempt to take Hannah Arendt's analysis further by considering the parable of the Good Samaritan and the use to which it has been put by contemporary jurists in founding what in French law is called the obligation to assist someone in danger.[14] The analysis of this paradigmatic situation will enable us to pose a third alternative which contrasts with both compassion and the politics of pity and, in addition, to reflect further on the relationship between spectacle and action.

Let us note at the outset that in its concision the story of the Good Samaritan, which is a secular parable in the sense that it does not employ the metaphor of the Kingdom to come but indicates the action that must be taken in this world,[15] gives a form to the principal features of compassion. Its real starting point is *the spectacle of suffering*. Three passers-by travelling from Jerusalem to Jericho *see*, one after the other, an unfortunate who has been left half-dead by robbers. The first two carry on regardless. The third 'exercises charity' towards him, dresses his wounds, gives him oil and wine, carries him on his horse to an inn and, the following day, provides the innkeeper with money for his care until the traveller's return. In this model, fortunate and unfortunate travellers find themselves face to face so that what is within the range of eyesight is also within reach of the hand. It is precisely this conjunction of the possibility of knowing and the possibility of acting that defines a *situation* characterised by the fact that it offers the possibility of being involved, of a *commitment*. This can be rejected, obviously, but only, as is shown by the example of the first two travellers, by looking the other way and quickly putting a distance between oneself and the sufferer. That is why, as Paul Ricoeur notes, the neighbour here belongs to 'the order of narration' as a 'chain of *events*': the parable converts 'the story told into a paradigm of action'.[16]

The second relevant feature is the absence of speech. Neither the indifferent passers-by nor the one who provides aid express the unfortunate's misery in words, nor do they seek to justify themselves. In short, we know nothing, or next to nothing, about the emotions and sentiments of the traveller who interrupts his journey. The 'pity' he feels at the sight of the unfortunate is immediately transformed into 'charity', that is to say into the 'objective disposition to relieve the distress of others' which incorporates 'the sentiment which prompts the act of pity'.[17] The ready availability of action does not free a space between seeing and acting within which an emotion or feeling could be displayed and expressed as such. The action, however, is described in detail. Its characteristic feature is its practicability. The person who practices charity does not accomplish the impossible. He sacrifices time, goods and money, but it is a limited sacrifice. The task that presents itself to him is not insuperable; he arrives on the scene after the struggle has taken place, for example, and he is not required to put his own life at risk by confronting the robbers.

Finally, coming upon the unfortunate one after the other, each of the passers-by comes to a decision as if they were on their own in considering the suffering. Significantly, this excludes a discussion of where the obligation lies for providing assistance. This last, and as we have seen, central feature of compassion, charity, is not put into action in wholly general terms but is inscribed in particular relationships between particular individuals: passers-by without problems and an unfortunate whose suffering manifests itself locally.

It should be noted that this kind of description of the form of compassionate relationships is realistic. It is realistic first of all because it focuses on the situation with its inherent constraints and on the ends with which individuals must come to terms if they are to commit themselves. It is also realistic because it places itself at the level of action, and specifically of an action directed towards the relief of the unfortunate's suffering which must consider both its practicability (taking into account the constraints on the person providing help) and effectiveness (the likelihood of effectively changing the condition of the suffering individual). Finally, it is realistic because it chimes with common experience. So, for example, the survey conducted by Kristen Monroe comparing a sample of non-Jewish people who helped Jews during the Second World War (identified and certified by Yad Vashem) with a control group, shows that explanations in terms of interests (linked, for example, to 'socio-cultural factors' or even 'psychical gratifications'), or in terms of political or religious affiliations, cannot account for the actions of those giving help (in whom only the cognitive framework, including a high sense of shared humanity, is specific).[18] At the same time the survey shows that those interviewed are usually themselves unable to attribute general motives to their action and they account for this by invoking a necessity inherent in the situation in which they found themselves involved without having wished to be, a situation which brought them into contact with individuals being hunted.[19]

1.4 The community bond

To elucidate the story of the Good Samaritan, however, it is not enough to oppose particularity to generality. Nor, it follows, can this opposition fully account for the structure within which compassion is inserted. If the various actors are all equally present in their particularity, an asymmetry is introduced by the different treatment of their definite statuses. The three passers-by are ascribed definite statuses which are necessary to the dynamic of the story because, as Jean Zumstein has shown, there is a tension between the expectations these statuses give rise to and the paradoxical outcome of the story.[20] The first two, a priest and a Levite, 'are defined by their social position'.[21] Being connected with the temple they occupy the summit of the religious hierarchy and it is precisely in order to avoid the ritual pollution involved in touching a body, and therefore in obedience to the law, that they pass on by. In contrast, as an enemy of the Jews the Samaritan represents the other pole of the moral and religious hierarchy, so that to the question posed by legal experts concerning the identity of one's neighbour, the story offers, as Mazamisa notes,[22] two answers depending on whether one cites the relationship of the Samaritan to the unfortunate – the unfortunate is the Samaritan's neighbour – or the relationship of the legal expert to the Samaritan – the Samaritan is the legal expert's neighbour (in conformity with the New Testament injunction to 'love your enemy').[23]

However, in contrast to the passers-by, the unfortunate has no definite status. Posited as a particular being, his role can none the less be filled by anyone. This lack of status cannot be attributed simply to a stylistic constraint that, out of concern for brevity, omits 'any description of the traveller fallen among thieves' as a 'secondary character', as Bultmann suggests.[24] The absence of status plays an active role in the story. Actually it makes possible a position in relation to suffering which does not entail any conventional, customary or contractual obligations. Thus, the paradoxical outcome rests on the unfortunate's lack of a definite status. And, in conformity with the structure of the parabolic statement, this outcome is paradoxical in the sense that the direction in which charity is exercised is not orientated by prior conventions. Compassion is thereby inscribed within a framework that is reducible neither to the universality of overarching law (to which Michael Walzer opposes a reiterative universality which can recognise the particular[25]), nor to a narrow communitarianism in which difference becomes endogenous.

If compassionate acts are distinguished from a politics of pity by their local and practical character, both of these possibilities together are opposed to a third and certainly more widespread alternative in which the relationship to the suffering of a third party is immediately identified as a function of the nature of pre-existing bonds connecting the unfortunate to the person who is aware of his misfortune. As in the well-documented case of systems of vengeance[26] and of relationships of honour in Mediterranean societies in particular,[27] such bonds enable obligations to assist to be ranked according to the status of the unfortunate and whether or not the offender belongs to the group.[28] Obligations depend in the first place on one's position within a kinship system which provides an answer to the question of who is responsible for helping someone. But by the same principle unfortunates are first of all divided into friends and enemies towards whom charity is far from being obligatory. In this instance, when confronted with the spectacle of suffering the moral attitude is not necessarily governed by the requirement to end it. One may come across an enemy who is suffering and do nothing to help him and nor yet hurry on to put a distance between this sufferer and oneself. The spectator may satisfy his legitimate desire for vengeance by gazing on the unfortunate's suffering and rejoicing in it, as when defeated enemies are tortured or simply put on show.

1.5 The question of commitment

This figure, that for convenience we will call *communitarian*, however different from compassion it may be, none the less shares with compassion a property which distinguishes both of them from a politics of pity. What they have in common is the reduction of the question of *commitment* which, while giving rise to a casuistry is none the less not posed in an unsettling, paradoxical or insoluble manner. We have seen that by bringing together particular individuals in a face-to-face situation compassion fills the space between sight and gesture, between knowledge and action, leaving only the alternative of flight or help, despite the indeterminate nature of the unfortunate who is *no matter who*. In a communitarian figure the unfortunate is immediately qualified in some way; by definition he is never just anyone. But because the properties which define him are *relational* in the sense that they establish his position in a structure, they also define, as we have seen, conventional courses of action which limit uncertainty about who must give assistance and the means to be used. Pre-existing conventions establish a precommitment that only has to be actualised when needed.

It is then only when suffering is considered from the standpoint of a politics of pity that the question of commitment appears as a problem. The reason for this is that a *politics* of *pity* must meet a double requirement. As a *politics* it aspires to generality. Its role is to detach itself from the local and so from those necessarily local situations in which events provoking compassion may arise. To do this politics may rely upon techniques for establishing equivalences, and on statistical techniques in particular. But in its reference to *pity* it cannot wholly free itself from the particular case. Pity is not inspired by generalities. So, for example, a picture of absolute poverty defined by means of quantitative indicators based upon existing conventions of equivalence may find its place in a macroeconomic treatise and may also help define a politics.[29] It will not, however, inspire the sentiments which are indispensable for a politics of pity. To arouse pity, suffering and wretched bodies must be conveyed in such a way as to affect the sensibility of those more fortunate. Clifford Orwin recalls that for Kant, pity possessed, amongst other things, the weakness of a lack of proportion: a suffering child fills our heart with sadness, but we greet the news of a terrible battle with indifference.[30]

However, these particular cases must be treated in a paradoxical manner. On the one hand, their singularity must be projected in such a way that suffering is made concrete. The unfortunate, or rather, every unfortunate, must therefore be conveyed as if they were there in person; as if one could touch their wounds and hear their cries. But going into details always runs the risk of collapsing the demonstration into the local. Now a politics of pity is not just concerned with one unfortunate and a particular situation. To be a politics it must convey at the same time a plurality of situations of misfortune, to constitute a kind of procession or imaginary *demonstration* of unfortunates brought together on the basis of both their singularity and what they have in common. The unfortunates conveyed in this way definitely must not be characterised in preferential terms. They are neither friends nor enemies. This is necessary in order to avoid the pitfall of the communitarian figure. They therefore must be hyper-singularised through an accumulation of the details of suffering and, at the same time, underqualified: it is he, but it could be someone else; it is that child there who makes us cry, but any other child could have done the same. Around each unfortunate brought forward crowds a host of replacements. The sufferings made manifest and touching through the accumulation of details must also be able to merge into a unified representation. Although singular, they are none the less *exemplary*.

The particular problem that a politics of pity must confront thus concerns this paradoxical treatment of *distance*. To avoid the local such a politics must bring together particular situations and thereby convey them, that is to say cross a distance, while retaining as far as possible the qualities conferred on them by a face to face encounter. This is not a new problem. In fact the hypothesis of this book is that the spectacle of suffering, incongruous when viewed at a *distance* by people who do not suffer, and the unease that this spectacle infallibly provokes – so evident today when eating our evening meal we see famished or massacred bodies paraded before our eyes in our home – is not a technical consequence of modern means of communication, even if the power and expansion of the media have brought misery into the intimacy of fortunate households with unprecedented efficiency. Similarly, the problems posed to the spectator (should he continue his meal, as if it was nothing?) are not, and this will be the argument developed in part I, absolutely new. They emerged at the same time that pity was introduced into politics. In fact, for reasons we will put forward, it is inherent in a politics of pity to deal with suffering from the standpoint of distance since it must rely upon the massification of a collection of unfortunates who are not there in person. For when they come together in person to invade the space of those more fortunate than they and with the desire to mix with them, to live in the same places and to share the same objects, then they no longer appear as unfortunates and, as Hannah Arendt says, are transformed into *'les enragés'*.[31] But then we leave the framework of a politics of pity. For what is in question, in the crisis, is precisely the division and separation of the unfortunate and the fortunate without which a politics of pity cannot be developed.

However, the distant spectator is not exempt from all moral obligation on the grounds that the unfortunate is not present. It is precisely to his moral sense that the demonstration usually appeals. For without morality there is no pity. But how can we specify and fulfill this paradoxical obligation which appears immediately obvious and at the same time profoundly obscure? We will rapidly examine some of the ways in which this problem has been posed in recent work which seeks to clarify the obligation to help and to extend it to people far away.

1.6 Distance and action

The Good Samaritan's charitable action may be seen to be good without it being treated as an obligation and so without it being liable to sanction when there is a failure to perform it. To make it into an obligation (the duty to give assistance and the liability to sanction in the absence of doing so, as in French law for example, when one fails to come to the assistance of someone in danger) the action of causing suffering and the action of giving assistance, as John Harris emphasises,[32] would have to be placed within the same framework (a view which is directed against the non-consequentialist thesis defended by libertarians and leaning on a Lockean theory of rights which separates the right to defend one's own life when it is threatened by others from the right to receive assistance from others when one's life is in danger).[33]

The obligation to give assistance to someone who is suffering may be based on a moral responsibility derived from a causal responsibility. The causal responsibility may itself be active or passive, through perpetuation or omission. If then moral responsibility belongs first and foremost to the person who caused the suffering, it can also be imputed to the person who knew about it but did nothing to prevent it. However, it is more difficult to determine where responsibility lies in cases of omission than in cases of perpetuation since, as Susan James notes when discussing the arguments of John Harris, candidates for passive responsibility are generally more numerous and indefinite than candidates for active responsibility.[34] According to A. Honoré, three instances of omission can be put forward.[35] Responsibility can derive from prior commitments which may be:

(1)   contractual – such as, for example, the professional commitments of a doctor who fails to help an injured person;
(2)   natural – like family commitments, which are close to the communitarian relationship. In both of these cases the candidate for responsibility is in the first instance someone 'specialised', that is to say someone one would expect to do something. But, there are,
(3)   other cases, of particular interest to us, where responsibility is sought among persons who are not specialised, either because the person usually responsible has not done anything or could not do anything (as when a disabled father watches his child drown for example), or because there is no one specialised and responsibility can then fall on anyone. As the jurisprudence of accusations of non-intervention shows,[36] judgements may take into account at least four dimensions as excuses which can be invoked by the accused: (1) the unintentional or 'non deliberate' character of the omission; (2) the weighing of the duty to intervene against respect for the other person's autonomy, especially in cases of suicide where the unfortunate voluntarily inflicts suffering on himself; (3) the material impossibility of giving help; and finally (4) the importance of the sacrifice which would have to be made in giving help.

The intentional or unintentional character of omission depends on the information available to the potential helper. This information bears on at least two different points: on the reality of the unfortunate's suffering and so on the urgency of the help needed, and on the possibility of help being provided by others and, in particular, on the existence of potential specialised responsible individuals whose obligation would be assured by a pre-commitment. This latter consideration is also involved in the second kind of excuse, since respect for the autonomy of the unfortunate is a more weighty consideration for an individual without precommitments than it is for a precommitted helper. Finally the material possibility of action is more likely to be weighed against the importance of the sacrifice demanded if the potential helper is not specialised. Jurisprudence here follows and reveals common sense. While from a contractual helper (a fireman for example), or from a natural helper (a father for example), an unlimited sacrifice may be expected, even to the point of a sacrifice of life, in the case of a helper without precommitments the expected, or normal, sacrifice, which is never nothing (be it only the loss of time), is always limited. When the obligation is juridically sanctioned, the sacrifice deemed normal usually concerns material goods, the property of the potential helper (thus, damage done to a new car may be weighed against the urgency of using it on poor roads to carry an injured person to hospital), but it does not involve risk to his own life or even his health. The fact of putting one's own life or health at risk is precisely what separates normal obligation, which can be expected of everyone, from heroism, which distinguishes only some people. A similar principle, while taking into account the common good rather than the helper's interests, is used to give a general moral foundation to the duty to give assistance by proposing, like Peter Singer for example in the article cited above, the rule that the sacrifice agreed to must be as important as possible without thereby sacrificing something else of comparable moral importance, that is to say, without failing in another duty and, say, depriving one's children of bread in order to feed a starving tramp. The example chosen by Singer, which is in some ways even less problematic than that of the Good Samaritan, is that of a man passing a shallow sea, with no one else nearby, who sees a child drowning and jumps into the water to help him, thereby running the risk of spoiling his new suit.

However, we cannot follow Peter Singer when he claims that nearness or distance make no moral difference and when he undertakes to extend his account to include giving aid to children dying of hunger in Bengal under the same obligation. Nor, to take another example, can we follow Gerard Elfstrom when, in relation to the problem of external intervention in response to a violation of human rights, he seeks to derive rules of international relations directly from interpersonal interactions on the grounds that moral constraints are in principle universal.[37] In fact, while there is an undeniable similarity between the vocabulary of sentiment, intention or action used to describe and judge moral relationships between persons within domestic units (friendship, squabbles, honour, duplicity, help, etc.) on the one hand and moral relationships between States on the other, this similarity assumes that each of the latter entities is treated as a *collective person* with its own will ('France does not accept that . . .'), or with a will delegated to a representative speaking in its name.[38] Now one of the most striking effects of the constitution of collective persons is precisely a reduction of the effect of size (does the telephone interaction between Kennedy and Kruschev during the Cuban missile crisis belong to the macro or micro order?) and, correlatively, a reduction of the dimension of distance. One of the dimensions of the collective person, or of its representative, is in fact action at a distance. It is this very attribute which describes in the most concise and striking fashion the intuitive content of the idea of *power.* It follows that one cannot tacitly slide from the treatment of distance in the description of relationships between States to the treatment of distance in the description of the way in which citizens of a State regard events which take place far away and which do not directly concern them.

In the case of ordinary persons, the question of distance is only raised when, as in Peter Singer's example, the sufferings of the unfortunate are visible, far away, to an informed spectator who cannot act directly. The disjunction between the possibilities of information and possibilities of action, and increasing uncertainty concerning the action needed, make the assimilation of not killing and not letting die defended by Peter Singer somewhat disturbing,[39] and provide stronger support to arguments which rank the obligation to help in accordance with a principle of distance (be concerned with those close to you first of all). Arguments in favour of ranking moral obligations to give aid according to the distance involved, arguments which are the legacy of debates on the extreme situations of famine within the natural law tradition which paved the way to a compromise between the contradictory demands of property rights and the right to life or survival,[40] can easily be used to reduce this moral obligation to one of communal solidarity.

How is a new situation created by distance? We will seek to describe this situation quickly by taking up again the dimensions involved in judgements of the obligation to give assistance already referred to. One effect of distance is surely that moral responsibility through omission becomes more uncertain and therefore difficult to establish when the causal chain is lengthened. The person who sees from afar is unaware of other people receiving the news, how near they are relative to the case, their readiness to act and whether or not they have precommitments. Each is thereby uncertain as to the existence of a ranked series of persons under an obligation to act to different degrees, as to their possible position in this series, and as to the failure to act of possible helpers higher up in the series for whom they would have to become substitutes.

Even when the unfortunate is strongly singled out, as for example in the case given by Susan James of a televised appeal for help on behalf of a young homeless Laotian girl dying of hunger, the distant spectator does not know whether others, and how many, will respond to the appeal.

When we examine the figure of *accusation* we will see that one way of consolidating distant responsibility consists in reinforcing the connection through omission (everyone has allowed something to happen, from the nearest to the most distant spectator) with a connection through perpetuation: the most distant spectator continues to draw a personal or collective profit from the suffering of the unfortunate to the extent that he is a member of a nation whose collective wealth is the result of the exploitation of poor nations (the argument is discussed in Singer).[41] The person who does nothing and fails to act is not only 'causally' responsible for an evil he could have prevented (which is what John Harris calls 'the marxist conception of violence' whose origin he traces back to Plutarch), but he does nothing because he has an interest in averting his gaze. The distant and passive spectator may actually be called an active accomplice of those who directly caused the sufferings of the unfortunate if the causal chain is extended to him. But for this complex figure to hold up it is necessary to construct a conception of responsibility through objective solidarity independent of the actor's intentions which, as we will see, presupposes a weighty systematic or structural armature which is itself hard to defend against criticism.

1.7 Paying and speaking

It is action above all that is the problem. The spectacle of the unfortunate being conveyed to the witness, the action taken by the witness must in turn be conveyed to the unfortunate. But the instruments which can convey a representation and those which can convey an action are not the same. Those who attempt to ground the obligation to provide aid to those suffering far away on the basis of face-to-face situations use examples in which only two forms of action are envisaged: paying and speaking. No one ever suggests, for example, that the spectator should drop everything and take himself to the unfortunate's side.

Both possibilities presuppose the existence of a chain of intermediaries between the spectator and the unfortunate. Payment at a distance cannot be made directly as to someone who offers his suffering to the gaze of every passer-by, as is the case with the beggar encountered in the street. To send a sum of money not only requires a banking system but also the existence of an institution – a State or supra-State institution or a 'non-governmental' humanitarian organisation – which can both receive the money and *forward* it to the unfortunate, as it is usually said, normally after having converted it into goods. Apart from the fact that such a medium may simply not exist, its action may be hampered or the way in which it uses the funds it receives may be challenged.

In the case of speech, the chain of intermediaries is formed in the first place by a series of interlocutors. But this is not enough, because it is not just a matter of conveying a *message* to the unfortunate (as it would be, for example, if all that was needed to help him was to send him 'the good word'). For speech to reduce the unfortunate's suffering, and for it to be regarded thereby as a form of action, in the sense that 'speaking is acting', a different kind of instrument is needed: *public opinion* engaging directly with political institutions. It is insofar as speakers are also citizens of a republic that they can express an opinion through elections or revolts and thus put pressure on governments reputedly inclined to intervene on behalf of the unfortunate, by laws or even by force, when those whose suffering is conveyed from afar are of another nation. To take the claim that speech is *effective* seriously, that is to say speech which, whatever the status of the person uttering it and the place or form of its expression, can be causally connected to the actions of others whose effect is felt *at a distance,* the first being in some sense the *authors* of the actions taken by *actors* to borrow the Hobbesian metaphor, we need the support of the complicated political construction of the City.

With regard to our problem, paying and speaking offer different advantages and drawbacks. The principal advantage of paying is that it is easier to see it as an *action* and, secondly, it makes the sacrifice made to benefit the unfortunate clearer and more easily calculable. But this quasi-action has two major drawbacks. On the one hand, it has the disadvantage of being realised by means of a general equivalent which, as such, obliterates the singularity of both the donor and the recipient. In sending a cheque, nothing remains of the singular suffering of a particular unfortunate. But we have seen that in one form or another the memory of the singularity of the person who suffers is indispensable to the existence and expression of pity. Similarly, the *commitment* of the donor is somehow hidden by the impersonal character of a medium which could be used for any other kind of purpose – buying a cooker or going on holiday for instance – so that giving money is often accused of being a 'way out', of being precisely a way to rid oneself of the burden of guilt, and of obligation itself, cheaply and without genuine involvement in the situation of the unfortunate's suffering. The money goes far away; but the donor does not follow it. The bond created between the donor and the unfortunate is therefore minimal and abstract (which is why organisations which collect money for children in the Third World, or in countries at war, often endeavour to organise a reciprocal arrangement, such as letters sent by the children to the donor).

On the other hand, a reproach just as often levelled against giving money is that it is an *individual* act. In fact, anyone can take this action regardless of whether there are other donors or who they are. By itself, if it is not accompanied by words, it is therefore insufficient for drawing that line in the collectivity which enables us to pick out what we call a *group*. Donations are aggregated, but not the donors. But a *politics of pity*, like any other politics, cannot do without the constitution of groups.

Compared with paying, the principal drawback of speech is that it seems to be detached from action and, without further clarification does not reveal what it costs. It is not enough by itself to reveal the existence and significance of the sacrifice. This is what is meant when it is denounced as 'costing nothing' or when we say ironically that it is 'just words'. For the sacrifice to be clearly apparent speech must come up against opposition and thereby introduce an uncertainty, a risk, which enables it to be described as 'courageous'. The paradox here is that it is precisely in regimes where speech or public opinion is the major means of orchestration, and so in regimes in which it is supposed to be most effective, that is in democratic regimes, that the exercise of speech appears to be the least costly and most distant from the idea of sacrifice. In any event it remains the case, and this is a considerable advantage for our purpose, that because it is communicated from one person to another and is expressed in public in front of others, speech constitutes the principal means for the manifestation and marking out of groups, as in the case of petitions, for example, which objectify units cut out from the continuum of the collectivity. It is by this means therefore that the politics of pity can develop, justifying the importance we accord it in the rest of this book.

We will now focus on the way in which the spectator can point towards action by putting himself in the position of having to report what he has seen and on the analysis of the constraints he must take into account in order to produce an acceptable report. This analysis requires us to return to the moment when the ideal of the public sphere as the transparent site of a generalised conversation was introduced into politics almost concomitantly with the introduction of the demand for pity. This will involve in particular a description of the tension produced by the conjunction of these two demands. We will then examine arrangements which can lessen this constraint.

2

Taking sides

2.1 The requirement of public speech

Let us consider the spectator's position. Take the case of a spectator contemplating a suffering unfortunate from afar, someone unknown to him and who is nothing to him, neither relative nor friend nor enemy even. Such a spectacle is clearly problematic. It may even be that this is the only spectacle capable of posing a specifically *moral* dilemma to someone exposed to it. In fact, when a spectator is faced with any other spectacle that he judges to be without interest, or even indecent, he has the easy option of withdrawing his attention: leaving the room, stopping reading, turning the television off, etc. But when he is faced with suffering such behaviour is not self-evident because in this case he could be accused, or may accuse himself, of indifference. Now, as we have seen, having knowledge of suffering points to an obligation to give assistance. Why else present a spectacle of suffering human beings to unconcerned people if not to draw their attention to it and so direct them to action?

If the spectator does not exit, which is already to take up a position, the least unacceptable option open to him is – following the famous distinction introduced by Albert Hirschman – to make his voice heard.[1] It is by speaking up that the spectator can maintain his integrity when, brought face to face with suffering, he is called upon to act in a situation in which direct action is difficult or impossible. Now even if this speech is initially no more than an internal whisper to himself (the spectator being alone in a room with no one else to speak to, for example), none the less in principle it contains a requirement of publicity. It is in some way already public speech addressed to an indefinite number of partners whose status is undefined.

The reason for this is the following. Until now we have been considering criticism of an essentially negative attitude: the indifference implied by the charge of guilt by omission. However, a different criticism is possible from which the spectator must exonerate himself or which he must forestall. Someone who observes the suffering of another without indifference but without lifting a finger to relieve it may be accused of being personally motivated or interested in viewing suffering, perhaps because it interests him or even gives him pleasure. The criterion of public speech or conversation is precisely what enables us to distinguish between a way of looking which can be characterised as disinterested or altruistic, one which is orientated outwards and which is motivated by the intention to see the suffering ended, from a selfish way of looking which is wholly taken up with the internal states aroused by the spectacle of suffering: fascination, horror, interest, excitement, pleasure, etc. While the first leads towards generalised communication, the second, when verbalised, which is not always self-evidently the case, can only be conveyed to people chosen on the grounds of some particular or specialist quality, either in terms of their tastes, like lovers of the same kind of pornography, for example, or their profession, such as when one confides to a confessor or to a doctor.

2.2 Fictional suffering and real suffering

The possibility that someone can be accused of having motives of interest or pleasure for viewing suffering raises the difficult question of the relationship between a fictional spectacle and one which refers to reality. The accusation may involve the charge that the spectator is taking an attitude towards a spectacle which refers to reality and includes real human beings really suffering which is like the attitude taken by a spectator towards a work of fiction. The stronger form of this accusation would raise the suspicion that the spectator's interest is intensified by his knowing that he is seeing something real. Its weaker form would be that he is unable to tell the difference between reality and fiction.

Actually we know that one of the main motivations of fiction is the staging of suffering and that the spectacle of suffering has been seen as a cause of the spectator's pleasure, something which has generally been held to be paradoxical or enigmatic. Moreover, for over 2,000 years and with astonishing persistence, the question of viewing suffering has been raised in relation to fiction, and more precisely to the theatre, as a moral problem of what J. Barish, in his study of its different but recurring forms, calls the 'antitheatrical prejudice'.[2] Surprise at the strange pleasure aroused by the spectacle of suffering is first expressed with regard to the pleasure taken in tragedy by the Greeks.[3] It is noticeable that the question of *tragic pity* is henceforth closely intertwined with discussions of 'human nature'. As with laughter, the pleasure of pity is sometimes interpreted as the result of imagination referring to the self something that happens to another person and enjoying its own felicity in the face of the other person's misfortune, (pessimistic interpretation), and at others, often at the cost of a mistaken interpretation of Aristotelian pity in terms of Christian compassion,[4] as a manifestation of what in the eighteenth-century will be called *sympathy*. This is how Saint Augustine, taking up this topic of the old rhetoric, tries to save certain manifestations of tragic pity which he characterises as merciful and contrasts with 'unclean' forms which are apparently erotic in tone but the precise nature of which unfortunately he does not explore.[5] However, an interpretation in terms of mercy which avoids the radical extreme of a condemnation of the theatre, and of representation in general perhaps, seems to be somewhat inconsistent with the starting point of the argument. This is particularly interesting from our point of view since Augustine links the question of mercy to an action which in the case of fiction lacks an object by definition: 'But what sort of pity can we really feel for an imaginary scene on the stage? The audience is not called upon to offer help but only to feel sorrow.'[6] By contrast, Augustine unambiguously condemns the cruelty of the circus games which offer non-simulated sufferings of real persons to the fascinated gaze of Alypius, a spectator despite himself, excited by passion against his will.[7]

The distinction between fiction and reality is not always so clear however. Thus, in his indignant denunciations Tertullian often mixes theatrical spectacle (where the sufferer is an actor) with circus spectacle (where the sufferer is a condemned person) as both equally *degrading*, without it seeming particularly relevant whether the action being observed is real or fictional.[8] Tertullian even thinks it worthwhile to get rid of the objection that the circus spectacle would be licit if those thrown to the lions were 'guilty' culprits.[9]

In the denunciation of spectacles, this mixing together of the real and fictional is found whenever the principal aim of moral criticism is the protection of the spectator's integrity against anything which might degrade him by provoking within him states that he had not necessarily sought (the theme of 'corruption'). In contrast, a concern for social protection leads to a sharper distinction between fiction and reality, finding fiction as such innocent but emphasising the risks of imitation or contamination. Examples of this can be found in the *consequentialist* arguments frequently advanced in the seventeenth-century debate about the theatre in France: 'What effect can these expressions accompanied by a real representation produce other than the corruption of the imagination, filling the imagination and then spreading into the understanding, the will and then into morals' the Prince de Conti writes in 1666 in his *Traité de la comédie et des spectacles*. Similarly, in 1694 the abbé Pégurier says about a young girl exposed to the spectacles: 'Whether she likes it or not she must put into practice what she has learned'.[10] We find these arguments again today in many studies on the effects on the real safety of individuals of fictional violence, especially violence on television (see, for example, discussions in the specialist literature concerning the 'Copycat Crime Phenomenon', that is real crimes committed in imitation of a simulated crime seen in a spectacle).[11] In this latter case, preoccupation with the civil protection of citizens may so prevail that it becomes lawful to conduct research which involves subjecting volunteers (usually psychology students) to the repeated viewing of (photographic, film or video) images of human beings suffering different kinds of violence in order to evaluate the effect these images might have on their disposition to carry out similar acts of violence in reality.[12] And this usually occurs without any deontological questions being raised about the possible effects of such experiments on the internal state and moral integrity of those who undergo them, or on the kind of self-image they might develop.

The fact remains that viewing suffering is especially problematic when the object of suffering is presumed to be real, as in the case of certain reports or televised current events for example, and it is all the more problematic the further away the unfortunate is and the more the possibilities of action open to the spectator are, as a result, uncertain. In fact, when the spectacle of the unfortunate and his suffering is conveyed to a distant and sheltered spectator there is a greater likelihood of this spectacle being apprehended in a fictional mode the more the horizon of action recedes into the distance. The distinction between reality and fiction loses its relevance for the utterly powerless spectator for ever separated from what he views. The demand for public speech and anticipation of an active attitude therefore constitute the minimal conditions of an appropriate relationship to reality.

2.3 The unacceptability of 'that's how it is'

If the spectator of suffering, especially of suffering which is presented as real, must adopt the position of speaking to someone else about it, if he is to avoid having to lower his eyes, in what style must he couch his report for it to be acceptable? Our hypothesis is that one possibility is excluded, that of a pure and simple factual description which aims only to state things as they are, just so. The spectator of suffering cannot speak about what he has seen in objectivist terms, even if in a great many instances this seems today to be the best way to warrant the seriousness of a description which aspires to the status of truth. We need only make a considered experiment to see how it would be considered out of place, 'indecent' or 'inhuman' to give a purely factual description of a hanging say, or of victims of a famine, with our main concern being to convey our words without deformation in the most exact and economical way possible (as when cataloguing an object or describing it so that it can be reproduced by someone else).

There is a clear reason for this which is that factual description exists and functions within a system of representation resting on a subject–object kind of set-up. This structure is appropriate for the representation of nature, but when persons are being described it can always be criticised in the name of common humanity because it is asymmetrical and distributes the humanity of the different partners unequally. It is particularly vulnerable to criticism when the persons described are suffering. The unfortunate who is the object or, as we say, the plaything of misfortune, is also the object of a realistic description in which mastery is distributed entirely on the side of the subject who is describing.

This difficulty that the spectator must overcome in order to put the suffering of a third party into words will be placed at the centre of our investigation. Actually, the relevance of the demand for public speech is due to the existence of a public sphere which is progressively constituted along with the conception of a politics of pity such that it is sometimes difficult to separate historically the two analytically distinct processes. The constitution of a public sphere and a definition of political legitimacy based on a conception of objectivity that emphasises the possibility of an observation without any particular perspective are strictly interdependent. We know today that, among other possible conceptions of objectivity, this conception (*aperspectival objectivity*) which is often associated with the development of the sciences, and of the experimental sciences in particular, actually originates in the political and moral philosophy of the eighteenth century – from where science will take it fifty years later – and especially in Adam Smith's attempt to reconstruct morality, together with the foundations of a morally acceptable politics, around the double figure of an unfortunate and an impartial spectator who observes him from a distance.[13] Thus we turn now to an examination of the relationship between public sphere, spectacle, and aperspectival objectivity. We will then take up again the position of the spectator and endeavour to understand how we might reduce the tension between the demand for public speech and the prohibition of a description without perspective.

2.4 Theatre and politics

How should we understand the importance given to the metaphor of the theatre and, more specifically, interest in the position of the spectator displayed in the moral, aesthetic, social and political speculation of the eighteenth century (in, for example, Rousseau, Diderot, the abbé Du Bos, Hutcheson, Hume and Smith, to cite only the most famous expressions of this commonplace)?[14] The metaphorical use of the theatre as an external support for a critical relationship to society is certainly not new. But the metaphor is no longer used in the same way. The emphasis is no longer solely on the *actor*, on the social subject as an actor and through this on the contrast between the simulated and the authentic (although this trope will continue to be widely used, as we will see), but also, or above all, on the *spectator,* on the social subject as a spectator. What particularly holds our attention in the character of the spectator is, on the one hand, the possibility of seeing everything; that is of a totalising perspective of a gaze which has no single point of view or which passes through every possible point of view and, on the other, the possibility of seeing without being seen. The two aspects are inseparable. The two components separate viewing and action. Action, as commitment in a situation, necessarily has a local character (the paradigm of Fabrice at Waterloo). On the other hand, someone who can be seen looking on can always equally be appealed to and involved, in spite of himself as it were, in the scene he views.

Until the eighteenth century, the use of the metaphor of theatre to define the essence of society is expressed essentially in the *topos* of 'the world is a stage' (*theatrum mundi*).[15] This commonplace, which is found in Hellenistic and Roman satirical poetry, in the Stoics, and in patristic literature, which disappears in the Middle Ages (or, with the decline of the theatre, is replaced by the image of 'the world is a dream'), and which again becomes widely used in the sixteenth and seventeenth centuries, has essentially four meanings. First, in its satirical or cynical use, which plays an important role in the history of Western criticism, it supports a denunciation of human hypocrisy and social inauthenticity: society is a stage on which everyone plays a role and from personal interest feigns a nonexistent reality. This critical position, which can be traced from antiquity to contemporary sociology (as in Goffman for example), can assume different forms which are more or less radical depending on whether the criticism is local (denouncing the theatrical character of a particular situation without questioning the very possibility of authentic experience) or general (the world is and can only be a theatre). There is a problem of logical coherence with the latter form since, like every extreme relativism or nihilism, it denies the existence of the normative basis of its critical position. Secondly, the Stoics employ the metaphor of the theatre of the world less to denounce the falseness and hypocrisy of the world in the name of authenticity and sincerity, than to emphasise its illusory character in order to reduce the hold of reality, to obtain a distancing effect and thereby promote detachment. Thirdly, this use is taken up again by patristics in particular, but now in order to compare the reality of the beyond to the unreality of the world. Fourth, and finally, in the neo-Platonists, the metaphor refers to the world as the stage on which the drama authored by God is played out. Contemplation of the *spectacle of the world* then becomes the way in which God's work is known.

In the sixteenth and seventeenth centuries, in Shakespeare, Calderon or Cervantes for example, these different interpretations, and particularly the satirical, stoic and patristic versions, are often blended together in a *melancholic* conception of life as both illusion and vanity. But the same underlying figure is found also in the anthropology developed in the second half of the seventeenth century which sees desire for recognition as the basic motive of human actions and which is expressed either critically (in the French moralists who denounce the inauthenticity of court society) or positively (in Hobbes who makes it the framework of a pacified political order). In the 'city of the famous'[16] each is great only to the extent that they can attract the attention of others to themselves, the greatest being the fictional person of the sovereign who, concentrating on himself the signs of honour, is to the people he personifies and represents like the actor to the author.

The tradition of *theatrum mundi* and the 'antitheatrical prejudice' which motivates it continue to inspire the moral imagination of the eighteenth century, particularly, as we know, in Rousseau.[17] But the metaphor of the theatre interests us here more particularly insofar as it undergoes a shift which enables it to take on new meanings. In fact, it is no longer uniquely centred on the actor, in order to denounce the deception of the world or provide political representation with an anthropological underpinning, but is applied also to the observing spectator. An important property attributed to the spectator in this political and social metaphor is his ability to see without being seen. In a famous passage of *The Tatler* (which was published from 1709 to 1711 to be followed, in 1711–1712 by *The Spectator*) cited by M. Ketcham,[18] Steele describes his greatest delight: to sit unobserved in the gallery and to observe the spectacle on the stage or what takes place in the audience.[19] From anywhere, the new spectator observes the actors and their spectators both of whom are involved in a common scene since the actors know themselves to be observed by the spectators and the spectators know that they know this. He is not absorbed by what takes place on the stage in that state of 'participation' or 'identification' so often described in the innumerable commentaries arising from the ambiguous notion of 'catharsis'.[20] Nor does he identify or thrill with the other spectators, but instead keeps control of his emotions.

Greuze's painting, analysed by Michael Fried, is also addressed to this spectator unexpectedly coming upon a scene which was not composed for him, and which is unaware of his presence.[21] In these often poignant scenes with their suffering suggested by tears, the 'absorption' of the principal characters of the drama, wholly involved in the common action (often highlighted by the distraction of a secondary figure, a child or a servant), breaks radically with the frontal theatricality and great spectacle of baroque painting. As on the stage where, according to Diderot, whose pictorial and theatrical conceptions Fried compares, to be convincing and arouse emotion the actor must act as if he is unaware of the public's presence, so too the painting can only convince and move the spectator if it is composed in such a way as to give the illusion that it was not conceived in order to be looked at. The absorption of the characters in the pictures by Greuze, who seem to be entirely taken up in the scene in which the painting has fixed them and who are not there for anyone outside that scene, allows the possibility of a pure spectator who is in a position to surprise them and, precisely, to get aesthetic pleasure from this effect of surprise.

2.5 The pure spectator

This spectator is a pure spectator because he is completely independent of the scene he views. His involvement in the figurative representation which stands before him is not symbolised by a vanishing point connected to him or by a frontality which as it were seeks to catch his eye. Nothing symbolises the *involvement* of the spectator with regard to the painting or even the involvement of the depicted characters and real spectators within the same scene, as was the case with the old devotional painting.[22] The painted scene is thus detached from the scene in which it is looked at. This is what enables us to conceive of someone as a pure spectator. He does not figure at all in the action shown. And at the same time this someone can be anyone. The spectator's place is imagined as one which is to be occupied by no matter who, that is to say by an individual who is in no way *affected* by the picture except insofar as just like anyone else he may occupy the spectator's place for a moment. Thus, he is not interested in the picture as he would be by a portrait (of, say, a close relative or hierarchical superior), or by a mediation with the supernatural world (an icon), or by a reminder of the homology between the political and divine orders, as in the paintings of Florentine punishments studied by S. Edgerton.[23] The works analysed by Edgerton, which represent the Last Judgement (or, in their upper part a Last Judgement and, in their lower part, a trial and execution) are not directed at a spectator who contemplates them for pleasure. These pictures, which are sometimes displayed in the rooms where tribunals are held or in the chapels of places of detention (like the Bargello in Florence), place the prisoner before the sufferings awaiting him in the hereafter and also – the demonic cruelties reproducing fairly exactly the procedures of interrogation and execution in force in Renaissance Italian towns – before those due to him and soon to be inflicted on him in the world below.[24] They have meaning only in an active relationship with the culprit who, exposed to what they illustrate, must find the way to contrition. The same is true of those pious images of saints undergoing torture for the glory of God that monks held constantly before the eyes of the condemned on the route from the chapel where they passed the night to the place of execution (often, in Florence, by hanging from the windows of a public building) in order to work for the culprit's repentance and so redemption.[25] In these different examples, the images of suffering, which usually establish a mediation between this world and the next,[26] dispense with the presence of outside observers. Rather than describe, they enable those involved as judges, priests, executioners, people, angels (like those who, in the anonymous panel of the sixteenth century devoted to the sacrilege at Santa Maria de Ricci, bear the soul of the execution victim to heaven) to circulate within a complex set-up which is inseparably judicial, political and spiritual.[27]

These different forms of viewing can be described as *committed* in the sense that both the illustration, inserted within mediating chains, and the person looking at it are equally active. The situation is modified by bringing the picture and viewer face to face, reactivating pre-existing commitments. Now the pure spectator has no prior commitment. As spectator, he is detached. This is again the ideal situation of *Mr Spectator*, the political hero of Joseph Addison and Richard Steele. The spectator's invisibility when he leaves the imaginary theatre for the microcosm of society constituted by the big city, and particularly for the cafés whose role in the formation of the 'public sphere' has been shown by Habermas,[28] takes the form of an ability to change identity according to the place in which he finds himself, passing from club to café, from inn to market.[29] Mr Spectator's primary quality is his invisibility. From his excursions he brings back reports on the portraits and topics of people and makes them known in a way that feeds an uninterrupted and general conversation which, in a circular fashion, will in turn feed the café topics he records day by day and puts back into the circuit of opinion.[30] As a systematic rumour-monger he creates a network of information, distributing it everywhere. In the absence of this network there would be the risk of information following pre-existing pathways, taking the obligatory routes, collecting in pockets and forming an incoherent mish-mash.

This ability presupposes someone vague, without definite substance, someone with no precise place or definite opinion, someone who has no *commitment* in the sense that no particular situation detains him or prevents him from moving on elsewhere and whose *raison d'être* is like that of a spy – to observe, listen and report. This vagueness, this detachment which a century earlier would have been a negative quality (since in a '*domestic*'[31] world someone without ties, with nowhere to lay his head, without hierarchical position, is nothing), is henceforth valued as a guarantee of *impartiality*. It is because the spectator is without ties and prior commitments that his report, his *testimony*, can be put forward as credible.

By means of unhindered movements, observation from an invisible position and close relationships with an indefinite audience, the spectator fashions the public sphere. In fact, the ideal of the public sphere is inseparable from the possibility of moving around in an open and homogeneous social space and of conveying 'without deformation', as Bruno Latour says of scientific objectivity,[32] observations made at any point in this space, within the exteriority of a relationship available to anyone. The public sphere thus presupposes the existence of a detached, casual observer who can survey the peculiarities of society in the way that the geographer, cartographer or painter inspired by the cartographic ideal[33] surveys the peculiarities of the landscape.

There is then interdependence between the constitution of a pure spectator and the separation of *contemplation* and *action* which, as Michel Foucault[34] and, more recently, Pieter Spierenburg[35] in his work on public executions, have shown, has an historical character. Until the end of the eighteenth century, public executions are not a spectacle in the modern sense which would presuppose a strict separation between the actions performed on the stage of the scaffold and the viewing of this by passive observers. Even the intensification of the public display of executions in the sixteenth and seventeenth centuries, which was linked to the demonstration of the State's power and its ability to secure justice and civic peace, did not succeed in expelling those present from the stage by tracing that invisible and uncrossable line which, in the modern theatre, separates the space in which the drama is performed from the space from which the spectators view it, and which confers on the actors that particular *aura* generated by the coexistence of proximity and untouchability. People came to see executions with their families and with children (in the Netherlands schools closed).[36] In some cases the public was permitted to throw rotten fruit and mud at the condemned man, and to abuse him.[37] The discourse of the authorities present was cheered or ridiculed. But the public's attitude towards the condemned was not always hostile. It could be touched by his repentance and pray for his redemption.[38] Praying was still a form of action, a way of committing oneself. Unlike today, prayer was not understood in terms of an opposition between passivity and action and denigrated as a hypocritical way of dispensing with action (as when Christians were reproached for being *content* to pray for the Jews during the Second World War).[39] Finally, it sometimes happened that, gaining strength from the courage of the condemned man, the public invaded the scaffold and brought the executioner to a bad end. The identity of the executioner, who was often a stranger, was ambiguous, and the satanic element of this identity favoured such reversals, he being the devil's assistant just as the judge was Christ's vicar. A reversal of this kind took place, for example, with the stoning to death of the executioner in Florence in 1503 when the crowd, already aroused by the courage of the tortured young man, learned that the executioner had executed Savonarola three years earlier.[40] Sympathy for the tormented victim is much more frequent when he is not a robber but a rioter or rebel identified as 'one of us' by those present, so that, as at Rouen in 1640, the population is prohibited, on pain of death, from witnessing the journey to the scaffold.[41]

2.6 Taking sides

In the literature on the constitution of the public sphere, particularly when viewed in its relationship with the formation of the modern conception of journalism,[42] it is generally accepted that there must be a connection between the insistence on the presence of an external and detached observer and a demand for neutrality, objectivity in the sense of impartiality, and consequently tolerance. This hardly seems disputable when the observer reports and circulates divergent opinions concerning, for example, economic or political measures. However, the public sphere is not only the site of reasonable debate on the important questions of the moment. The public sphere is not constituted solely around such matters as call for deliberation but also around *causes*. Now nothing promotes the formation of a cause more than the spectacle of suffering. It is first of all around the suffering of unfortunates that the *precipitate* is brought about which launches people who were previously indifferent into a cause.[43] It is through the cause that the public sphere and a politics of pity are connected to each other. A public sphere therefore is not only turned towards the ideal of an aperspectival objectivity, as the laboratory will be later. Consideration of suffering modifies the conditions of debate especially by imposing on it an *urgency* which demands a *commitment* from people for a *cause*. In this configuration the critical moment of the *swing to commitment* is, precisely, the *grand moment par excellence*.

There are two different states then in which people may exist within a public sphere: a state of noncommitment and a state of commitment. But for commitment to be valid in the public sphere it must be purely *moral*, that is to say free from any determination by interests and consequently from any prior communal ties. It follows that in shaping a common space the separation of *actor* and *spectator*, of viewing and acting, is inseparable from the conception of an unspecified individual, that is an individual detached from any communal tie. The model of the 'public sphere' is precisely that network which to start with does not have laid down pre-existing pathways and within which people can subsequently group together around causes. But because actors are always qualified, at the least by what they do, by their prior involvement in actions already under way, only spectators, by definition inactive observers, can make acts of commitment. Because *commitment* is only authentic in this political figure when it marks the moment at which uncertain individuals take up a position. But the realisation of this moment requires that at the outset all the individuals within a network, between whom in principle every connection is possible, have the same information at their disposal and are aware of the same causes. What constitutes the network is precisely the shared character of the information. Without this precondition, those making up the network would be separated from and unaware of each other, or else they would reconstitute stable and reciprocally opaque communal spheres. The crucial moment in this topic is then the moment of *commitment* understood as the moment of transformation from the state of being a receiver of information, that is to say, of being a spectator, observer or listener, into that of being an actor. But insistence on this moment, understood as the political moment par excellence, by the same token inevitably accentuates the separation between *viewing* and *acting*, as we shall see when we consider the critique of sentimentality. It leads in particular to a distribution of passions and emotions between the spectator (who experiences 'sympathy' or 'horror') and the actor (who, involved in scenes, is given over to 'jealousy', 'fear' or 'discomfort').[44] Or again, it gives rise to the question of whether 'feelings' can be evaluated morally, in other words, whether they can be wicked in themselves regardless of their consequences in the world of action.[45]

So in the ideal of the public sphere a local suffering can be conveyed without deformation in such a way that it is there for anyone to examine it, that is to say, for all those who, from the fact of their receptivity arising from their lack of prior commitment, are free to examine this suffering and find themselves sufficiently affected by it to become committed and take it up as their cause. Consider the case of Voltaire in the Calas and the chevalier de La Barre affairs, both studied by Elisabeth Claverie.[46] Voltaire takes up the suffering of the Calas family, Toulouse petits-bourgeois for whom he has no personal sympathy or prior feelings apart from a certain condescension tinted with contempt for their narrowness as local protestants attached to a faith and a community, and he turns this suffering into a general cause to which he devotes himself with the determination one usually exerts in pursuit of one's own affairs, those which concern you personally. We must follow Elisabeth Claverie when she stresses the novel character of this way of *taking a stand*.

In this new political figure suffering is no longer conveyed as it is in a communal relationship. In the latter, suffering is normally conveyed from person to person by word of mouth and so at the cost of a reappropriation and usually transformation of the narrative[47] recounted in the presence of particular addressees by someone involved and affected by the suffering of those close to him (like, for example, the survivor of a battle who has returned to his village). In this situation, voice, accents, emotions, anger, tears and, in a word, the *presence* of the speaker, involves the audience in a shared scene, and every member of the audience, each of whom could have been in the place of the person telling the story, through the expressive manifestations of their affected bodies will convey that suffering to others, who will in turn be drawn into it. Conveying suffering in a public sphere takes a different form because the public sphere constitutes itself against a communitarian sphere.[48] In contrast it must establish a representation of suffering which is presented as *falsifiable* (through the elimination of rumours or mendacious presentations) and it must convey this representation with the least modifications possible to the greatest number of people possible. The real or potential spectator of someone else's suffering being anyone, their reactions are no longer motivated by a natural commitment so that there is uncertainty regarding the identification of the unfortunate which may, as will be seen, give rise to controversy. Why this unfortunate rather than another? The selection must be justified.

2.7 Detachment and commitment

But if, in contrast with the community relationship, the public sphere really is characterised by the ideal of an aperspectival objectivity which favours the publicity of matters of debate, how will it admit the integration of diverse and local sufferings within a general picture nourished on the particular examples required by the demonstration of a politics of pity? Specifically, if the public sphere requires communication without deformation, how will it lend itself to distantly observed suffering being conveyed by the speech of spectators who in the fabrication of their account are subject, as we have seen, to the constraint we have called, for convenience sake, *the prohibition of the 'that's how it is'*. It is just this tension that the metaphor of the theatre highlights. The theatre arena, which brings together unconcerned spectators at the same time as appealing to their emotions, enables the tension within a politics of pity to be handled. We have seen that this tension arises from two contradictory requirements. On the one hand there is a requirement of impartiality, detachment (no prior commitment) and a distinction between the moment of observation, that is to say, of knowledge, and the moment of action. This requirement points towards the possibility of generalisation. On the other hand there is a requirement of affective, sentimental or emotional investment which is needed to arouse political commitment.

One way in which this tension is expressed in a report on suffering with a political objective consists in the alternative of a general presentation and going into particular cases (which, moreover, poses different problems depending on whether the picture of suffering is given in the form of an image or by means of written statements). In fact, while it is easier to integrate general forms of presentation into the logic of political programmes (like the definition of a threshold of poverty for example), nonetheless it is necessary to go into particular cases, that is go into details, in order to arouse pity, involve the spectator and call on him to act without delay. But then the question arises of how far it is appropriate to go in the description of wretched details, and the desire to arouse pity comes into conflict with the contrary demand of respect for the person of the unfortunate. A picture which goes too far in the realistic description of details, one which might be described as repulsive, may actually be denounced as on the one hand *reductive,* inasmuch as the person is entirely defined by their suffering, and on the other hand as taking the suffering away from the person inflicted by it in order to *exhibit* this suffering to those who do not suffer. Consider the case of public campaigns to raise awareness of the AIDS epidemic. Numbers alone won't do because, as the communication experts charged with the problem say, 'they do not speak'. These campaigns therefore rely on the presentation of particular cases, of real persons really ill. But in what state should they be shown? Should seemingly healthy people be shown and the demonstration be judged not 'effective'? Or should sick people in the final stages of their illness be shown, with the risk of being accused of taking from these people something which belongs only to them, their illness and their death,[49] as well as of infringing the implicit rule to which photographic humanism seems to conform: not to show others as one would not wish to be shown oneself?

A politics of pity, that is to say a politics which takes hold of suffering in order to make of it a political argument par excellence, must therefore be able to be orchestrated by a formula which enables this tension to be overcome by combining within a single statement both a realistic world reported by an uninvolved spectator observing from anywhere and, in view of the ban on pure factuality, a world of people who are affected and whose concern promises commitment. We will try to isolate this formula by leaning heavily on the construction by means of which Adam Smith seeks to derive the coherent model of a moral society from the relationship between an unfortunate and a spectator.

3

The moral spectator

3.1 The impartiality of the spectator

The introduction of the metaphor of the theatre into moral argument is not peculiar to Adam Smith, even though the figure of the spectator assumes a particularly prominent form in his work, especially in his innovation of the internalised spectator ('the man within'; 'the man in the breast'; 'the internal voice'). The metaphor is found in Hume, in his predecessor and master Hutcheson and, as we know, in a great many English and French writers and essayists of the eighteenth century. Besides, as D. Raphaël notes, Smith borrowed the term 'spectator' from the title of the famous paper brought out by Addison and Steele almost forty years previously.[1] But there is no question that the figure of an uninvolved spectator observing a suffering unfortunate is employed in Adam Smith in the most rigorous and systematic way to found a moral theory which also appears as an empirical social psychology and a political philosophy since it opens out into a construction which sets its sights on the possibility of harmonious and peaceful relationships between human beings in society.

Adam Smith appreciated the theatre and was interested in astronomy (in his youth he wrote an essay on the history of astronomy).[2] *The Theory of Moral Sentiments*[3] sought to transfer the method used by Newton in the domain of natural philosophy to the treatment of moral problems, with the same requirements of simplicity and familiarity, that is to say in a way both economical and directly accessible to the imagination. Newton, Smith wrote, made the 'greatest, and most admirable improvement in philosophy . . . when he discovered that he could join together the movements of the planets by so familiar a principle of connection, which completely removed all the difficulties the imagination had hitherto felt in attending to them'.[4] In *The Theory of Moral Sentiments* the equivalent of this principle of simple and economic connection, 'the simple and familiar fact of gravitation' on which Newton succeeded in constructing a logically coherent system which at the same time could account for the most familiar experience, is the relationship between an *unfortunate* and a *spectator*.

Adam Smith's problem is the convergence of the judgements of two separated observers who *look at* the same object. But (in section 1 of part I) the problem is posed in different ways depending on whether we consider objects 'without any peculiar relation either to ourselves or to the person whose sentiments we judge of' (p. 19) or objects 'which affect in a particular manner either ourselves or the person whose sentiments we judge of' (p. 20). In the first category Smith puts 'all the general objects of science and taste' (p. 19). These objects 'we and our companion regard as having no peculiar relation to either of us' (p. 19). In this instance judgements naturally converge (provided that information is equally available to each): 'We both look at them from the same point of view, and we have no occasion for sympathy, or for that imaginary change of situations from which it arises, in order to produce, with regard to these, the most perfect harmony of sentiments and affections' (p. 19).

A question arises concerning the convergence of judgement with regard to objects which relate to each 'in a particular manner' (p. 20). 'My companion does not naturally look upon the misfortune that has befallen me, or the injury that has been done me, from the same point of view in which I consider them. They affect me much more nearly. We do not view them from the same station, as we do a picture, or a poem, or a system of philosophy, and are, therefore, apt to be very differently affected by them' (pp. 20–1). Now it is precisely in this case that there is a risk of dissension due to the absence of converging judgements, because judgement applies to objects which affect us personally. The question Adam Smith poses then is that of the 'correspondence of sentiments between the *spectator* and the *person principally concerned*' (p. 21). This is a fundamental political question since it concerns the possibility of an agreement between unequally *affected* or unequally *concerned* persons which does not rely on force.

It is therefore absolutely necessary for Smith's argument that the spectator be defined as someone *uninvolved*, as someone personally sheltered from the adversity which produces the unfortunate's suffering. Although in the original position the spectator is not explicitly specified as someone fortunate, there is here a radical distinction between someone who suffers and someone who does not, between an unfortunate and someone else who is sometimes referred to as a *beholder*, someone who sees, sometimes as a *bystander*, sometimes as a *spectator*, which emphasises the distant and even theatrical character of the relationship, and also sometimes as 'every indifferent person', 'a third person' or just 'another man'.[5] The coexistence of these different terms, and particularly of the most frequently used terms *bystander* and *spectator*, which seem to be used as equivalents for each other, suggest that Smith did not seek to emphasise the tension between a necessarily local face to face encounter, as in the figure of compassion, and the conveyance over distance of a representation of suffering that is required by a general politics of pity, as if the second figure could be directly derived, smoothly and uninterruptedly, by extension of the first. By the same token, the problems raised by the separation of the moment of observation from the moment of action usually remain implicit. None the less, the insistence on the spectator's non-involvement, as well as on the fact that he is 'well-informed',[6] suggests that this model can be compared with the kind of set-up on which a politics of pity is based and consequently that we can treat *The Theory of Moral Sentiments* as a modelling of moral relationships between persons when the political order incorporates a reference to pity. Distance is rarely taken into account explicitly precisely because it is introduced straightaway in the original face-to-face situation.

The unfortunate who suffers and the person who views him are, on this account, nothing to each other. Neither family nor community ties nor even interest bring them together. The person looking on is thus characterised by the absence of already existing commitments which, as we have seen, is one of the spectator's principal characteristics. Smith describes his spectator as 'impartial'. The attention he gives to the person suffering is disinterested. The misfortunes which affect the suffering person have no effect, in the present or the future, on the spectator's condition (on his mode of life, for example), so he could safely ignore them. And yet the spectator sympathises with the suffering of the patient. With this premise Smith places himself in the current of Scottish moral philosophy which, in reaction against anthropologies based on selfish interest, especially those of Hobbes and Mandeville, and also in seeking to overcome interpretations of Lockean sensualism which lead towards sceptical subjectivism, makes the 'moral sense' (Shaftesbury) a 'faculty of the human mind' (Hutcheson). *Sympathy* is the natural faculty without which an individual could not know or be interested in someone else.[7]

In his account Smith distances himself, however, from the sentimentalism of his predecessors (to whom we will return when we come to deal with the topic of sentiment). There is nothing in his writing to suggest the idea of an intuitionist transmission from sentiment to sentiment, from interiority to interiority, and still less, in contrast with Hutcheson, the idea of an emotional 'contagion' or 'infection', or of identification with someone else in their misery. Sympathy does not presuppose empathy.[8] In this sense Smith holds to sensualist empiricism as to something fixed that cannot be

superseded.[9] The moral mechanism must be established within the limitations imposed by a society formed from a collection of separate individuals and without recourse to notions of tribal solidarity or emotional
community. Smith is ironical about 'the force of blood' which exists, he
says, only in tragedies and romances. 'In some tragedies and romances, we
meet with many beautiful and interesting scenes, founded upon, what is
called, the force of blood, or upon the wonderful affection which near relations are supposed to conceive for one another, even before they know that
they have such connection. The force of blood, however, I am afraid, exists
no-where but in tragedies and romances' (*The Theory of Moral Sentiments,*
p. 222). The figure of the spectator and the metaphor of the theatre give a
precise expression of the distance which characterises the original social situation.[10]

3.2 The powers of the imagination

The obstacle this distance creates can be overcome by means of a faculty
however: the imagination. In the original situation the spectator is not
involved in the scene of suffering he observes. Like the spectator affected
by the sentiment of the sublime in the account given by Burke considered
below, he is sheltered and fears nothing for himself. It is by incorporating
distance that the possibility of aesthetic sentiments and moral sentiments
(still partially mixed up with each other in Hutcheson) must be understood.
In Smith, as in Hume, distance is overcome by a deliberate act of imagination. The spectator represents to himself the sentiments and sensations of
the sufferer. He does not identify with him and does not imagine himself to
be in the same situation. As Smith remarks in the chapter of *The Theory of
Moral Sentiments* in which he criticises Hobbes and Mandeville, the spectator imagines what the woman in child-bed may feel, but does not imagine
himself actually in the process of giving birth, and this excludes a
Hobbesian interpretation of pity which is based upon the possibility of
experiencing the same reversals of fortune oneself and consequently on
selfish interest.[11]

   The mediation of the imagination is important because it supports the
moral and social edifice without recourse to communal identification or to
an Edenic fusion. In Smith's account, which has political pretentions and
is therefore directed towards the possibility of a harmonious City, the relationship between the spectator and the unfortunate is still symmetrical.
This will no longer be the case in later formulations which insist upon the
aesthetic dimension of the relationship to suffering that we examine later.
On the one hand, the two roles are not allocated once and for all to differ-

ent persons. The same person may be sufferer and spectator in turn.[12] Smith defines a model, or a structure, that is a system of places comprising positions whose occupants are not specified. On the other hand, the unfortunate is not placed in relationship to the spectator as an object to a subject. If the spectator imagines the sensations of the suffering unfortunate, the unfortunate also imagines the spectator's sensations imagining his, the unfortunate's, sensations. This reflexive, mirror relationship is not sequential. Each anticipates how he will be imagined by the other and the composition of these anticipations generates an equilibrium.[13] Sympathetic equilibrium is based upon the loss of intensity that occurs during this imaginative exchange. The spectator imagines the suffering of the unfortunate, but he is not the one suffering. The suffering is therefore represented in an abated form in his imagination. But the unfortunate anticipates, in imagination, the abated form in which the spectator imagines his suffering. He therefore abates its expression so as not to exceed the possibilities of the specatator's attention and so as not to exhaust his patience. Sympathetic equilibrium is achieved when concord is formed between the imaginative supply of the spectator and the unfortunate's demands for attention. This mechanism introduces an element of moderation into society since the unfortunate, who is each one of us at certain times, voluntarily limits the expression of his suffering. Although Smith does not present his schema in the form of a sequence, it is reasonable to think that the realisation of equilibrium is greatly facilitated if spectator and unfortunate are in each other's presence. They can then, as Hume explains when he describes the mechanism of sympathy,[14] regulate their reciprocal expectations by interpreting external signs accessible to sight (attention, boredom, exasperation, etc.). It is in this sense especially that we can see a prefiguration of social psychology in *The Theory of Moral Sentiments*. But then we are returned to the face-to-face situation.

3.3 The spectator of the spectator

However, the apparatus set up by Smith to establish the natural laws of morality contains more than just an unfortunate and a spectator detached from any pre-existing commitment. At least two other actors are needed to pursue the demonstration. On the one hand we require an *ideal* and *internalised spectator,* and on the other someone whose dealings have a direct action on the unfortunate and who for this reason we will call the *agent*. By this departure from Smith's demonstration we will attempt to show how a new formula can be developed by means of these two new actors which enables us to overcome the tension identified in the previous chapter.

With regard to earlier uses of references to a spectator in the construction of models of moral judgement (by Hutcheson and Hume in particular), we know that Smith's principal innovation essentially consists in
adding to the model a mechanism for securing the spectator's reflexivity.[15]
The spectator is thereby split. To the *ordinary spectator* who, as we have
seen, is by definition an uninvolved spectator with no personal commitments at stake in the situation he observes, is added an *ideal spectator*[16] who
is the spectator of oneself and of one's own conduct.[17]

The construction of the ideal spectator derives from two premises. The
first is that the desire for approval is an irreducible feature of human nature.
'He desires, not only praise, but praise-worthiness; or to be that thing
which, though it should be praised by nobody, is, however, that natural and
proper object of praise' (*The Theory of Moral Sentiments,* p. 114). The
second is that this desire for concord with the other can only be satisfied by
adopting a point of view on oneself and one's own sentiments that would
be adopted by an impartial spectator. It is this *internalised* ideal spectator,
a spectator without any particular perspective, who Smith calls 'the representative of the impartial spectator, the man within the breast' and makes
the moral guide of the conduct of each.[18]

So as to accord the spectator an ability to depict the unfortunate's suffering and to communicate it in an acceptable way to someone else, we retain
from this analysis the need to endow the spectator with a reflexive ability
and, more precisely, the ability to consider himself as a speaker. To be sure,
Smith does not deal directly with the question of language in *The Theory
of Moral Sentiments.* But the least that can be said is that linguistic activity
was not far from his concerns since he added to the second edition of *The
Theory of Moral Sentiments* his essay 'Considerations Concerning the First
Formation of Languages'.[19] At face value the subject of this essay seems
unrelated to the arguments developed in *The Theory of Moral Sentiments*,
since it is a 'conjectural history' of different kinds of words, but one cannot
help but be struck by the structural analogy involved between the opposition between the particularity of the ordinary spectator and the generality
of the ideal spectator in *The Theory of Moral Sentiments* on the one hand,
and the major concern of the 'Considerations' on the other, which is to
show how abstract, that is to say *general* terms, are generated from *particular* terms.[20] This common concern is especially apparent in the analysis of
the word 'I' which is 'a general word, capable of being predicated, as the
logicians say, of an infinite variety of objects', that

differs, however, from all other general words in this respect; that the objects of
which it may be predicated, do not form any particular species of objects distinguished from all others . . . It is far from being the name of a species, but, on the

contrary, whenever it is made use of, it always denotes a precise individual, the particular person who then speaks. It may be said to be, at once, both what the logicians call, a singular, and what they call, a common term.

Like the self in *The Theory of Moral Sentiments,* divided between an ordinary and an ideal spectator, it joins 'in its signification the seemingly opposite qualities of the most precise individuality, and the most extensive generalization'.[21]

3.4 The emotive style

We will argue that if one shifts the description of the spectator's internal states and applies it to the formation of statements about suffering, then the introduction of a mechanism of reflexivity into the model makes it possible to introduce a symmetry which reduces the tension between an aperspectival objectivism and moral involvement. A discursive apparatus is brought into the process. This consists in inserting and giving prominence to the person speaking within what is said, within the statement.[22] Very generally this discursive apparatus is that of opinion. By rapidly reviewing the properties of the discursive forms in which opinion is conveyed we will be able to see the particularities of a morally acceptable formula for the communication of suffering.

As O. Ducrot has shown, the peculiarities of statements of opinion are actually established by contrast with statements reporting knowledge.[23] The validity of knowledge is established by means of demodalisation 'which suppresses the particularity of the point of view in favour of an absolute predication'.[24] Their validity is subordinated to evaluation by reference to a criterion of truth which depends upon a test against reality. By contrast, statements of opinion (*I find that . . . I think that . . .*) retain the trace of an original predication. The judgements they include cannot be separated from the subject of their enunciation and so from the perspective from which they were stated.

Although the reports which interest us obviously arise from a problematic of public opinion, since their communication marks out the contours of groups, their peculiarity, comprising a reference to suffering, is not exhausted by this contrast. Someone, for example, who says 'it is inhuman and scandalous to let children die of hunger in Somalia', and who shows by this that they are 'distressed', modalises neither the second part of the statement 'children die of hunger in Somalia', nor the first, 'it is inhuman and scandalous' that this is the case. Louis Quéré's comment concerning factual statements can be transposed. To say 'I think children die of hunger in Somalia' would introduce reference to an uncertainty about the information, not to a modalisation reintroducing the person speaking into the statement. As for the first part, 'it is inhuman and scandalous', this does reintroduce the person speaking within the statement, but modalisation arises from the affective dimension, not from opinion. It would be bizarre and even shocking to say 'in my view, it is inhuman and scandalous to let . . . etc.', for this would involve relegating to a point of view, and so relativising, an assertion which gets its force precisely from its absolute character and which thereby excludes the possibility of a contrary assertion (there is no point of view from which it would *not* be inhuman and scandalous to let children die of hunger).

Here, it is not by way of a 'modalising style' but by way of an 'emotive style' that the trace of the person speaking is inserted within the statement. In fact the emotive style 'emphasises the speaker in the relationship between the speaker and the reference of the discourse. The clearest example is provided by interjections: *Ah!* does not evoke the object provoking the astonishment, but rather this astonishment itself on the part of the speaker'.[25] Thus '*evaluative* and *emotive terms* (terms containing semantic features that imply a judgement or a particular attitude on the part of the speaker)'[26] appear here which will flesh out and give substance to the speaker when he undertakes to communicate to others the suffering he has witnessed.

We note that this exchange does not take the form of discussion but functions in the mode of an assertion which calls to be taken up again and asserted in turn to a third person by the interlocutor. One of the properties of these statements, on which the presence of suffering confers as it were a sacrosanct character, is actually that of presenting themselves as indisputable, and it is precisely in virtue of this that they do not belong to the sphere of opinion *stricto sensu*. The exchange brings about the 'sharing of emotion'. Communication consists here in a coordination of affects. It follows that there are only two ways in which its emotional force can be lessened. Either by challenging the reality of the *fact* in reference to which emotion is displayed; there was no famine, the information was 'doctored'. Or by questioning the speaker's intentions, by challenging the *authenticity* of the emotion displayed by the speaker and which he proposes to share. To sustain the first challenge there must be an *investigation* seeking to establish the real facts of the matter. This presupposes therefore that emotion is mastered and stifled for a time so that one can turn to the objects which must be assembled in the form of a proof. But this takes time and the need for an investigation can easily be countered by an appeal to the *urgency* of a suffering which cannot wait. To sustain the second challenge the interlocutor must be found at fault by showing that there is no correspondence between his external emotion and his internal intentions: the emotion is 'affected' or 'superficial', it has no basis within. This unmasking of hypocrisy is usually based upon a criterion of action; the proof of the inauthentic character of the emotion is that it is not followed up with action. In the following chapters we will see how each of these two criticisms is put to work to reduce the force of statements about suffering, the first when they are transmitted in the genre arising from the emotive style that we will call the *topic of denunciation,* and the second when they take the forms of a *topic of sentiment.*

3.5 The requirement of symmetry

We have seen that for reasons of symmetry, that is to say in order to respect a rule of common humanity, the spectator of suffering cannot adopt the stance of a subject describing an object and speaking of what he has seen as a simple reporter. He cannot describe the execution of condemned persons, or the bodies of dead children during a famine, with the same kind of precision and detachment one would use to speak of a system of economic regulation, a policy of regionalisation, or a plan for a road network. It is difficult to convey human bodies in representations, that is it is difficult to convey them in accordance with a requirement of truth regardless of how their display affects the spectators to whom they are exposed to view. We have seen that human bodies repel the 'realism' of the 'that's how it is' of representations which claim to reproduce an external reality with no additional intention, freed from moral constraints and, in the case of literature, from the constraint of pre-established discursive conventions.[27] Or rather, their reproduction as they are makes them repugnant.

To get around the prohibition of a description without a point of view, while maintaining the hypothesis of a disinterested spectator observing from anywhere, there is then a discursive solution which consists in introducing into the same report a description of the suffering unfortunate and a description of the spectator who observes him and who would have to be absent from his account if he were a pure subject of truth. The person speaking reveals himself and describes not only the spectacle but also its effect on the spectator. The process presupposes a split self and as a result requires a supplementary actor to be added to the set-up. To the observing spectator must be added an *introspector* who can enter within the person looking to consider the effects on him of what he is seeing, to become aware of his feelings and to inscribe them within the final account which is to be communicated to others. The person who reports and the spectator are no longer one and the same. The former is detached from the latter. Actually he reports both on what the spectator sees and the spectator's impressions faced with what he sees; on how he is affected by it.

This reflexive apparatus, which serves no purpose in the case of compassion since the helper immediately goes into action without being encumbered by discourse, reduces the tension confronting a politics of pity which cannot do without the conveying of distant suffering. It affects, albeit not to the same degree, the two constraints which have to be taken into account by someone who considers the unfortunate from afar. On the one hand it affects the constraint of symmetry, as we have seen. The asymmetry of the report is reduced since the spectator himself becomes an *object* of description like the unfortunate who is suffering. On the other hand the apparatus also affects, although less convincingly, the constraint of having to act. In fact, if the spectator always remains really inactive, nonetheless by making himself present within his report he demonstrates his awareness of the fact that one should act. By involving himself as *subject* in his own story he takes a step in the direction of involvement within a situation and points the way to action.

The splitting of the spectator which is a central element in Adam Smith's argument is itself based upon a topography of interiority developed since the sixteenth century and which, having become a theme in the psychology of sensualist philosophies, with Locke's distinction, for example, between an acting self and an observing self, is displayed in the new literary forms of the same period: the essay as a conversation with oneself;[28] the novel with a character split between 'an observed, struggling, idiosyncratic element acting in the world and a reflective self which observed it';[29] and, above all, the autobiography as public confession.[30] The triangular structure we have identified in Addison and Steele is found again in these different genres: a reporter who embraces spectacle and spectator in a single gaze. But here it is internalised. The spectator looks on the suffering of the patient; the introspector observes the effects of this observation on the spectator and blends these different accounts together in a composite report.

The result of this mixture combining different ways of seeing cannot be truly coherent. But it can certainly be more or less apt, different realisations being distributed around a balancing point that is always fragile and hard to achieve. If, as we have suggested, we may readily judge a description directed wholly towards the detailed reproduction of the object (centred on the report of a detached spectator) to be embarrassing and even unbearable or cruel, such a description may none the less be acceptable in certain cases, like that of medicine in particular, where factual description can be justified as contributing to the alleviation of the patient's suffering, that is to say by its involvement in the action. But even this justification is only valid if the description passes only between specialists, actively intervening practitioners, and this places these cases at the extreme limits of our concerns.

Naturalism or realism, in the literary sense, are not however the only dangers which threaten the aptness of the report. As we shall see more clearly further on, it may have other defects which are linked instead to a weakness of the introspector. Two examples of this can be indicated quickly. We will come back to them later. The first is that of an over-zealous introspector whose report on the spectator's interiority overwhelms the spectator's report on the external suffering of the unfortunate to such an extent that it takes its place entirely. We know everything about the state into which the spectator is thrown by the spectacle of suffering, but we no longer know anything about the person suffering. This kind of report can be interpreted in two different ways: we may regard the spectator as having let himself be imaginatively taken over by the patient in a way which could easily be described as 'hysterical'. Or else the spectator could be reproached for complacently being more interested in himself than in the person suffering. These attitudes can thus be criticised either as 'vicarious possession' or as 'self-absorption' according to Adrian Piper's distinction.[31] In the second case, the introspector who is usually absent from the report, since he only reports on the internal state of the spectator, makes himself present in the report as such. The process consists in going up a notch in the (unlimited) series of persons speaking. The spectator regards himself in the process of describing his own feelings; he considers his own introspective activity from outside. An example of this is found in certain pages of Laurence Sterne's *A Sentimental Journey*. This distancing, which usually employs the means of irony and humour, is equivalent to self-criticism in which the spectator unmasks the inauthenticity of his own states.

In our view, there is only a limited number of ways of composing this mixture so as to obtain a broadly satisfying result. We will try to describe the most successful mixtures and to identify the topics in which they are stabilised. However, even the relatively harmonious solutions we examine are still quite fragile because they cannot wholly suppress the tension engendered by contradictory demands: to tell the facts about suffering; to show how one has been affected by it; to avoid the reproach of impassivity (treating suffering and the unfortunate experiencing it as external objects) and the accusations of hysteria (letting oneself be taken over and contaminated by it) or hypocrisy (feigning nonexistent internal states). They will thereby be subject to criticism, as we will see below, which will encourage the formation of new topics which are no less problematic themselves.

3.6 Justice and beneficence

To isolate the first solutions given to our problem we start with the second of the actors Adam Smith adds to the unfortunate-spectator couple, the one we have called the *agent* because his dealings have a direct effect on the fate of the unfortunate. In the second part of *The Theory of Moral Sentiments*, which analyses the 'sense of merit and demerit' of our actions, Adam Smith complicates the picture of sympathy by showing that it is a 'compounded sentiment'. To do this he has to introduce an *active* character, 'the person who acts', which indicates the unfortunate's passive character by negative implication. Two cases are examined corresponding to merit or demerit. They are presented by placing beside the unfortunate firstly someone beneficent who obliges the unfortunate and for whom this unfortunate feels *gratitude*, and then someone treacherous who is the cause of the unfortunate's suffering, and towards whom this unfortunate, now characterised as a *victim,* feels resentment. In these two cases the spectator's sentiments may be experienced either directly for 'the person who acts' or indirectly for 'the person who is . . . acted upon'.

When the person who acts is beneficent, the spectator's sentiments will be a compound of direct sympathy with regard to him and indirect sympathy with the gratitude of the unfortunate who has been obliged, which corroborates the comment made concerning 'social passions' to the effect that we sympathize with the pity someone feels for a third person.[32] But when the person who acts is treacherous or perverse, the spectator's sentiments will equally be composite. They will be in part composed of indirect antipathy toward the person who acts, the persecutor.[33] They will also be in part composed of 'indirect sympathy with the resentment of the sufferer' (*The Theory of Moral Sentiments,* p. 83). In developing this idea, Adam Smith speaks of the 'just resentment' of 'innocent sufferers' and makes his style seethe with the 'sympathetic indignation' which naturally boils up in the breast of the spectator of injustice:

When we bring home to ourselves the situation of the persons whom these scourges of mankind insulted, murdered, or betrayed, what indignation do we not feel against such insolent and inhuman oppressors of the earth? Our sympathy with the unavoidable distress of the innocent sufferers is not more real nor more lively, than our fellow-feeling with their just and natural resentment . . . Our sense of the horror and dreadful atrocity of such conduct, the delight which we take in hearing that it was properly punished, the indignation which we feel when it escapes this due retaliation, our whole sense and feeling, in short, of its ill desert, of the propriety and fitness of inflicting evil upon the person who is guilty of it, and of making him grieve in his turn, arises from the sympathetic indignation which naturally boils up in the breast of the spectator, whenever he thoroughly brings home to himself the case of the sufferer.' (*The Theory of Moral Sentiments,* p. 76)

These remarks suggest that the spectator's sentiment, how the introspector will describe his internal states, whether seething with indignation or gentle with tender-heartedness, and so the genre in which the report on the unfortunate's suffering will be produced, depends essentially on how the description of the actor we have called the *agent* is filled out, that is as either helper full of pity or as cruel persecutor. These genres of the report on suffering correspond to the distinction made by Smith in the next section (section 2 of part II) between *beneficence* and *justice.* While the always voluntary actions which arise from the former are alone worthy of reward and 'excite the sympathetic gratitude of the spectator' (p. 78), actions connected with the latter may be 'extorted by force' and are, in cases where justice is violated, the 'proper object of resentment' which all 'mankind go along with' (p. 79).

With this distinction Adam Smith revives an old opposition, but it is given a new colour by the introduction of the spectator. The traditional opposition between *justice* and *charity* still belongs to a world in which the separation of contemplation and action is not a problem of great concern. Justice is an art of action, a prudence, devised in situations where a dispute must be brought to an end by a judgement. As for charity, it is conceived of in a world in which the presence of the hereafter, the communion of saints, the system of prayer and of grace do not allow a clear distinction to be made between contemplation and action. We will give a rapid description of the emotions by which pity is specified depending upon whether the spectator sympathises with the unfortunate in his relationship to a persecutor or, to the contrary, to a benefactor, that is the emotions of *indignation* and *tender-heartedness (attendrissement)*.

Consider a spectator moved by pity at the spectacle of an unfortunate. The impossibility of acting *illico* frees a space in which this emotion can be displayed, expressed verbally and transformed. In fact it is part of the definition of pity that it is transient. Pity passes through a state orientated towards the satisfaction of one's own needs and a state in which the needs of someone else are considered. Therefore, as we have indeed seen in the case of the Good Samaritan, it must rapidly give way to action. When that action is delayed or mediatised, particularly by being put into discourse, the spectator affected must extend his emotional state and take up a posture which indicates, in words but also by the way in which the emotion is expressed, how he will act when he can (or how he would act if he could). He must therefore enter into emotional states which are more specific than pity, in the sense that the type of action indicated is itself more specific.

With the entry of pity into politics two kinds of emotion are freed which specify and extend the states of feeling pity. These two kinds of emotion call upon different resources and point towards different levels of action. *Tender-heartedness* brings into the political world, that is to say into the world of considerations and actions at a distance, resources drawn from compassion, it extends over a range of *sentiments* and it points towards *beneficent* action. *Indignation* is supported by justice and, more precisely, by political constructions which establish the possibility of a just world and, in a style which can be called *pamphleteering* (since it has to combine both a reference to equivalence, necessary for the unmasking of injustice, and the expression of violence, in order to display the spectator's emotion), it points towards *denunciation* and *accusation.* As we have seen with regard to Adam Smith, the difference between these two ways of specifying pity will depend on whether the spectator sympathises with the unfortunate's feelings towards a persecutor (the unfortunate's *resentment* entailing the spectator's *indignation*) or with those he has for a benefactor (the unfortunate's *gratitude* arousing the spectator's *tender-heartedness*).

These remarks suggest two consequences which we will have to consider. The first is that in order to specify the state of the inactive spectator we have had to introduce a third place which is occupied by an agent who acts directly on the unfortunate. The second is that the triangular character of the system makes it possible to introduce effects of dissemination and therefore of the mapping of groups around causes which would not be possible if we were dealing with only an unfortunate and a bystander. The spectator can be overcome by tender-heartedness because the unfortunate's state is specified by his relationship to a beneficent third. Similarly, he can be seized by indignation to the extent that the unfortunate is specified by his relationship to a persecutor, that is to say he is specified as a victim. The spectator's tender-heartedness towards an unfortunate puts him in the position of benefactor regarding a fourth thief who is in turn affected by him, and so forth.

3.7 The coordination of emotional commitments

Until now we have interpreted Adam Smith's construction in the sense of a restricted interactionism. Essentially we have taken the elements which would enable us to draw out an analytic schema for clarifying the dyadic relationship between spectator and unfortunate. Smith's ambition, however, is much wider than this since as we know he aims to establish the possibility of a generalised social bond. But this cannot be achieved by the serial juxtaposition of pair relationships. To pursue the wider aim we must replace the dyadic schema with a triadic schema by introducing another spectator and we must consider not only the coordination between spectator and unfortunate (the sympathetic equilibrium) but also the coordination between two distinct spectators in their relationship to an unfortunate. Besides, we have done this tacitly by giving ourselves a spectator who, in order to respond to a moral demand, must not only observe on his own but also put himself in the position of someone reporting to a third party both what he has seen and the emotion the spectacle aroused in him, how he was affected by it.

It is this very requirement which determines that the spectator must be split into an empirical and an impartial spectator. The impartial spectator, the spectator of the spectator, who is posited in order to take into account the spectator's judgements on himself, is this very third party who brings others into the schema.[34] We saw that the basis of the impartial spectator was found in an essential feature of Smith's anthropology which is the desire to be praised by others. But the impartial spectator does not represent only the synthesis of the actual opinions of other empirical spectators. In fact, if this was the case we would still have only a restricted interactionism, each spectator's opinion of himself depending only on his perception of the opinions of those around him who influence him by their proximity. Now what interests Smith is the possibility of accounting for a sympathy which can overcome the obstacle of distance, as is shown by the pages devoted to the possible reactions of the inhabitants of England to news of a terrible earthquake ravaging China.[35] Coordination between the reactions and emotions of distinct spectators cannot then be imputed solely to the gradual contagion of opinions and affects. It is precisely because the impartial spectator is not the synthesis of the opinions of others that he can secure this coordination.[36] Actually the impartial spectator is internalised in each of us in the form of an ideal spectator who is not just another empirical subject and who observes from the point of view of aperspectival objectivity. It is to the extent that everyone, in the original state of separation in which the postulate of solipsism places them, falls under the gaze of the impartial spectator that a coordination of the modes of emotional concern and commitment can be effectuated.

But when it comes to identifying how this coordination is carried out, as in the coordination between the spectator and the unfortunate, an essential role is played by imagination. Each spectator makes what we will call a *proposal of commitment* to the person he addresses and to whom he conveys the spectacle of suffering and how it concerns him. For the proposal of commitment to be recognised and accepted (or rejected) we must postulate a common ability to imagine the suffering of the unfortunate as well as the sympathetic effects that consideration of this suffering has had on the person who observed it. It is then firstly by means of a coordination of imaginations that Smith's schema can be extended.

How can we imagine distinct persons being able to converge through reliance on their imagination? Imaginative capabilities are not produced fully fledged as a result of some kind of spontaneous generation. Imagination, as we say, must be *nourished*. Thus to a considerable extent the answer to our question will depend on how we view the way in which imagination is fed. Nourishment can come from personal experience provided that this experience is shared with others to a greater or lesser extent. Adam Smith considers this possibility but judges it insufficient to secure the kind of extended coordination he wishes to account for. Actually, particular personal experiences – and Smith takes the example of love – will nourish the imagination in a way that we are hardly able to share because our imagination has not 'acquired that particular turn'.[37] 'Our imagination not having run in the same channel with that of the lover, we cannot enter into the eagerness of his emotions.' The suffering of the lover seems to us 'entirely disproportioned to the value of the object' and 'love . . . is always laughed at, because we cannot enter into it. All serious and strong expressions of it appear ridiculous to a third person.' By contrast, if 'our friend has been injured, we readily sympathize with his resentment, and grow angry with the very person with whom he is angry. If he has received a benefit, we readily enter into his gratitude, and have a very high sense of the merit of his benefactor', and this is why, Smith adds, in works of fiction love 'interests us not as a passion, but as a situation that gives occasion to other passions which interest us', 'the distress which that love occasions' and which will be the occasion of resentment or gratitude.[38]

In order for imagination to play its role in the coordination of emotional commitments, different persons must be able to nourish their imagination from the same source. To illustrate this topic, Smith frequently refers to works of fiction and, in particular, to the feelings inspired in us by the heroes of tragedies and romances.[39] In an article devoted to the links between impartiality, imagination and compassion,[40] Adrian Piper calls *modal imagination* that ability to imagine what is impossible and not only what actually exists (or what has been directly experienced), and he considers this ability indispensable to the formation and sharing of pity in the face of the suffering of someone else.[41] To understand this ability we must have recourse to the 'forms of expression' of myths, tales, historical narratives, novels, autobiographies, songs, films, television reports or fictions, etc, in which in particular we find descriptions of the internal states of other people to which we can have no direct access and which by that fact *nourish the imagination* of spectators when faced with distant suffering.

3.8 Nourishing the imagination

We can be a little more precise than Adrian Piper in the identification of these forms of expression.[42] On the one hand, the appropriate forms must include a declarative dimension. They must actually be able to nourish the imagination by not only directing it towards objects about which one can think – in the sense of *thinking of* – that is, as it were, with the aim of enjoying oneself but without considering these objects to be possible in the real world (like Robert Desnos' ant, eighteen metres high with a hat on its head which, as the next verse says, does not exist), but also by fleshing out the form of expression with objects we can reasonably conceive of – in the sense of *thinking that* – which assumes that one considers them to be possible in a real universe by putting oneself in the state of mind of someone who makes judgements concerning them. This is what is required for forms of expression to be able to inform evaluations and strengthen beliefs by establishing a connection with real situations, either directly experienced or known through person to person oral communications.

On the other hand, these forms of expression must be sufficiently detached from precise empirical contexts and must include sufficiently supple descriptions to allow for their reapplication to a fairly extended range of concrete situations whose imaginative fleshing out they will promote. That Captain Dreyfus was unjustly condemned in Paris in 1894 is not enough to nourish our evaluative imagination. This particular circumstance must be extended into an entire flow of stories – some presented as real and others, as we say, embroidered – which when brought together make possible the crystallisation of a vignette – the innocent person who is accused and then exonerated – which can function as a scheme that can be reapplied to a number of situations.

The forms which interest us must therefore occupy an intermediate position between two extremes. Extravagant forms are not suitable (such as, for members of our societies, the myths and legends which still fill the imagination of other societies), those we call, precisely, purely 'imaginary' when the imaginary is identified with the fictional or even the fabulous and phantasmagoric. Such forms are constructed precisely to challenge reality and too much work is needed to reestablish their connections with the world of experience. But no less unsuitable for nourishing the evaluative imagination are forms which offer themselves as strict reports of existing situations with all the features (places, times, proper names, etc.) which particularise them and so make difficult their reapplication. In fact reapplication to an unlimited number of different concrete situations assumes that the beings and events which nourish the imagination are 'set at a distance from the spectator' by gaining a distant ground from where they can be re-employed to draw out the meaning and consequences of actual circumstances.[43]

Between these two extremes there is a rich array of forms to fill the imagination of the spectator of distant suffering. There are, for example, forms which situate themselves in relation to reality while transforming it into intrigue and dramatising it in a story, as in those works half-way between plea, testimony and fictionalised history which are almost contemporary with the events they report (often *affaires*). Or, again, there are novels which present themselves as fiction but contain 'states of affairs' 'compatible with real life'[44] or, more precisely, stage characters and circumstances which when viewed in the right way can be seen to correspond to persons and situations which were the subject of strict reports (in up to date daily newspaper reports concerning particular events for example).

However, as we have already brought out in the preceding paragraph, with the introduction of those actors posited by Adam Smith we have called *agents* into the analysis, the pity of the spectator of suffering may split in two directions to which correspond different modes of emotional and (since they point toward action) intentional commitment. There must be a corresponding split in the imagination which itself may also follow different paths, that is to say, fill the system of places by reference to which the state of the unfortunate with whom one sympathises will be specified, either by favouring identification and description of the persecutor or, on the contrary, of the benefactor. These two forms of imagination are as far from each other as are the corresponding emotions of indignation and tender-heartedness.

Wholly distinct and to some extent even contrary resources must be activated depending on whether we commit the imagination in the direction of denunciation, which requires a fairly detailed description of the unfortunate's scandalous ill-treatment, and accusation, which assumes, in particular, revealing the persecutor's often dissimulated actions and intentions, or whether we turn instead towards the benefactor in order to gain imaginative access to the frequently restrained and reticent internal states of benevolence which guide his action, and to the states of gratitude which fill the heart of the unfortunate in turn.

These remarks suggest the existence of a plurality of forms of expression necessary to nourish the imagination of the spectator of suffering by directing it in different directions. Even if these different forms of expression are not realist, their *basis* is one and the same actual world. But each of them describes a different possibility of the world by establishing a correspondence between elements of a 'primary universe' and those of a 'secondary universe' set out in the narrative. Using different languages, these secondary universes 'articulate only approximately with one another' so that it is utopian to imagine that they could all be brought together within a *magna opera* which ignores the 'irreducible plasticity' of the real world with 'no privileged vantage point' on the basis of which the alternatives offered to the imagination could be reassembled in a coherent totality.[45]

We must therefore consider each of these forms of expression separately by acknowledging their relative autonomy and coherence which derive moreover from their conventional character and the functions of coordination they perform. In fact, they further an imaginative convergence between the person who proposes commitment and the person to whom the proposal is made. This takes place in the way in which literary *pre-conventions* – which lack the stability of institutionalised conventions (like metrical conventions in poetry for example) and so do not determine 'uniform conformity' – emerge from the regularities of coordination established between the author's and reader's horizons of expectation.[46]

Different forms of expression thus propose different coordination games[47] which allow for a coming and going between statements and the emotions.[48] Some 'paradigmatic scenarios' elaborated from 'everyday life' and 'literature' (in the broad sense) further the identification and labelling of emotional experiences which, by being recalled to mind, are stabilised and become common property.[49] In our case, coordination bears first of all on the formation of common *sensibilities*. It is to the extent that they are aware of a problem, that they are *sensitised*, that persons exchange with each other accounts of the spectacles which have outraged, shocked or amused them. But, as A. Greimas and J. Fontanille show, this *sensitisation* is the support and first stage of a *moralisation* because, being manifested by 'the presence of pejoration and melioration, generally through the intermediary of judgements of excess' it 'inserts a configuration of passions within a communal space'. It follows that 'the study of moralisation presupposes that of sensitisation (*sensibilisation*)'.[50] This is in fact the direction in which we would like to orientate our work. By describing the different ways of transmitting the spectacle of suffering to another person, of sharing the emotional experiences it has aroused, and of making perceptible how one is both *affected* and *concerned*, we would like to suggest that the persistence of these ways trace relatively stable facilitating paths. They pick out common *sensibilities* on which prereflexive agreements – of the order, if one likes, of prejudice if not prejudgement – can be sustained between persons who recognise if not the same ethical values then at least a community of reactions which can often be called 'visceral' in expression of the fact that they preexist as it were their principled justification. As we will attempt to clarify at the end of this work, it is also on this basis that sensibilities are formed which, when projected on to a political sphere, oppose each other like the Left and the Right.

To describe these forms suitable for feeding the imagination and the pre-conventions which enframe the emotional coordination between the sender and the receiver of a distant suffering, we will take up the old term of *topic*. Although the term is not entirely satisfactory for our purposes, inasmuch as it does not suggest the dynamic and distributed character of semantic equipment, and also inasmuch as, at least in its modern connotations, the discursive aspects of coordination are better captured than its emotional and affective dimension, we will use it nonetheless to highlight the idea of closure around a coherent form producing considerable redundancy, as well as the idea of the conventional in the sense of the ordinary, common or banal that this term evokes better than any other.

In the following chapters we will sketch out a description of these topics in the form of a series of pictures or vignettes. We look first at the topics of *denunciation* and *sentiment* (corresponding to indignation and tender-heartedness in the emotional order), and we then examine a third topic which calls on resources of an aesthetic order and which establishes itself a bit later on the basis of the criticism of, and in reaction against, the two previous topics. As this comment suggests, the kind of conventions we explore, like literary or narrative conventions, obviously have an *historical* character, even if some of the resources which support them and, in particular, certain emotional resources, have a wider and even anthropological validity. Athough we do not entirely eschew historical references, this is not the aspect we privilege. Rather we focus on those aspects which, taking the term in its weakest sense, may be termed structural, by emphasising relationships of homology and opposition which, once pity has been introduced into politics, organise different forms of emotional commitment in the face of distant suffering.[51]

These pictures are far removed from social history in yet another respect. Insofar as we seek to identify ways of being concerned and affected and not, for example, to describe the formation of public politics, in drawing these pictures we have called above all on literary documents, whether the works referred to narrativise reality (as in the case of Voltaire in chapter 4) or offer themselves as realist fictions (as in the case of the novel in chapter 5). These forms actually seemed to be especially suitable for the description of affective states which do not normally figure in juridical, economic or political documents.

PART II

The topics of suffering

4

The topic of denunciation

4.1 From indignation to accusation

Faced with the spectacle of an unfortunate suffering far away, what can a morally receptive spectator do when he is condemned, at least for the moment, to inaction? He can become *indignant*. Becoming indignant passes through pity, for if one does not feel pity why would one become indignant (just as the revolt of someone who feels himself to have been offended passes through self-pity, which helps explain the constraints on its public expression). But pity is transformed by indignation. It is no longer disarmed and powerless, but acquires the weapons of *anger*. It is in this sense that we can say that it points toward action since anger, which is an emotion of actors, prepares or – as might be said in the Sartrean terms of a denunciation of emotional bad faith[1] – simulates commitment in a situation in which it could be realised in actions. What kind of actions would these be? Quite clearly, of a violent kind. But this violence at a distance, and so without any physical contact, is condemned to remain verbal. The speech act which expresses it is an *accusation*.

Clearly, the accusation is not addressed to the unfortunate himself. The transformation of pity into indignation presupposes precisely a redirection of attention away from the depressing consideration of the unfortunate and his sufferings and in search of a *persecutor* on whom to focus. It could by this be said to be encouraging. Following the model set out by Adam Smith, it is when the spectator sympathises with the unfortunate in his *resentment* that he can give way to indignation. Is not this precisely what Smith himself does in the passage cited in the last chapter when his previously strictly argumentative style of discourse unexpectedly takes on an angry tone when he invokes the resentment of the unfortunate?

4.2 Identification of the persecutor

The first question posed to the spectator by indignation is that of who occupies the place of persecutor. Three possibilities offer themselves. First, a persecutor may be proposed to the spectator. This is what happens, for example, in the two sadly famous photographs studied by Vicky Goldberg in her book, *The Power of Photography*, devoted to the history of photographic images which have had a political influence in the United States in the nineteenth and twentieth centuries.[2] The first of these images shows American soldiers pushing Vietnamese children in front of them. The second shows a prisoner being shot at point blank range by the Saigon Chief of Police during the Tet offensive. Clearly, by refusing to become indignant the spectator can refuse the *proposal of commitment* offered him. But then he must put forward a counter-proposal, by denouncing the photographs as 'propaganda images' for example, or by seeking to prove that they have been 'tampered with', which involves taking the argument further.

The second possibility is that the spectator may identify the persecutor or select him from among several possible candidates. A third possibility emerges when this process fails and it is said that a clearly identified agent cannot be established for a sufficient length of time in the place of the persecutor. There are too many candidates none of whom will really do; the roles of unfortunate and persecutor constantly change places, etc. This eventuality, which can be characterised as a crisis of the representation of suffering, will be left for the final chapter. For the moment we will stay with the less problematic cases and attempt to clarify some of the constraints on the identification of the persecutor.

Like any spectator within the framework of a politics of pity, the indignant spectator must start from an uncommitted standpoint. If his commitment is to have general validity it must not be dictated by personal or group interests. He must therefore demonstrate that he is free from any prejudice towards the designated persecutor and, in particular, from any negative investment in their relationship which could lay him open to the charge of pursuing an old quarrel by means of the present act of accusation. As can be seen in the course of the Dreyfus affair, for example, one of the most effective ways of discrediting public support (by means of a petition, for example) is to reveal the existence of a hidden link between the unfortunate and the person taking his side, or even to merely suggest the possibility of them having a common status (they are all Jews, communists, homosexuals, etc.). Léon Blum seeks to show this in his book on the Dreyfus affair, when he says that no preexisting link brought together those ranged behind the Dreyfusard cause, which meant that their adhesion to the cause was not predictable.[3]

But the same also holds for the relationship between the spectator and the unfortunate. For if the spectator harbours a favourable prejudice towards the unfortunate, he will naturally sympathize with his resentment and will accept without proper examination the candidate for the place of persecutor proposed by the unfortunate. We have already suggested that this clause of disinterestedness in the original position is necessary for the commitment to have proper weight and in order to clearly distinguish taking sides in a cause from communal solidarity. The constraints on the identification of the persecutor therefore have a wider scope since they weigh equally on the selection of the unfortunate himself who will fail to satisfy the requirement of an absence of preexisting concern if he is a close relative.

Consider the case of someone who takes sides with a 'fellow countryman' (*the unfortunate*) offended by a 'foreigner' (*the persecutor*). His indignant attitude can easily be imputed to a communal identification involving a xenophobic 'reflex'. He is connected with other members of his peer group and adopts what might be called a 'contagious' indignation. This form of *unanimous indignation*[4] is denounced by Svend Ranulf[5] when he generalises the results of a study undertaken five years earlier on the criminal law at Athens.[6] A large part of Ranulf's descriptions are devoted to the Nazi regime (his book was clearly provoked by the rise of Nazism in Germany) and to Protestant puritanism, particularly in the English Levellers and Calvinists. What he calls 'moral indignation', a social attitude he identifies as an essential attribute of the 'petite bourgeoisie' which he endows with a transhistorical existence, and which recalls the '*ressentiment*' described by Max Scheler following Nietzsche,[7] manifests itself in a readiness to inflict punishment and to 'witness the punishment of criminals'. The tendency is a collective one. The group reinforces its cohesion by exalting the morality of its members and by accusing others of immorality and imputing to them the very acts they themselves commit. Collective fault is thus thrown on to a scapegoat who is always characterised as foreign to the group (Jews, Irish Catholics, etc.), or as a foreign body in the group, like the idle and depraved vagabonds and poor stigmatised by Calvinist asceticism. When someone who cries shame is accused of 'blaming the victim' the target is always moral indignation.

4.3 The '*affaire*' form

Elisabeth Claverie's study of the chevalier de La Barre affair (*affaire*)[8] provides essential elements for describing how indignation and accusation must be fashioned to make them acceptable within a public sphere by distinguishing them from unanimous indignation and accusation. Her study is of particular interest to us because it concerns an event – the last public execution for blasphemy in 1766 – in relation to which a new social logic was established, that of the *affair,* to which we will return. As a first approximation, the *affair form* – which assumes its typical shape with the Dreyfus affair about 150 years later and which is one of the forms used today to bring people together and to set them against each other[9] – can be defined as the form into which a sequence of events based upon the unmasking of a suffering easily slips when it is set out in a public domain. To make an event an affair, there must be an unfortunate whose defence constitutes the cause around which the social bond is both forged and torn apart. The chevalier de La Barre affair is interesting precisely because of its pivotal position. It is actually the occasion of an unprecedented confrontation between two forms of accusation and defence. The first invokes tradition, follows ready-made communal paths, and is inserted within the judicial forms of the old regime. A crime is discovered and almost immediately a culprit is identified by rumour, accused, condemned and executed. The second form of accusation and defence is orchestrated by Voltaire and appeals to the commitment of impartial spectators. A new trial, with no institutional legitimacy, is established by enlightened opinion. The cause is turned around and the occupants of the place of the unfortunate and the place of the persecutor are reversed.

This thus enables two different ways of constructing an accusation to be compared. An initial action immediately follows acknowledgement of the blasphemy (a Christ has been disfigured). This initial verbal trial 'preserves a spontaneous, natural and emotional character and tends to give depth to the action and impart to it a plurality of voices unanimously expressing the same feeling of offence'. It is fed by 'rumour,' by the 'judgement of the street'. It 'aims for a homogeneous and total subject, "the whole town", and a judicial judgement which appears as its direct expression and simple extension'. 'Things, persons and institutions henceforth form a continuous line orientated towards a single commitment, a single sentiment, a single end, and identify a culprit, a plaintiff, a victim, an injured party, an accusation, a demand for reparation, and a punishment.' In fact, in unanimous indignation, indignation immediately turns 'towards the culprit' and is 'directed towards the search for punishment'. Unanimous indignation can thus be characterised by strict agreement between leaders and led both of whom speak with one voice and together designate the culprit. The indignant people are a crowd massed behind local authorities who, not meeting with opposition, can narrow the field of inquiry, limit the preliminary investigation and advance directly to punishment. Indignation takes the form of 'moral indignation' in Ranulf's sense: the collective reaffirms its values by stigmatising the immorality of the isolated culprit. The moment of indignation – which includes the identification of both the victim and the persecutor – and the moment of punitive action coincide.

The defence mounted by Voltaire results in a reversal of the 'system of accusation and of the places of executioner, victim and offended party'. The chevalier de La Barre dies, Voltaire writes, a victim of the intrigues of an 'old rascal of Abbeville named Belleval, the lover of the Abbess of Vignancourt . . .'[10] As this example suggests, how the persecutor's place is filled is an important feature for distinguishing communal indignation from what Elisabeth Claverie calls 'enlightened indignation'. Enlightened indignation, as expressed in the *affair form*, reverses the occupants of the places of unfortunate and persecutor. It is an indignation on the rebound which needs to affirm itself against and to oppose unanimous indignation. It is by choosing as the unfortunate someone – an individual or collective person – who was previously *accused* and, more precisely, someone who has been accused by his own group, that the perfectly disinterested character, free from any prejudice and commitment, can be demonstrated in a striking way. In a topic of denunciation, the unfortunates of choice, those who can occupy that place for the longest time by successfully resisting attempts to eject them into the indistinct chaos where individuals are sometimes unfortunates and sometimes persecutors, sometimes good and sometimes wicked, are therefore persons previously accused by members of the group, perhaps even by the whole group, to which the accuser himself belongs. Like the unfortunate who must be rescued, the denouncer appears therefore as a man alone opposed to a collectivity. And if he makes an *accusation*, it is, and it is only, he says, to exonerate an isolated unfortunate who has been made the crowd's *scapegoat*. The violence of the accusation is thereby toned down and justified.

4.4 Social denunciation

The reversal of the occupants of the places in 'enlightened indignation' is the *critical* operation *par excellence*. We can see in this one of the devices which has helped to maintain the political division between *Left* and *Right* in France. The enlightened indignation of the Left which *deconstructs* unanimous indignation with the weapons of criticism is constituted against the communal indignation affected by the Right in order to defend culprits that this indignation exposes to public prosecution and punishment. Up to the present day the topic of denunciation has kept this political colouration which in the nineteenth century was asserted in defence of the oppressed, and of impoverished workers in particular. The defence of the working class often takes on the form of an immense and grandiose *affaire*.

But the work of accusation and the identification of the persecutor come up against different degrees of difficulty which call upon different resources depending on the length of the causal chain which needs to be established between the unfortunate and the agent who causes his suffering. It is much more difficult to create an affair when the unfortunate and his persecutor are far apart and the connections to be established and stabilised have to extend so far as a result. In fact, to construct an accusation a causal connection must be established between the happiness of a wicked person and the misfortune of his innocent victim. This is relatively easy when both the innocent and the wicked are seen together by eye witnesses in a situation of aggression (as, for example, in the Rodney King affair, when King was filmed being beaten with batons by police officers who were later brought to trial in Los Angeles in 1992). The situation becomes increasingly delicate the greater the distance between the persecutor and his victim. To take another contemporary example, that of an unfortunate who dies of hunger in a shanty-town. His persecutor, who has never seen him, occupies an office in Paris or New York at the head office of a holding company from where he works on the financial markets. How can the connection between unfortunate and persecutor be made to stick? To extend its operations to cases in which those occupying the place of the unfortunate and those occupying the place of the persecutor are very far apart, the topic of denunciation must avail itself of a theory of *power*. It must be able to provide an explanation of the way in which the persecutor's action has affected the unfortunate's destiny, that it is to say it must reveal the links in the causal chain. Moreover, it is better if it can establish the non-circumstantial nature of this causal connection and show that the persecutor's good fortune is the result of the unfortunate's suffering. To be more precise then, the theory of power must be a theory of *domination*.

In relying upon a sociological theory of exploitation and social classes, especially in its Marxist form, the workers' movement has provided itself with powerful tools for distinguishing, within the immense universe of human suffering, between suffering for which there is a political and social cause, and consequently political and social remedies as well, and suffering which, however distressing it may be, is inherent in the human condition, or, to reinforce this contrast by using Pierre Bourdieu's terms, between 'generic alienations', such as those linked to sex or age for example, and 'specific alienations' linked to class.[11] Whereas the first are by definition apolitical, so that their treatment is left to private institutions like the family or to charitable organisations and, at the intellectual level, to philosophy as traditionally defined,[12] the second are political through and through in the sense that they result from the power of a dominant class which is wielded over an exploited dominated class. That being the case, action directed towards halting the latter kind of alienation cannot then take place at once at a precise moment but is undertaken case by case on a local basis. The point of application of public and collective action is the political regime and it is based on a science of society which is none other than sociology. Now this detour of action, which must be orientated towards the future and follow a general direction in order to turn later to the relief of individual miseries, is also a detour through denunciation. This is because collective mobilisation presupposes that the division between generic alienations against which it is pointless to revolt and social alienations to which a remedy can be brought by political action is internalised by each of those who are dominated and who, avoiding acceptance of their condition as an ineluctable destiny, find a motive for action in the hope of change. But this very division assumes that sufferings produced by exploitation are identified and imputed to a persecutor, either to an individual person like a boss, policeman, or master, etc., or to a collective person like a social class, the system or the structure. Here denunciation therefore constitutes a necessary mediation of the orientation to action. But because this action is action in the long-term and requires a detour through mobilisation and strategy, it presupposes the stifling of those sentimental emotions which lead one either to turn to immediate and local palliatives (like giving alms to beggars, for example, or the aid offered to the poor by local authorities or the parish) or to a gratitude towards equally local benefactors which masks the reality of class antagonisms (as in denunciations of paternalism).

However, the borderline between generic and specific alienations is not fixed once and for all. Quite the opposite is the case; the borderline is constantly being drawn and redrawn. It is part of the logic of denunciation, particularly in its theoretical expressions, to demonstrate its power by extending its domain, that is to say, by shrinking the field of generic suffering in order to show that they are specific by inserting them within a structure of domination and exploitation, as we can see from the belated extension of denunciation to the school, to medicine, and then to the couple and to the family as mechanisms of exploitation and domination. One result of these processes, to which we return below, is to increase the number of unfortunates and the diversity of their suffering (which may not be recognised as suffering by those who endure it, or, as it is said, may be unconscious) which, by removing their particular prominence ultimately risks blurring the borderline between generic and specific suffering.

4.5 From revolt to investigation

In a topic of denunciation, how does the spectator reporting to someone else affirm his presence in the utterance? By giving free rein to his indignation. It is through indignation that he renders himself present in person, because indignation cannot be impersonal. As an *emotion* indignation implies a being with a body, and so an individual being. The expression of indignation thus brings out the denouncer's individuality – someone who by taking sides against communal opinion or rumour stands *alone*, someone who has received no mandate from anyone. In order to express himself in his statements the denouncer has a particular resource available to him. This is the pamphleteering style as Marc Angenot has described it on the basis of a corpus of texts going back no further than 1868, but whose elaboration from satire, lampoon and *factum*, particularly by Voltaire in France, accompanies the development of political argument calling upon pity.[13] The speaker truly expresses himself as an individual in the pamphleteering style. Breaking with his group, breaking the 'conspiracy of silence', he speaks from 'nowhere' (what Marc Angenot calls *exotopia*) but is none the less 'fully involved in the event'.[14] To unmask the 'deception' he allows himself a personal obviousness, a 'heartfelt conviction' affirmed in a discourse of *anger* – of indictment or plea – the emotive dimension and so embodied nature of which frequently shows through in the metaphors used to describe it: a discourse expressing a 'gut wrenching' 'visceral reaction' which 'comes from inside' and the criterion of which, as Angenot says, sometimes comes down to the question of either "having it or not".[15] A form of agonic discourse, the pamphlet is *antymémathique*. In relation to the speaker, Marc Angenot writes again, the addressee is split into a 'universal audience' which must be convinced and 'incited to action' on the one hand and, on the other, an 'adversarial listener' whose refutation involves the deployment of dialogical or ironical figures. The 'open letter', for example, that missive fictionally addressed to an adversary but also made public, is addressed to both of these figures inseparably.[16]

In the topic of denunciation the spectator's attention does not dwell on the unfortunate. As we have seen, it shifts from the pitied unfortunate's place to that of the accused persecutor. Indignation is addressed to the persecutor in the first place. If the unfortunate's suffering releases the 'reflex' of 'anger', this anger is expressed against the persecutor as soon as he has been identified. But the would-be persecutor himself can also be the subject of a *defence* which, basing itself upon the suffering inflicted upon him by the very fact of being accused, puts him in the unfortunate's place in turn. In a topic of denunciation then, the statement is inserted within a structure of controversy. The speaker's words must be more than just invective. Meeting with resistance, the statement must equally appear in a *debatable* form. It must set out and argue its positions. The violence of accusation must be justified by proofs. Assuming 'a *strong* and explicit presence of the speaker in the statement', the denouncer's accusation must at the same time include 'a search for the truth, or at least for what can be agreed to' which seeks to 'strengthen mental adherence to a chain of propositions'.[17] In a topic of denunciation the spectator cannot linger on the emotional therefore. He must come to terms with the injunctions which require a separation between the *subjective* emotion and the *objective* causes which are capable of backing them up. He must therefore master and stifle his emotion in order to turn to things, because to gather proof he must direct his attention to the world of objects in order to base the accusation in reality. In fact, the purely subjective – impassioned, ideological, illusory, fantasmatic, etc. – character of the accusation may be invoked as an objection to it. In contrast to what will be seen with the topic of sentiment, the spectator must quickly eschew the description of his inner states when faced with someone else's misfortune in order to provide proofs of the reality of the suffering and, above all, of good grounds for the accusation. In this topic, precisely because there is an accusation, the authenticity of an inner state, the strength of conviction, are not sufficiently firm bases for maintaining an acceptable discourse. To support an accusation we must leave the domain of inwardness for the external world and lean, more precisely, on objects. It is in objects, that is to say in *objective* beings, in the sense here that they are reputedly impartial and have no interest of their own, that the trace of the crimes which must be denounced can be lastingly inscribed. These proofs must be established at a general level and consequently must not depend on personal interest or even on a perspective or point of view. The topic of denunciation thus abandons indignation to be deployed in an investigation.

Once again, to illustrate what is required by accusation we can take up Elisabeth Claverie's description of the way in which Voltaire intervened in the affair on the side of an isolated unfortunate who was the victim of apparently unstoppable conspiracies. After a moment of great emotion, indignation and, in the chevalier de La Barre affair, fear (the *Philosophical Dictionary* was burnt with the body of the Chevalier), Voltaire starts his investigation to give an objective basis to his intuition of the victim's innocence, and to identify and confound his persecutors. He 'sends a series of letters in which he requests information' from 'enlightened magistrates' of his friends, from 'local judges' and also from some old friends living in the region of Abbeville (the town where the chevalier was judged) on the 'hidden agenda of the affair' and 'gossip (in which, he says, the truth of the judgement will doubtless be found)'. Relying on the information gathered by this investigation he undertakes to 'deconstruct' and 'reconstruct' the narrative of the event, retaining the system of actors but changing the occupants of the different places by basing his new version on 'an empirically demonstrated description of the facts'. Indignation now 'falls on the victim'; the 'people' are henceforth entirely on his side; responsibility for the chevalier's accusation and condemnation is attributed both to the personal vengeance of a jilted lover (Belleval, the lover of the chevalier's aunt) and to the fanaticism of the religious party.

It is the tension between this double requirement then – indignant presence of the speaker and cold, or at least controlled, observation – which characterises the report of the misfortune when it functions in the denunciatory mode. The indignant presence of the speaker of the pamphleteering style must be linked to an argument modelled on genres characterised by the *speaker's effacement*: on that of the essay, which presupposes a high level of generality and a subject of idealised abstractions,[18] on that of scientific discourse in its positivist forms, and even, at times, on that of the police investigation. The discourse of denunciation thus appears as at the same time indignant and meticulous, emotional and factual. It overflows with details, objects, places and dates. The rhetoric of investigation, which facilitates the transition from indignation to denunciation, is worked out, at least in part, in the detective novel, which links the question of justice to the unmasking of a truth hidden beneath illusory appearances.[19]

The tension between these two contradictory requirements is found in the letters and testimonies (275 packets) received by *Le Monde* in which ordinary people try to make a public denunciation of an injustice or scandal which has outraged them.[20] When protesting against an injustice of which they have been the victims or that they have witnessed, these people spontaneously, and more or less deftly depending on their level of education, adopt the pamphleteering form whose historical genesis and scale Marc Angenot brings out and which, far from being the preserve only of writers, is today a common resource. But they strive also, and sometimes with a persistence and thoroughness which lends a strange character to the denunciation, to set out the proofs of their case, going into infinite detail and accompanying their letters with a multitude of exhibits – trial reports, legal documents, personal letters, acknowledgements of the receipt of registered letters, etc. On the other hand, so as to give their denunciation a general validity, they endeavour to de-individualise the actors by substituting abstract synecdoches for physical individuals (sometimes using an identifying nickname, for example, and sometimes an idealised abstraction like 'the bosses' for the superior who occupies the persecutor's place). Finally, to magnify the drama which preoccupies them and to make it clear that their plea is disinterested and undertaken for the common good, frequently they compare what they call their 'personal history' to the series of great affairs whose scale touched the whole social body and thus assumed an explicitly 'political' form. Through these connections they seek in particular to link themselves with the Dreyfus affair, which is today the paradigm of the affair form and which, as Elisabeth Claverie notes, is prefigured by the affairs taken up by Voltaire.

4.6 The metaphysics of justice

In orientating itself towards an investigation, denunciation must also mobilise those resources which are put to work by people acting in situations in which their sense of justice is questioned. In fact, as we have seen in denunciation the unfortunate is constituted as a *victim*. The sufferings which overwhelm him are imputed to a third person. It is by this very process that, in this topic, the distinction essential for a politics of pity can be made between two kinds of suffering. On the one hand, there is ordinary suffering with as it were an anthropological dimension and, as we say, inherent in the human condition, like the death from old age of a loved relative for example. We may regret such suffering while recognising the inevitability which makes it politically irrelevant. On the other hand, there is suffering we consider to be avoidable, like the death of a previously healthy child due to famine for example, and for which it therefore seems legitimate to search for someone responsible.

On its own investigation cannot establish and ground a connection between the unfortunate's suffering and the persecutor's good fortune, especially when the person identified as being responsible is far away and the accusation is based on lengthy causal chains. Investigation must then call upon a *principle of equivalence* which makes possible a higher level of generality that enables two *apparently* distant conditions to be brought together. The rhetoric of denunciation thus makes great use of a comparison based upon an equivalence which may remain implicit. Consider, for example, a televised report on life in a Rio de Janeiro shanty-town. The proposal of commitment addressed to the spectator is particularly clearly orientated towards indignation if representations of poverty are contrasted with images of idleness and good fortune in the luxury apartment blocks on level ground adjoining the hillside shanty-towns.

The equivalences needed to establish these links may be taken from the system in which people are inserted when in the course of disputes in which violence is kept at bay they engage in criticism or justify themselves against criticisms, that is to say when they find themselves within a *regime of justice.* Justification in this regime is based upon a metaphysics of the City which contains two distinct levels[21] and whose framework can be extracted from, as one among many examples, Rousseau's *The Social Contract,* especially with its distinction between the will of all and the general will.[22] In *The Social Contract* legitimate political relations cannot be established directly on the basis of concrete interactions between people characterised by their affiliations and interests. In fact at this level, which is wholly subject to the realm of force, no interaction or arbitration is possible. To install just relationships between individuals their interactions must be mediatised by the relationship to a second order totality. This detour, and the sacrifices it calls for, are the only conditions which make civil peace possible without the domination of one party by another, that is to say, a civil peace which is just. The principal object of *The Social Contract* is to provide a rational foundation for this second order totality. It cannot be based upon a natural transcendence (as in the *domestic city*[23]). But neither can it be wholly identified with the statistical sum of empirical subjects defined by the set of their affiliations and interests, and nor yet can it be identified dynamically with the composition of their interactions. The solution, which serves as a model for most constructions of society established in the nineteenth century and for that of Durkheim in particular, consists in founding the possibility of a natural transcendence by defining two possible states of persons and, thereby, two possible ways of conceiving the whole formed by their joining together. The joining together of persons characterised in terms of the first state gives a sum of particular individuals defined by multiple affiliations and interests and immersed in antagonistic relationships.

However, individuals have the ability to escape from this selfish and wretched state and gain access to a second state in which they look not to their own interest but to the interest of all. The possibility of installing a just order depends on putting to work this ability which individuals can either cultivate or leave dormant. The system at the second level is actually the one in which the general will is formed. It contains the same human beings as at the first level, but in a different state in which each man turns towards the common good and puts aside the concerns and interests peculiar to himself as a particular individual.

In *The Social Contract,* the general will is not reducible to an adding together of particular wills. Particular individuals are committed neither by a pact of submission to whoever they choose as their chief, nor by a series of mutual pacts as in Hobbes, but by a 'reciprocal commitment of the public with particular individuals'. As Robert Dérathé emphasises, the 'same men' thus constitute 'the two contracting parties, but seen under different relations: as members of the sovereign and as particular individuals', so that 'everything takes place as if each contracted with himself'.[24] In Rousseau, the law is the expression of this disembodied sovereign:

law . . . considers subjects *en masse* and actions in the abstract, and never a particular person or action. Thus the law may indeed decree that there shall be privileges, but cannot confer them on anybody by name. It may set up several classes of citizens, and even lay down the qualifications for membership of these classes, but it cannot nominate such and such a person as belonging to them.[25]

This model can be generalised by replacing law, the canonical form of equivalence in what we have called a *civic city*, with the more general notion of *convention,* which enables us to shed light on the architecture common to different (merchant, industrial, opinion-based, etc.) cities all of which establish the political bond on a two-tiered metaphysics with a level above that occupied by individual beings and where there are conventions making equivalence between them possible. When the coordination of actions is broken by a disagreement, individuals can seek to return to agreement by making the conventions explicit in an argument and by verifying the state of equivalences by means of a reality test in the sense of a test whose validity depends on reference to objects, whether these be material objects like machines or trees, or immaterial objects like rules or customs. It is the connection between persons and objects under a single convention of equivalence which allows disputes to be settled by enabling agreement to be reached on the relationship of order between different persons faced with the same reality. Convergence of judgements is only secured to the extent that objects are regarded as being external to persons. The regime of justice thus rests on this convention of objectivity. In particular, it enables disputes to be settled by dispensing with reference to persons' internal states which are considered to be irrelevant insofar as they cannot be used in support of a common judgement.

But as these comments suggest, convergence of judgements in a test is not readily available to spectators. In fact it presupposes involvement in situations stabilised by the presence of objects to which the spectator does not have access. What we have called the *topic of denunciation* thereby presents a composite character. As we have seen, to a large extent it relies on the form of justification which prevails in a regime of justice. But, on the one hand, its slide towards the reality of an 'objective' world is carried out from a position of indignation the trace of which must be preserved in order to reduce the asymmetry of the report on suffering. On the other hand, in the rhetoric of the test it deals with elements of a world which, not being ready to hand, constantly elude the test. It follows that in the absence of a principle of closure, there is a risk of the controversy becoming interminably unstable.

4.7 Criticism of denunciation

The indignant denunciation of a spectator who accuses is therefore open to criticism. We will quickly examine these criticisms. For the most part they turn on the question of the relationship between *denunciation* and *action*. But these criticisms go in different directions depending on whether we see denunciation as a form of *inaction* (speaking is not the same as acting) or *action* (speaking is acting).

Denunciation can be criticised as an empty substitute for action. At little expense, someone who makes a denunciation spares himself the costs of action. His commitment is not genuine. It is commitment only in *words*, which cost nothing and appease the spectator's moral unease without reducing the unfortunate's suffering in any way. Actually, two arguments are mixed together here. On the one hand there is an argument concerning the sacrifices accepted by someone who makes a denunciation, the costs or risks of the denunciation. On the other hand there is an argument concerning the effectiveness of denunciation, its ability to lessen the unfortunate's suffering. The first kind of argument seems to be fundamental. Above all, without necessarily taking into account its effectiveness, denunciation is recognised as a genuine commitment and thereby a respectable moral attitude if it can be shown that it represents some cost or risk to the person making it, as might be the case in a totalitarian regime for example. It would seem that denunciation is more often denigrated as empty words in democratic regimes where logically it would otherwise seem to have a greater chance of being effective since its diffusion is easier and the political authorities are supposed to be more sensitive to public opinion. No doubt the reason for this is that, in the former case, distant sympathy is as it were relayed by commitment in situations in which the spectator appears to have the features of an actor because he faces difficulties (in listening to Radio London under the Occupation one was no longer a 'passive' audience because listening broke a ban and involved risks).

Conversely, denunciation which encounters no resistance can easily be discredited as 'superficial', 'conventional' or 'ritual' because it can be reduced to a clandestine form of unanimous indignation disguised as enlightened indignation. The criticism of empty words finally comes down to revealing the hypocrisy of the person making a denunciation whose indignation cannot be authentic because he is not really *affected* by the unfortunate's suffering. This criticism is more likely to be considered if it can be shown that the denouncer does not *share* the unfortunate's suffering. He does not live the same life as the unfortunate and does not have the same experiences. In this case it is precisely because the denouncer has nothing in common with those he seeks to defend and is not directly affected by their suffering that his commitment may be suspected of being phoney. His simulated concern is motivated solely by the desire for social esteem. The denouncer, especially when he is distant from the unfortunate, may additionally be charged with 'irresponsibility' in the sense that his accusations cost him nothing because he is safe but may provoke reprisals on the unfortunate whose cause he claims to defend.

As we see in the case of Tolstoy, which Robert Wuthnow refers to in the introduction to his book on voluntary action in the United States,[26] the question arises of how far we must go in our identification with unfortunates before our concern is seen to be genuine. Is it enough to dress like a peasant for example? To bake our own bread? Or (the question comes up with respect to Gandhism) should we weave our own clothes? Or again, to take a more recent example, should we live in a shanty-town? But the question can be pushed even further. Should we live in the centre of the shanty-town or on the edge? Should we live in a cardboard hovel or in prefabricated shacks? And so on. There are no limits to that form of criticism inherent in the operations of a politics of pity which denounces false concern on the grounds that the committed volunteer does not truly experience the unfortunate's suffering. It cannot be brought to a conclusion by a test. Either the witness is himself an unfortunate and he can always be accused of basically acting 'just like everyone else' in defending his selfish interest. Or a distance is maintained between his fate and the unfortunate's for whom he testifies and the charge of falseness can always be revived. This can be seen, for example, in the Jacobin and then the Marxist version of this argument which has served as a prop for an unlimited politics of suspicion. The unmasking of a trace of privilege secretly inscribed in the innermost part of individuals who 'apparently' have the greatest devotion to the cause of the people has always been used to discredit, exclude or condemn militants on the grounds of their real bourgeois origins or, as in the case of the kulaks for example, on the grounds of origins which have been invented to serve the needs of accusation.

But there is a more direct way to link denunciation to communal indignation by unmasking the hidden link which connects the denouncer to the victim in a way which shows that his claim to be an impartial spectator actually disguises a clannish solidarity. One will then endeavour to show that far from the denouncer being as he claims concerned by the unfortunate's suffering, he is in fact filled with the passion for denunciation. This criticism holds at least implicitly that it is an established fact that denunciation is not 'innocent' and that it has real effects. In this case criticism will focus not so much on the denunciation's effectiveness or ineffectiveness in improving the unfortunate's lot, as on the accusation. Denunciation is criticised in terms of its connection with accusation. The reproach may be that under the cover of reducing the suffering of unfortunates denunciation permits an acceptable and hypocritical expression of the spirit of revenge, of envy or, as in Nietzsche's *On the Genealogy of Morality*, of the resentment felt by the weak toward the strong. The principal argument is then that under the appearance of struggling against suffering denunciation actually succeeds only in increasing it and disseminating it throughout the social body, since its accusations create other sufferings and other unfortunates.

A well-known figure of the counter revolution can be detected here[27] and, in particular, the argument developed against *les enragés,* the *sans-culottes* and even more frequently against Saint-Just and Robespierre, whose discourses are for Hannah Arendt the most striking demonstration of the political use of pity, with their references to '*le peuple*' who are identified with '*les malheureux',* to the 'compassionate zeal', to 'that imperious impulse which attracts us towards *les hommes faibles*', to 'the capacity to suffer with "the immense class of the poor"'.[28] We need think only of Chateaubriand's portrait of 'Saint Robespierre' in his *Mémoires d'outre-tombe*, describing this 'executioner who speaks with tenderness of God, misfortune, tyranny and the scaffold in order to convince people that he kills only the guilty, and then only out of virtue'. The transformation of pity into indignation, and then into denunciation and accusation, is linked to its consequences at the level of action, that is to say to the processes of the Terror, to the 'government of fear, which Robespierre portrayed in theory as a government of virtue'.[29] One of the legacies of the Terror, which 'poisoned all subsequent revolutionary history and, beyond that, all political life in nineteenth-century France' until in the 1870s the republicans 'conquered their own demons and presented a pacified version of their great ancestors from which the specter of the guillotine had been exorcised',[30] was to set off a first, deep and lasting crisis of denunciation to which we will return when we examine the formation of an *aesthetic topic* in the nineteenth century. (The second crisis of denunciation, at work today, followed the collapse of the communist regimes.)

4.8 Denunciation and its critics

It will be noticed that the stimulus of criticism has not been without effects and that it helped give rise to the formation of secondary elaborations which have made the position of denunciation more complex and so at the same time both more defensible and solid (arguments have been forged to respond to detractors), but also more fragile, because the extension of networks, the lengthening of connections, and the multiplication of mediations which have to be secured in order to make an accusation stick, increase the number of points on to which doubts and challenges can be hooked.

One way to parry the criticism that denunciation of a victim's ill-treatment is *in fact* subordinate to an accusation (rather than seeing accusation as a secondary consequence of the defence of a victim) and the principal effect, indeed hidden 'function' of which is to create new victims and thereby increase and disseminate suffering under the guise of wanting to relieve it, consists in desingularising the accusation. In this figure, accusation is shifted from *persons* on to larger de-individualised entities such as *systems* or *structures*. This form of accusation, which is found already in Rousseau and revolutionary discourse, is formulated most explicitly in Marxism. Its advantage is that by means of a requirement of *generalisation* it is connected to a politics of pity without too much difficulty. The retention of singularities, which are necessary to achieve an effect of pity, is justified within a logic of *representation*, in the sense both of an exemplification and of the political representation of a collectivity by an individual. Particular unfortunates who arouse pity, and particular persecutors against whom indignation is directed, are staged as extremely general representatives of an unjust system. Moreover, the transformation of an individual or communal accusation into a general denunciation referring to a supra-individual entity is of particular interest to sociology inasmuch as it doubtless plays a not inconsiderable role, at the very origin of our discipline, in establishing the notion of society which was distinguished from the old understanding (the good society) at the end of the seventeenth century and comes to designate a collectivity which can be spoken about without referring directly to the individuals who compose it.[31] However, a number of obstacles have to be overcome for such a construction to stand up. Without any attempt to be exhaustive (a task which would fill a library), we can recall some of the objections, particularly relevant to our subject, which have frequently been made either against the generalisation of accusation as such or to one or other of its supporting segments.

As once again Hannah Arendt suggests, with reference to Hegel, this construction presupposes a considerable enlargement of the spectator's perspective to the scale of a history which is observable from outside.[32] The principal reference of the spectator is always the suffering of human beings. However, he is no longer faced with an identifiable suffering individual but with an historical plan of systems from which can be drawn, for example, the representation of multiple sufferings (as when Marx and Engels, at the beginning of *The Communist Manifesto*, set out the procession of slaves, serfs and proletarians). The possibility of access to an external vantage point – which characterises the modern spectator as we have seen – remains central in the conception of the spectator of universal history whose strength of commitment for a cause rests always on an initial uncommitted position. However, with the extension of the area embraced by the spectator to the totality of historical time it becomes difficult to identify, the place from which access to this external vantage point is possible. It no longer suffices, as in Steele's metaphor, to hide oneself in the gallery of the theatre or to stroll through salons and inns in order to hear what is being said about town. As we know, *science*, *social* science, will be progressively recognised in the nineteenth century, especially in Marx and Durkheim, as precisely the only instance on the basis of which such *detachment* is possible and consequently as the *critical* instance *par excellence*.

But it turned out to be difficult to hold the bastion. In fact, a choice has to be made between two options, both of which provide weapons for a counter-attack. Either, in the first option, science is treated as an instance of truth which escapes both social criticism and history. The externality of the critical observation of society is thus secured. But by the same token large areas are subtracted from critical observation and the entities accused can find refuge in these areas. In fact, to shelter them from critical observation it is sufficient to increase the number and length of connections joining them to the sphere of scientific legality. Social science no longer has a hold on them. In the second option, which moreover is above all developed precisely in order to follow the accused entities into the city of knowledge in which they have found refuge, historical criticism is brought into the sphere of scientific legality and the external position on the basis of which criticism is carried out is itself quickly threatened. The external position is no longer protected, in fact, except by a frontier between *science* and *ideology* drawn within the sphere in which the claim to scientific legality is demonstrated in such a way as to distinguish between what is due to a *true* science from what is due to a *false* science. But this frontier is difficult to maintain, on the one hand because it must be consolidated with the same epistemological arguments as those of the adversary, and on the other hand because the isolation it secures lays it open to the accusation of it having the sole *function* of protecting the local interests of those who defend it. The unmasking of the interested character of the claim to universality is turned back against the instance from which it was effected.

The reorientation of accusation from *persons* to *systems* gives rise to a different order of difficulties linked to questions of the *subject* and *responsibility*. On the one hand it requires an anthropology of splitting based on complex mechanisms which are difficult to conceptualise and, above all, to reinforce against doubt. Individual persons become *agents* who, somewhat in the manner of the Hegelian hero, actually serve the system while thinking they are realising their own ends. They must therefore be split – the right hand not knowing what the left is doing – by means of an internal device which can take different forms: the unconscious, bad faith, etc. The relationship between their actions and their intentions is loose and even nonexistent. The bearers of the structure are not personally responsible for the entities of which they are the props. One of the principal advantages of the transition from persons to the system is precisely that it reduces the weight of accusation on persons. But accusation cannot abandon all orientation towards responsibility without falling into self-contradiction. It is the very possibility of things happening otherwise and, consequently, the existence of responsibility, which distinguishes the denunciation of suffering about which it seems reasonable to be *indignant* from the attitude of *resignation* which prevails in the case of sufferings about which nothing can be done.

The kind of responsibility most easily connected with a systemic accusation is *collective responsibility*. But it is difficult to stabilise this ambivalent figure which we have already come across in connection with the passive responsibility of the distant spectator. If the accusation really is *collective* and equally addressed to all simply by virtue of their participation in a system, then one tends to get away from the register of responsibility. To keep one foot in this register, we must allow the possibility of individuals escaping the constraints of the system which introduces at least two classes of agents, those fully responsible and those either not responsible or less so. Responsibility is saved, but at the cost of a reduction in its collective character.

On the other hand, this solution requires that we hark back to the anthropology of splitting by implanting mechanisms within the interiority of individuals enabling bad faith to be overcome through knowledge and an *awareness*. Knowledge may lead to either a passive or an active responsibility although the difference between these two forms tends to diminish when one extends the links which attach the agent to the unfortunate. Passive responsibility: certain agents close their eyes to the existence of suffering; others keep them open (which gives them the status of actors).

Active responsibility: certain agents *realise* that they are themselves in a causal relationship with this suffering as agents of an oppressive system. If the idea of collective responsibility is to stand up then we must presuppose a division between culpable agents and those who escape accusation. But one thereby loses the principal advantage of a systemic derivation of the accusation. As Paul Ricoeur wrote in 1949 on the appearance in French of Karl Jasper's work on *German Guilt* and the problem of collective reparation, 'the accusation of collective guilt always ventures into an uncertain zone where it is caught between the two dangers of legal arbitrariness and moral phariseeism'. The danger of legal arbitrariness arises from 'a lack of reference to a definition of what is immediately connected with the crime without being itself criminal'. With regard to the 'otherwise indefinable moral signification' of collective sanction, 'it strikes in a statistical manner the individual acts of the preparation, complicity and tolerance of the crime which cannot be assessed in their individuality'. Accusation is only sound, Ricoeur adds, 'if it is restricted to the definite and limited plane of a *criminal* accusation against individuals'. Beyond that the problem arises of 'guilt in history' which ought not to be approached from the point of view of a 'single public' which ponders 'the misdeeds of history in general' as if we could abstract from 'historically concrete situations' and forget that such a public cannot be detached from the 'plane of *argument*', that is to say from a 'context where there are accused and accusers'.[33]

5

The topic of sentiment

5.1 The unfortunate's gratitude

We come now to the second possibility for the spectator of distant suffering when he no longer goes down the road of *indignation, denunciation* and *accusation* in his sympathy with the *resentment* felt by an unfortunate towards a persecutor, but takes the other route set out by Adam Smith and sympathises with the unfortunate's *gratitude* inspired by the intervention of a *benefactor*.

Like the persecutor, the benefactor does not need to be present in person in the picture in order to lend his weight to the orientation of commitment. In the case of indignation we saw that it is precisely the processes of denunciation by which indignation, as emotion, is orientated towards an action, which make necessary the search for a persecutor whose true nature (individual or system) may be uncertain and subject to debate and dispute. The moment pity takes the definite form of indignation therefore is the most important moment of bifurcation setting off the sequence which leads to the identification and accusation of a persecutor. Likewise, the moment pity takes the definite form of *tender-heartedness* the route is marked out which turns away from the search for a persecutor, and so from accusation, and directs attention to the possibility of *an act of charity* performed by a *benefactor.*

Let us note at the outset that orientation towards either one or the other of these alternatives can neither be thought of as an entirely unconstrained choice nor as wholly determined by the guidance of a programme inscribed once and for all in the spectator's bodily objectivity (as would be the case if his attitude depended only on 'internalised values' or 'unconscious interests' for example). Without a doubt, if we are to understand how the spectator's commitment is specified we must take account of the way in which the actor we have called the *agent* is picked out in the scene in which the unfortunate's suffering is *shown*. The benefactor may be represented and given prominence, as, for example, when a doctor or a nurse, voluntary workers and disinterested people, are filmed or photographed leaning over the body of a wounded unfortunate or giving a starving child the food which will ensure its survival.

Let us open once more Vicky Goldberg's book, this time at p. 183.[1] The photograph is taken from a report published in *Life* in 1951 on the charitable action of itinerant midwives who work among the poor populations of the Southern United States. It shows a woman in a nurse's blouse, a stethoscope around her neck, leaning over the body of a black woman who is giving birth. However, the scene is unusual because we are not in a hospital but in an improvised dispensary set up in a Baptist church. A simple curtain separates the scene of childbirth from the space given over to religious activities, visible in the background, with a crowd of faithful blacks seated on wooden benches (the photograph was taken from above, no doubt from the gallery which is traditional in Protestant churches). The proposal of commitment is fairly precise here. However, although it is focused on the description of the poverty of Blacks in the South – the cause of which we might well seek to discover in order to identify and accuse those responsible – it includes no direct reference to denunciation or accusation. In this case the spectator's sympathy is thus clearly directed towards the benefactrice, towards the charitable action she performs for the unfortunate woman to whom she gives her most urgent care and, as a result of this, at least indirectly, to the gratitude the unfortunate may show her in return. But the place of the benefactor is not always so clearly defined, so that its display must make a stronger appeal to the spectator's tendencies which may lead him either to an emotional state pointing in the direction of charity – which puts him as it were in the position of ensuring its performance himself – or, through the transformation of an initial pity, to indignation, pointing towards the identification and denunciation of identities and causes.

This is the case with two other photographs appearing in the same chapter on the use of photography to advance social reform. The first, on p. 165, dating from 1863, shows emancipated slaves who Colonel George A. Hanks has snatched from their fate in Louisiana. It represents a black child in the middle of white children, but the Colonel, the child's benefactor, does not appear in the photo. This leaves open the possibility of being moved by this peaceful scene and, indirectly, by the Colonel's kindness or, on the contrary, of being indignant at the inhumanity of the great landowners of the South. The same openness is found in a very famous photograph taken by Lewis Hine in 1908 which represents a little girl of about eight years old working in a cotton mill (p. 175). The charm of her face, her pose, and her wretched clothes may evoke tender-hearted sympathy while, by contrast, the inhuman force of the immense job of weaving to which she is in some sense chained, may move the spectator to indignation against mechanisation and, extending the chain of imputations, against the inhuman capitalism which devours children. Finally, the little girl's manifest resignation, her apparent lack of revolt, is what leaves open the possibility of different ways for the spectator to become emotionally involved. In fact, in order to introduce the possibility of someone filling the benefactor's place, it would be sufficient perhaps for the unfortunate to be shown as open to gratitude or, in an even clearer way, as expecting a benefit, as when he begs, or as the recipient of help which must reach him. Staying with *The Theory of Moral Sentiments*, we turn then to an interactionist schema by approaching commitment as an *event*. Using the same approach as the one we adopted for the topic of denunciation, we confine ourselves for the moment to a description of the resources available to the spectator when he takes this path, and to some hypotheses on the way in which these resources have been fixed in forms and, specifically, in literary genres.

5.2 The sentiment of urgency

As we suggested in our reading of *The Theory of Moral Sentiments*, when the spectator who sympathises with the unfortunate's gratitude goes down the road of sentiment, the political emotion which is proposed to him, that is to say pity, is not given in the form of indignation but in the form of *tender-heartedness*. Just like indignation, this emotional posture can open the way to the deployment of a form of public speech which avoids the *ban on the that's how it is*. At first it even seems particularly favourable to the speaker's implication in the report given by the spectator of the spectacle of suffering. Actually, in this instance the spectator does not let his indignation speak but expresses the concern aroused in any *sensitive* being who considers the suffering endured by an unfortunate. In the account he gives he must therefore finely blend the representation of the person suffering and the representation of a third person who recognises, shares and responds to that suffering.

The means available to the spectator for setting out a discourse of tender-heartedness are radically different, however, from those available to someone who speaks out of indignation. In fact he cannot resort to denunciation and accusation. A first consequence of this, which may seem to be an obstacle to the politicisation of suffering within the framework of this topic, is that outside of the topic of denunciation it is not easy to draw the line separating generic suffering, inherent in the human condition as it were, from those scandalous cases of suffering which deserve to become causes. Take, for example, the case of an old internee of the camps, an elderly woman who is now struck by cancer and who attributes her illness to the suffering she endured in the camps. If we go along with her interpretation, and if doctors support her claim, her illness could give rise to political indignation which woud not be the case if her interpretation was rejected by experts and, like any other sick person, she could reasonably only expect the concern of her close relatives. Nonetheless, the distinction is not abandoned in a topic of sentiment, only now it is marked by the intensity of concern and by a discursive attitude which points bluntly to action in such a way as to break clearly with the sad resignation which might prevail in the face of inevitable miseries.

An essential figure for the expression of this posture is that of *urgency*. Whereas in indignation bodily resources are brought together to express an *anger* which overcomes the muteness of raw emotion by pointing to the demonstration of threat and force – which gives a real presence to accusation by making the possibility of reprisals palpable – in the topic of sentiment bodily resources are mobilised for an expressionist gesture of urgency. The emotion which betrays pity in the intonation of a voice breaking between sobs is mastered by a speed of delivery and a contraction of expression and of the whole body, which is ready as it were, from within the calm immobility of a television panel, to leap to the aid of the unfortunate whose suffering cannot wait, completely tensed in an imitation of action. There is no time to lose.

In contrast with indignation, the topic of sentiment dispenses with denunciation and accusation. Even if the unfortunate's suffering is not held to be fatal (which we have seen would lead to resignation and political inaction), and even if it does not fall outside of the world of responsibilities and causes, it is not part of this topic to track down and punish those responsible. Because it does not insist on accusation, the topic of sentiment, unlike the topic of indignation, is not constrained therefore to unravel an apparatus of objective, material proofs and so does not attach great importance to things. More centrally, it is not deployed within a metaphysics of justice of the kind rapidly summarised in the previous chapter, in which the need to ground criticism by revealing what turns an unfortunate into a victim leads to an ascent from the logical level occupied by persons and objects to the level of conventions of equivalence which stabilise their relationships and which when activated allow the equitable or unjust character of these relationships to be checked.

5.3 The metaphysics of interiority

Nevertheless, the topic of sentiment is not foreign to all metaphysics, but its metaphysics is a metaphysics of *interiority*. In this it is distinguished from a metaphysics of justice in which internal states cannot be the objects of truth. Reference to these states cannot then be taken into account in a judgement in the absence of an instance external to persons – like grace, for example, from which great inspiration may be drawn – from which these states or some of them proceed. In this case the internal state is treated as the internal inscription of an exteriority, as testifies the possibility allowed the inspired subject to report on his own states as if they were foreign to him. Only constructions of this kind, whose paradoxical character makes them quite fragile (particularly in view of the fact that their main convention is the rejection of conventions), enable reference to these states to be included within a judgement, relations of equivalence to be established between them and their insertion into ordered relationships.

Like a metaphysics of justice, a metaphysics of interiority also contains two levels. But the second level is not one of relations of equivalence with a bird's-eye view of people beset by disputes and threatened with dispersal. In a metaphysics of interiority the surface level is one of *superficial* relationships between people immersed in artificiality, illusion, conventional society life and, above all, separation and coldness. It is underpinned by a *deep* level to which anyone can gain access by looking inside themself. This is the level of the *heart*.[2] The spectator must not only be faced with unfortunates and see them from outside to be moved by their suffering, at the same time he must also return into himself, go inwards, and allow himself to *hear* what his *heart* tells him.

In a topic of sentiment the relationship of spectator and unfortunate is real, authentic and thereby *touching*, not when it is established superficially with regard to appearances, but when it is heart to heart, going from interiority to interiority. It is by leaving open the route to his heart, by not closing his heart, that the spectator can gain access, not to the manifest suffering of the unfortunate – without relevance and if it comes to it without reality – but to the suffering as it is gathered within the unfortunate's own heart. The relationship between spectator and unfortunate is established through the intuition which passes between hearts (mocked by Adam Smith in his opposition to Shaftesbury's sentimentalism[3]). It is also by reproducing this process that the spectator interests others in the unfortunate's suffering, others with whom he shares his emotion, who he *touches* in turn by evoking everything which *touched* him. Coming together in a group around a cause, the formation of a collectivity, does not take place

therefore through a convergence of *judgements*, as in a topic of denunciation, but through an emotional contagion which transmits the *sociable*
from interiority to interiority. It is precisely because emotion submerges the
person speaking who makes himself present in the report, that the spectator transmits by touching.

Thus, emotion creates truth. If it does not need to ground accusations on
material proofs, the topic of sentiment none the less does not hold itself
outside of reality. But access to truth in this topic is arrived at neither by
the argued exploration of conventional principles nor by connection with
generalisable objects, but by a revelatory externalisation of interiority.
Truth is *manifestation*. When the spectator opens his heart to accept the
trace left by suffering in the unfortunate's heart, it is at the same time a
moment of the greatest *emotion* and the moment of truth. The quality of
the emotion, which does not deceive, is the test of reality which makes it
possible to allay an always possible doubt about the authenticity of the
suffering endured by the unfortunate.

Emotion, and specifically that particular emotion we have called tender-
heartedness, therefore plays a central role in this topic. Taking on the role
which is played by a judgement which descends from equivalence to cases
in a metaphysics of justice, in a topic of sentiment emotion assumes the
entire weight of the relationship between the two levels of exteriority and
interiority. Emotion here is understood as an *externalisation of the interior*.
What is inside, that is to say real, *manifests* its *presence* in the exterior. This
manifestation possesses the ambiguous and almost contradictory character of an epiphany.[4] It is actually *manifestation* in one domain using the
means of this domain, that is to say the means of the body (its agitation,
its secretions, its tears, its nerves, its sweat, etc.), of a reality of *a different
domain*. Now this manifestation is not at all an objectification. Interiority
is not separated from its origins when it reveals itself. It does not rejoin the
world of objects even as a species of signs. It is not inscribed within the
world like a text which is available to everyone through a reading, interpretation or decoding. It is only ever by making the detour through one's own
interiority, by following the *route of the heart*, that one can put oneself in
the presence of an interiority which manifests itself.

5.4 The welling-up of emotion

Because emotion establishes a paradoxical link between two separate
orders it is also understood by a topic of sentiment to be by definition *unintentional*. Intention, which manifests itself in plans of action, is a state
which is directed outwards and arises from the level of exteriority. The

externalisation of interiority projects emotion on to the plane of intentions and submerges or overwhelms it. The not merely involuntary but above all unintentional character of emotion which eludes expectations in principle, which cannot be anticipated and still less desired, and whose mode of appearance is to *well up*, is thus our only guarantee that it truly comes from the heart, from within, and consequently that it is really genuine.

Subject to the test of the heart, we can only declare the externalisation of interiority to be realised through experience of its internal effects. It follows that in this topic the characteristic of being *moving* cannot be attributed to objects and discourses in the way that properties like colour, clarity or precision can. In fact the quality of being moving cannot maintain stable relationships with other attributes (like age, sex or even the presence of a reference to suffering and death for example). A person cannot be said to be 'moving' in the way they are said to be 'dark haired'. It is appropriately attributed not to objects but only to what are by definition uncertain *events* constituted by externalisations of interiority, and consequently to the tests themselves.

The constraints governing the test in a topic of sentiment have a paradoxical effect on the use of the qualifying term *moving* when it is applied in a judgement concerning a representation or a report. The most radical criticism of a representation or a report in this topic consists in showing that its moving character has been written into it in the fashion of an attribute (like the colour red of a car for example), which amounts to disclosing an intention to move. This is especially the case for representations of suffering affecting real persons, as is clearly shown by an analysis of the criticism of television journalism which condemns, for example, contrived 'effects' or 'the amassing of means' (*Le Monde,* 5 October 1992), the 'sensational' (*Télérama,* 12 September 1992), 'miserabilist images' (*Télé Loisirs, 10* October 1992), and praises, on the contrary, 'a camera which knows how to be tactful, which is what gives [this report] all its emotional force' (*Télérama,* 30 September 1992), and which 'shows modestly' (*Télérama,* 12 September 1992), etc. Representation designed to move fails in its aim because emotion is anticipated by the 'visible strings' fixing it to the images, sounds and words in the way a property is attached to a product. Deciphered as an attribute, or as a code, and as a result set at a distance in an object, the *moving* is no longer something which manifests itself; it blocks the event constituted by the paradoxical presence of interiority in the exterior.

Criticism of the sensational or emotional, which we will come across again when we consider the problem of sentimentalism, clearly depends on the spectator's ability to decipher. Here again we can turn to Thomas

Pavel's analysis of narrative conventions (see section 3.8. above). The reader's expectations are guided by preconventions which generate regularities. A competent reader of the novel is familiar with the regularities associated with a genre and knows that only expectations orientated in a certain direction will be satisfied. Coordination thus depends upon a prior familiarity with these regularities. But when, as in the present case concerning emotion in the presence of suffering, the preconvention is the refusal or superseding of conventions, critical vigilance will depend on the spectator's ability to identify regularities (pathetic music accompanying a picture of an unfortunate's distress, for example) and will be sharper the more the spectator is 'informed', the more able he is to identify conventional effects which go unnoticed by a 'novice' spectator. The critic will be all the more inclined to reveal the 'strings' behind the representation if he thinks he is addressing a more sophisticated reader, that is to say, generally one with a higher level of education. The same report may be judged differently in different magazines, 'tactful' in one and 'sensationalist' in another, according to the spectator's presumed degree of competence. It will be noted that these comments are as valid for works of fiction as they are for reports which, like documentaries, claim to represent reality, except that the unmasking of the *artifice* employed to arouse emotion is only condemned on aesthetic grounds in the first case whereas it is also, or above all, condemned morally in the second, for reasons to which we will return when we consider the criticisms to which a topic of sentiment must respond.

Only the analysis of the metaphysics of interiority underlying the topic of sentiment enables us to reconstruct the common sense meaning given to the emotions – and especially to so-called altruistic emotions – and to appreciate their coherence rather than consigning them to physiological automatism, irrationality or, alternatively, denouncing them as indirect and so hypocritical means of acting strategically towards someone. The latter approach, however, is the only one usually adopted by sociological attempts to apprehend emotions and rescue them from the monopoly of physiology and even psychology. Sociologists have arrived at definitions of emotion which, while different in different traditions, share the fact of breaking with the meaning that common sense recognises in emotion, and in that kind of emotion in particular – tender-heartedness – which is the focus of our interest here. Sociological efforts in the domain of the emotions effectively concentrate on two points. On the one hand, the essential aim is to show, against physiological interpretations, that emotions are socially constructed and consequently are socially and historically variable.[5] This is a compromise solution that consists in identifying primary emotions with a universal character (fear, anger, depression, satisfaction) which function as the basis for the elaboration of secondary, historically and socially variable emotions.[6] This is also the compromise solution which concludes H. Wallbott's and K. Scherer's great study of students from twenty-seven different countries which, while recognising considerable stability in emotions in the different countries studied, brings to light significant differences, especially in their intensity and duration.[7] The second axis of sociological activity and social psychology concentrates on questioning the spontaneous, unintentional and, as it were, gratuitous character of emotions in order to highlight their strategic aspects. Far from escaping the will, the emotions are presented in these works as managed and even manipulated by actors who have undergone an implicit or systematic apprenticeship. This is the conclusion, for example, of Arlie Hoschild's research, inspired by Ervin Goffman, on what must be called a very particular population, that of air hostesses, for whom emotional control is part of their professional training.[8] The same strategic aim, but in this case directed towards someone else, inspires recent research in which the emphasis is placed on the *rational* character of emotions in the management of interaction in situations where conscious interest presupposes that directly selfish tendencies be overcome.[9] These different approaches share a semiological definition of emotions which can be traced back to Darwin, since they are basically interested in the emotions inasmuch as they constitute signs of a language for producing a perlocutory effect. If they have the advantage of connecting the question of the emotions to an already established problematic like that of rationality, their limitation is that they no longer allow actors to grasp the meaning of emotions which these approaches denounce as illusion. For if, for example, we hand over the tears of love to disillusion when we link their volume and rhythm to hormonal changes, we have not advanced beyond the thematic of illusion when these tears are described as a language or as a code made up of recordable, interpretable and manipulable signs within communication strategies aiming, either consciously or not, to produce perlocutory effects. Semiological interactionism is, in this sense, no better than physiology for enabling us to stay close to people's intuition while setting it in an analysis which is subject to the constraints of internal coherence, that is to say for treating it within an anthropological perspective.

5.5 A window on the place of the heart

How will the spectator who has taken the route of sentiment give free rein to his tender-heartedness and convey it in public speech? By blending two kinds of report, one which describes the unfortunate's suffering and which, turned towards the outside world, can be termed an *external report*, and another which can be called an *internal report* in the sense that, devoted to inner life, it seeks to depict what takes place in the heart of the reporter, the states through which the heart passes (sadness, tender-heartedness, hope, joy, etc.). Thus, it is in a mode of expression which mixes a depiction of inner life and a description of the outside world that the person speaking figures in a statement which expresses the suffering of a distant unfortunate without infringing what we have called the prohibition on realism.

Where will the speaker find the discursive resources required for this process? Not in the pamphlet or political essay, as was the case for the topic of denunciation, but in a form which first developed at roughly the same time as the entry of pity into politics, that is to say in the novel. It is by work on the form of the novel that discursive techniques were established whose novelty did not so much consist in opening up the field of a representation of inner life (which other forms, and especially mystical writing, made possible with a high degree of precision and complexity) as in harmoniously mixing together different registers whose markers are progressively effaced so that they can be smoothly and uninterruptedly linked together; the register of narrative for example, which reports a story (the deeds and gestures of characters cast into the world), of inner life (the thoughts and inner states of these characters), or even of digression which, deriving from the essay, allows the opinions and generalisations of the narrator to be inserted within a narrative.

Without going into too much detail, we can remind ourselves of some of the solutions brought to this problem by calling upon the meticulous description given by Dorrit Cohn in her book on 'narrative modes for presenting consciousness in fiction'.[10] Studies of the novel are often underpinned by an implicit evolutionist scheme which, by according a privilege to the representation of 'facts of consciousness', ranks the forms of the novel along an historical vector going from narration, of the story or of history, to the techniques of the 'stream of consciousness' developed by James Joyce after Edouard Dujarlogue (*Les Lauriers sont coupés,* a novel written in 1887 and republished with corrections and a preface by Valery Larbaud in 1924). But the forms which interest us are neither the utterances characterised by the third person and past tense that Emile Benveniste calls 'historical' and which are narratives and objective (in contrast with 'discourse' in which a speaker seeks to influence a hearer),[11] nor the wholly subjectivist forms – with their unknowable external world – like the interior monologue in which an absent narrator's mental states are set out, but rather those intermediate forms which set reports of inner life within histories or tales.

The technical problem is posed differently depending on whether we are dealing with a history in the third person, with its omniscient narrator who is not represented within the work, or with a narrative in the first person (fictional biography or epistolary novel). In the novel in the third person, the omniscient narrator acts as if, taking up the myth to which Laurence Sterne refers in *Tristram Shandy* and that Dorrit Cohn puts in the introduction of her book, Vulcan had opened a window 'on the place of the heart' when modelling his clay statue. To gain access to the inner life of a human being it is enough 'to have taken a chair and gone softly, as you would to a dioptrical bee-hive, and looked in, – viewed the soul stark naked; – observed all her motions – her machinations; – traced all her maggots from their first engendering to their crawling forth; – watched her loose in her frisks, her gambols, her capricios; and after some notice of her more solemn deportment, consequent upon such frisks, &c – then taken your pen and ink and set down nothing but what you have seen, and could have sworn to'.[12] Dorrit Cohn describes three major procedures for opening a window on the heart in the novel written in the third person. *Psycho-narration*, which is the narrator's discourse on the character's inner life: *he knew that he was late*; *quoted monologue*, which is the character's mental disourse: *(he thought) I am late;* and finally, *narrated monologue,* a character's mental discourse taken over by the narrator's discourse: *he was late.* The intermediate form, narrated monologue, is distinguished from psycho-narration by 'the absence of mental verbs' and 'tense and person separate it from quoted monologue, even when the latter is used in the Joycean manner, without explicit quotation or introduction'.[13]

Methods for entering into inner life appear relatively late in the novel in the third person and develop above all in the second half of the nineteenth century. In the eighteenth century, novels in the third person, in which 'a hyperactive narrator deals with a multitude of characters and situatons', are devoted most of all to the 'manifest behaviour' of the characters. In Fielding, for example, the narrator displays a 'refusal to look inside'. Speaking about the feelings of one of the female characters in *Tom Jones,* Fielding writes: 'these words, which perhaps contributed to form a dream of no very pleasant kind; but as she never revealed this dream to any one, so the reader cannot expect to see it related here.' The inner life of characters is constantly covered over by 'the presence of a vocal authorial narrator', of a narrator who puts his own comments and generalisations into his story as he would in an essay. With regard to the fairly rare quoted monologue, it is often preceded by the phrase 'he cried' which transposes into the novel the theatrical convention of the monologue, uttered by an actor who speaks for himself (*in petto*), alone on the stage. Actually, in the period with which we are particularly concerned, it is mostly narrations in the first person, fictional autobiographies or epistolary novels, which contain extended forays into the inner life of the characters.[14] We will focus on those forms in which a language for describing inner life is established together with a genuine pedagogy of feelings and introspection. These forms are worked out in the essay,[15] and the autobiography,[16] but are diffused most of all through those novels constructed on the model of the autobiography which were extremely successful at the end of the eighteenth century.

The first-person narrator in fictional autobiography has the double privilege of being both subject and object at the same time and he can therefore question himself and play the role of what Dorrit Cohn calls a 'lucid narrator turning back on a past self steeped in ignorance, confusion, and delusion'.[17] The result is a composite flux or, as Jean Starobinski says of Rousseau's *Confessions* (but which is also valid for fictional autobiographies), a 'mixed entity' which he dubs, taking up the categories of Emile Benveniste already referred to, a 'history-discourse',[18] which is half-way between impersonal memoires and pure monologue. It is this kind of form that we find in Sterne's *Tristram Shandy* (an autobiography which is so fictional that it ends with the birth of the narrator) and which, endlessly mixing narration, digression and forays into the narrator's thoughts, comes close to being an immense and delirious monologue.

Take, for example, chapter 2 of book II in which the narrator answers an imaginary critic who reproaches him for having introduced confusion into the description of the mental states of his uncle Toby:

– How, in the name of wonder! could your uncle Toby, who, it seems was a military man, and whom you have represented as no fool, – be at the same time such a confused, pudding-headed, muddle-headed fellow, as – Go look . . .
– Therefore I answer thus:
Pray, Sir, in all the reading which you have ever read, did you ever read such a book as Locke's *Essay upon the Human Understanding?* – Don't answer me rashly – because many, I know, quote the book, who have not read it, – and many have read it who understand it not; – If either of these is your case, as I write to instruct, I will tell you in three words what the book is. – It is a history. – A history! of who? what? where? when? Don't hurry yourself. – It is a history-book, Sir, (which may, possibly recommend it to the world) of what passes in a man's own mind; and if you will say so much of the book, and no more, believe me, you will cut no contemptible figure in a metaphysic circle.
But this by the way.
Now if you will venture to go along with me, and look down into the bottom of the matter, it will be found that the cause of obscurity and confusion, in the mind of man, is threefold.
Dull organs, dear Sir, in the first place. Secondly, slight and transient impressions

made by objects when the said organs are not dull. And, thirdly, a memory like unto a sieve, not able to retain what it has received. – Call down Dolly your chamber-maid, and I will give you my cap and bell along with it, if I make not this matter so plain that Dolly herself should understand it as well as Malebranche.[19]

Lockean psychology, a comical description of which is given here, is also the construction which underpins the associationist unravelling of the work and the relationship the narrator has with himself. In the English novel of the middle of the eighteenth century, the relationship to interiority is carried out – as Morris Golden has shown[20] – within the framework of the Lockean scheme of the divided self: one self acts in response to the way in which he perceives signals coming from the external world, beset by the uncertainty and contingency of empirical situations; a reflexive self observes these processes, records them and questions them, often from a distance and with irony. By the same process the unity of the self is pro-blematised. It no longer derives from the position occupied in the hierar-chical order or chain of beings which makes up the universe. The search for the true self thus becomes a central task of this literature which is realised precisely in the to-ing and fro-ing between sensory experience and the inter-nal sense – *moral sense* or even *personal genius* – which both takes up and modifies experience. This is the way in which Richardson's *Clarissa* is sen-sitive both in the sense that she receives stimuli from the outside world with a particular acuteness which increases her suffering, and in the sense that, withdrawing into herself, she subjects these stimuli to the reflective judge-ment of her moral sense which is, as we know, particularly developed. The authentic self is the self which, in the manifestation of *sentiments*, carries out the synthesis of the divided selves.[21]

It is without question in Sterne's *A Sentimental Journey* that we find the most striking illustrations of the division of the self between an active self, orientated towards the external world, and a reflective self which, turned inwards, passes through the different states of a sensitive heart. Two exam-ples have the advantage for us of relating scenes in which Yorick, the nar-rator, comes face to face with misfortune. In the first, a 'poor monk of the order of St. Francis' comes begging into the room of the Calais inn where 'I had got sat down to my dinner upon a fricassee'd chicken.' The acting self closes his purse. 'The moment I cast my eyes upon him, I was predeter-mined not to give him a single sous; and accordingly I put my purse into my pocket.' The reflective self distances itself from the hardness of the acting self: 'there was something, I fear, forbidding in my look'; and without deviating from the line of conduct he had taken, already regrets it: 'I . . . think there was that in [his figure] which deserved better.' A touching description follows of the wretched state and modesty of the monk. But

Yorick's acting self remains inflexible; he accompanies his refusal with acerbic words. When the monk has left the scene, the reflective self takes charge of the narration once again to describe how his harshness had troubled Yorick's heart:

My heart smote me the moment he shut the door – Psha! said I with an air of carelessness, three several times – but it would not do: every ungracious syllable I had utter'd, crouded back into my imagination: I reflected, I had no right over the poor Franciscan, but to deny him: and that the punishment of that was enough to the disappointed without the addition of unkind language – I consider'd his grey hairs – his courteous figure seem'd to re-enter and gently ask me what injury he had done me? – and why I could use him thus – I would have given twenty livres for an advocate.[22]

In the second encounter with poverty Yorick shows himself to be more generous. Leaving the Montreuil inn, about to board his chaise, Yorick is surrounded by unfortunates and forced to deal with 'the sons and daughters of poverty'. Poor himself, he has little to give: 'A well-a-way! said I. I have but eight sous in the world, shewing them in my hand, and there are eight poor men and eight poor women for 'em.' A portrait of the different unfortunates follows and of the different ways, some more sensitive than others, in which Yorick is charitable to them. The narration proceeds in a constant to-ing and fro-ing between the description of the acts and an exploration of the *intentions* within each of the actors which qualifies the acts and, in departing from their external factuality, gives them their true meaning and value. In the charitable act the inner experience of the donor is brought into line with the inner experience of the recipient. The first 'poor tatter'd soul' immediately withdraws his claim. Yorick insists 'upon presenting him with a single sous, merely for his *politesse*'. The involvement with the second unfortunate is more complex since the donor modestly hides his generosity by becoming recipient: 'A poor little dwarfish brisk fellow . . . took his snuff-box out of his pocket, and generously offer'd a pinch on both sides of him . . . The poor little fellow press'd it upon them with a nod of welcomeness – *Prenez en – prenez,* said he, looking another way; so they each took a pinch – Pity thy box should ever want one! said I to myself; so I put a couple of sous into it – taking a small pinch out of his box, to enhance their value, as I did it – He felt the weight of the second obligation more than that of the first – 'twas doing him an honour – the other was only doing him a charity – and he made me a bow down to the ground for it.' All the sous are distributed when the most interesting character in the scene appears in the narration: a *pauvre honteux*, characterised, as such, by a discrepancy between the external action and the internal sentiment. The donor therefore must not only respond to a solicitation but also decipher intentions and explore inner states. This unchains his heart:

But in the eagerness of giving, I had overlook'd a *pauvre honteux*, who had no one to ask a sous for him, and who, I believed, would have perish'd, ere he could have ask'd one for himself: he stood by the chaise a little without the circle, and wiped a tear from a face which I thought had seen better days – Good God! said I – and I have not one single sous left to give him – But you have a thousand! cried all the powers of nature, stirring within me – so I gave him – no matter what – I am ashamed to say *how much*, now – and was ashamed to think, how little, then.'[23]

5.6 The vocabulary of sentiments

As we have just seen in Sterne, self-reflection is applied first of all to the exploration of sentiments and of sentiments of a *tender-hearted* kind in particular. To bring it into play within a narrative requires not only the establishment of new discursive structures, but also the creation and fixing of a new vocabulary which will permit an almost technically precise description of psychical facts and, of particular interest to us, of the different states which affect a heart sensitive to the spectacle of suffering. To describe this vocabulary we have an irreplaceable tool at our disposal: *Le vocabulaire du sentiment chez Jean-Jacques Rousseau*, produced under the direction of Michel Gilot and Jean Sgard.[24]

From the enormous vocabulary meticulously listed in all its occurrences by Gilot and Sgard, we take three terms to illustrate our theme: *to move (emouvoir), tender-heartedness (attendrissement), and tears (pleurs)*. In Rousseau, emotion is a fact of interiority, an 'internal agitation' which, as in Condillac, is like a movement of the senses brought about by an internally excited sentiment. It is involuntary, wells up, and takes hold of the subject like a force which upsets all his senses and completely overwhelms his entire being. However, on this very general conception which connects emotion to the whole universe of passions Rousseau particularly develops the analysis of the gentle, tender and altruistic emotions: those which engender pity, recognition, sensitivity to the grief of someone else, the act of receiving a service and more importantly of rendering one. The emotion in the forefront of Rousseau's interest is therefore *tender-heartedness*. Tender-heartedness is the sympathetic emotion par excellence, a 'gentle emotion' which tends to be contrasted to the *indignation* aroused at the sight of injustice, both being different responses to the spectacle of 'human miseries'. As the 'imagination of the heart', tender-heartedness consists in 'feeling oneself in one's fellow man', in recognising in a gesture of 'humanity' 'the common interest' which links the one it touches to others. Most of all it is associated with *pity* 'before simple suffering humanity' (in *Emile*, for example) or with *gratitude* (as in *La Nouvelle Héloïse*): being moved to tears, Julie experiences 'a kind of consolation in feeling that these gentle movements of nature are not completely extinguished in her heart'.

Tears play a central role in the mechanism of sentiment since, along with other bodily expressions such as sighs, moans and cries, they point to the process by which interiority is displayed in the external world (what Gilot and Sgard express by saying that for Rousseau they are both 'natural facts and cultural realities'). As the expression of emotions whose site is the heart, authentic tears are by definition *involuntary* and *irrepressible*. Actually, tears only establish communication in the world insofar as they manifest a connection already realised within the *intimacy* of *consciences:* 'The stakes of tears are always what is most intimate in the human being's relationship with someone else and with himself.' This is why upstream of tears and as it were more powerful than them, there are *silent embraces* which are 'more eloquent than cries and tears', as Rousseau writes in *La Nouvelle Héloïse,* because they make present a coordination of inner states which not only precede language but even every external expressive sign. In the order of sensibility, the silent and those who hear the voices of silence thus precede those who 'can only be moved' by tears and who are thus unable to recognise the distress of those who cannot cry themselves.

The tears which most interest Rousseau, like those which concern us here, are not the expression of suffering, resentment or even less of impotent rage, but *tender-hearted tears.* Now what characterises tender-hearted tears is that within them a certain *joy* is mixed with *sadness.* The connection between these two contrary emotions manifests their role as a relay or, to take a term from semantics, as a *shifter* between different states. The moment tears spring forth involuntarily can actually be described most concisely as the moment of transition from the *irreversible* to the *reversible.* Misfortune, misdeed, death and egoism plunge a conscience or, in Rousseau's vocabulary, a soul, into the repetition of the evil and grief from which it is suddenly snatched by the welling-forth of *liberating*, redemptive tears, like the 'purifying tears of Mama' in the *Confessions*, which 'relieve the heart', snatching it from 'despair', restoring 'confidence' to it, acting in it in the fashion of a grace, restoring it to the side of life. Sudden, often following fury or rage, tears thus procure a *respite* and a 'moral liberation': 'Instead of the dry pain which consumed me before, I had the sweetness of being moved to tears.'

5.7 Virtuous young women in distress

What empirical characters occupy the unfortunate's place in the novels with which these are concerned?, As in the example from Sterne cited above, it may be a matter of the poor and of beggars. But this is not most frequently the case. In many French and even more so English novels of the second half of the eighteenth century, the plot is tied to the destiny of a *female unfortunate* who, usually expressing herself in the first person, recounts her misfortunes to the reader. What is more, the suffering of 'virtue in distress', as Brissenden puts it,[25] has, in short, a social character which makes them open to political investment. Pamela and Clarissa in Richardson and the heroines of Mrs. Radcliffe are so many young girls of the provincial petite bourgeoisie abandoned with neither fortune nor protector, yet none the less educated and virtuous, who are abducted, ridiculed and handed over to evil in an aristocratic and libertine society in which their very virtue increases their suffering.

In both *Pamela* and *Clarissa*, which were among the most widely read and appreciated novels of their time, almost as much in France as in England with the translations, or rather adaptations, of the abbé Prévost,[26] the occupant of the unfortunate's place is not a problem: the place is filled by the heroine, the daughter of poor peasants who is confided to a benefactor who dies in the case of Pamela, and the young daughter of the petite bourgeoisie who is sacrificed to the ambitions of her family who want her to marry the infamous Somes in the case of Clarissa. On the other hand, how the persecutor's and the benefactor's places are filled is more complex. In both cases the persecutors are what Anglo-Saxon criticism calls *demon lovers,* Belfart in the case of Pamela, the libertine Lovelace in the case of Clarissa. But their allocation to one or other place is relatively unstable. This instability is encouraged by the characteristic techniques of the epistolary novel. In fact, if the epistolary novel, like fictional autobiography, is at least usually written in the first person, the relationship of the narrator to the temporal unfolding of the action is established in a different way. In the autobiographical novel, the narrator writing the story of his past life adopts a point of view on the events making up this life which takes into account their connectedness and their outcome. In contrast, in the epistolary novel the narrator describes day by day the events which have happened to her (with Pamela this is most often done in letters to her parents for example). Sticking to the present, the epistolary novel thus sustains uncertainty on the direction of events and the nature of the characters which favours description of the ambiguity of situations and the ambivalence of sentiments.[27] In both of these novels the heroines are virtuous young girls who consequently do not have evil thoughts – so that they are inclined to interpret any apparently generous action at face value where the reader accustomed to the conventions of the genre immediately suspects a devilish ruse – and who because they lack malice and spite are by defini-tion, as it were, inclined to forgiveness. However this instability of the agent, which will help give rise to the criticisms of sentimentalism we examine in the next chapter, is somehow inherent to the topic of sentiment which, in order to provoke pity, must pick out the figure of persecutor and then, abandoning the chase, shift attention towards the gentle emotions which move the unfortunate and touch the spectator.

Lovelace is thus a benefactor first of all, before becoming the very model of future persecutors: trustful Clarissa places herself under his protection so that he can snatch her from the claws of Somes before making her his prey. In *Pamela*, the heroine puts Belfart, the son of Pamela's protectress, in the benefactor's position: remember poor Pamela, she says to him on her deathbed. At the start of the novel he seems to fufill this role honourably and gives her many presents which Pamela delightedly accepts. But seized by passion the benefactor is quickly transformed into a terrible persecutor in order to get Pamela to forget her virtue. The narration of the outrages to which he subjects her comprise most of the first volume. However Pamela never shows any resentment or desire for vengeance towards him. She never proposes a form of involvement which would incite the reader to expect punishment of the persecutor as the favourable outcome of the novel. A passive subject, she suffers his assaults in tears. The same structure is repeated with the secondary characters. In the eyes of the naive Pamela most of them appear in the role of benefactors. Some, like Mrs. Jarvis, remain so. Others, like the horrible sister of Mrs. Jewkes (or even like the Reverend Williams) soon reveal their true nature. In spite of everything, and against (a naive reader's) every expectation, the novel has a happy ending: Belfart gives half-way signs of humanity. Pamela recognises that he is not indifferent to her. The persecutor is newly transformed into that par-ticular kind of benefactor who makes an excellent husband.

The difference between the conditions of Pamela and Belfart enable contrasting individuals to sustain a permanent ambiguity. A young girl and an older man; but also rich and poor:

O the unparalleled wickedness of such men as these, who call themselves gentlemen! who pervert the bounty of Providence to them, to their own everlasting perdition, and to the ruin of oppressed innocence!

But now I will tell you what has befallen me. And yet how shall you receive what I write? Here is no honest John to carry my letters to you! And, besides, I am watched in all my steps; and no doubt shall be, till my hard fate ripen his wicked projects for my ruin. I will every day, however, write my sad state; and some way, perhaps, may be opened to send the melancholy scribble to you. But when you *know* it, what will it do but aggravate your troubles? For what, alas! can the abject poor do against the mighty rich, when they are determined to oppress?'[28]

Diderot, whose theory of the novel emphasises the moral effects which may be produced by the emotions this genre arouses in the reader,[29] praises Richardson: 'Until now a novel has been understood as a web of chimerical and frivolous events which it was dangerous for taste and morals to read. I truly wish that a different name could be found for the works of Richardson which elevate the mind, touch the soul, breathe throughout with the love of good, and which we also call novels.'[30]

6

The critique of sentimentalism

6.1 The indulgence of sentiment

Descriptions of the heart touched by an unfortunate's suffering, or of tears shed on hearing a story of an act of kindness, are not confined to the novels of Richardson. By becoming linked to the social question with the development of pauperism, such descriptions continue and even flourish in the next century. The privileged objects of tender-hearted tears are always innocent and persecuted young girls in distress, but their misfortunes are now placed in an urban setting. Similarly, their condition of economic poverty prevails over their domestic dereliction. They suffer because they are poor, lacking resources, lost in the jungle of the towns, like Eugène Sue's heroine Fleur de Marie, of whom Anne Vincent-Buffault justly remarks that she 'is almost always in tears, either because she is moved by the kindness of her benefactors or because she is tormented by the memory of her past life. Naive and melancholic, her angelic figure is never more touching than when she is bathed in tears'.[1] But without doubt it is Dickens who establishes the closest connection between sentimental tender-heartedness and social denunciation by placing creatures with a natural capacity for sympathy in the hostile and artificial environment of the big industrial town. As a reader of the moral literature of the previous century who is concerned to bring out the benevolent capacities of human beings, Dickens also seeks to use realism to open the eyes of his contemporaries to the bleakness of the world which is revealed in an often humorous treatment of the discrepancy between sentiments and action, between sentiments stamped with *sentimentality* and actions dominated by motives of interest.[2] This also explains why the abundant representations of the poor in his work have met with such contrasting judgements, sometimes praise for its realism and ability to arouse indignation, and sometimes criticism of its lack of understanding of social class, its moralism and its preference for the 'deserving poor' (an expression not found in Dickens and which, according to G. Himmelfarb, is unjustly attributed to him by a kind of retrospective failure to understand the moral dimensions of the social criticism of his time).[3]

At every stage, however, sentimentalism survives by winning out over criticism. It is remarkable then that from the second half of the eighteenth century the vogue for the sentimental is accompanied by an extensive ironic and critical literature. Publication of *Pamela* in 1740 is immediately followed by the publication of several parodies, two of them sharing the title *Anti-Pamela*, in which the final success of the heroine is the reward of vice rather than virtue,[4] and more importantly by Fielding's *Shamela* and then *Joseph Andrews*, the first of which relates the stratagems employed by a domestic to excite her master and get him to marry her, and the second the misfortunes of a young servant, a kind of masculine Pamela, constantly in danger of being raped by his mistress. But more remarkable than parodic reversal which follows in the tracks of a century old debate and reveals the hypocrisy behind virtue and the interested motives behind apparent disinterestedness, is the progressive appearance of works which, as already sketched out in Sterne's *A Sentimental Journey*, combine 'sensibility and comedy',[5] and which then bring the gothic novel or gothic parody (like Jane Austen's first novel), sentimentality, the tender-heartedness of a spectator faced with an unfortunate young woman's suffering and its ironic unmasking together within a single genre.

The developing criticism of sentimental tender-heartedness at the end of the eighteenth century takes up the arguments which, from Aristotle to Hobbes, seek to base pity for someone else on the selfish sentiment of one's own vulnerability and so on personal interest.[6] Mandeville, whose *The Fable of the Bees* is one of the principal sources for criticism of sentimentalism, always invokes the same type of argument when he strives to unmask the hypocrisy of altruistic sentiments: 'There is no Merit in saving an innocent Babe ready to drop into the Fire: The Action is neither good nor bad, and what Benefit soever the Infant received, we only obliged our selves; for to have seen it fall, and not strove to hinder it, it would have caused a Pain, which Self-preservation compell'd us to prevent.'[7] However, ironical deconstruction of the sentimental novel does not stop there and the joyful ease with which this charge is developed and the future stability of the figures on which it is based, brings to light other reasons for the fragility of the topic of sentiment at the very moment of its greatest success. Its weak point is first of all the narrator's difficulty in maintaining a balance between the report on the external world describing the unfortunate's suffering and the report on the inner world containing the account of the spectator's agitations.

Actually, in this topic the report on the external world quickly comes up against a limit. The description of the unfortunate's suffering is blocked by the impossibility of developing the picture into an accusation and denunciation without changing its genre and falling back into that of the pamphlet for example. The description is cut short if it is not enriched by presenting not just a display of the objects which are causes of suffering – rats, jailers, cellars, etc. – but also of the investigation undertaken to accuse and unmask the persecutor. The logic of investigation takes us beyond the universe of sentiments to a link with systemic connections beyond interiority: the display of objects indicates responsibility – the jailer obeys orders, the rats are part of a system, etc. – which causes emotional investment to swing towards indignant denunciation. The shadow of the persecutor is then cast on references to the benefactor and resentment prevails over tender-heartedness. We have to make a choice: rats or gratitude?

If description of the unfortunate's suffering encounters its limits too quickly in the topic of sentiment, then the main inconvenience of the internal report is that its development is potentially infinite. It is constrained only by the nature of the available discursive resources. With the adoption of narrative techniques which favour the representation of mental life (the vocabulary of sentiment, interior monologue quoted directly or indirectly in the story, etc.), there is nothing to stop an endless display of sentiments, a burgeoning description of the emotions aroused in the spectator's heart by contemplation of the unfortunate's suffering.

The person speaking does indeed figure in the statement; the unfortunate is not an object described by an omniscient subject. However, this does not ensure symmetry. The affected spectator is in danger of swamping the statement, of being too prominent within it and so upsetting its balance. We no longer know anything about the unfortunate who takes second place as it were, but we know all the feelings he provokes in the spectator. The spectator can thus be accused of surrendering to an introspective description of his own affliction. What to start with appeared as disinterested attention directed towards someone else is denounced as exclusive attention to oneself, as interest only in oneself, as *indulgence*. Thus Henry Mackenzie, who was himself one of the most appreciated representatives of sentimental literature after the publication of his short novel *The Man of Feeling* in 1771, warns the reader, fifteen years later in his periodical letter *The Lounger*, of the moral danger represented by a too refined description of *impressions* and an 'enthusiasm of sentiment' which, like 'the enthusiasm of religion', runs the risk of substituting illusory feelings for real actions.[8]

6.2 The duplicity of sham emotions

From the end of the eighteenth century, *sentimental* and *sentimentalism* are especially singled out for criticism. At roughly the same time in France, the term *sensiblerie* (oversensitiveness, squeamishness) appeared which protected only the word *sensibility* from the discredit it suffered in England. To understand the success of the criticism of sentimentalism and of the charge of indulgence this criticism laid against it, we must remind ourselves of the philosophical background on which the sentimental novel leant. The moral idealism, especially of Shaftesbury and Hutcheson, in reaction against the pessimistic accounts of human nature in Hobbes,[9] as in Bayle, Mandeville or La Mettrie also, and perhaps also against the Puritan idea of a world abandoned by grace, undertook to constitute benevolence as a faculty of the human mind and even, in its most radical versions, as the clearest expression of the humanity of human beings.[10] The distinction between *human* and *humane* dates from this period. It is only when individuals are 'humane', in the sense of full of 'humanity' for fellow human beings, that they manifest and realise their full membership of the 'human kind'. It is in the presence of suffering that this full humanity manifests itself in pity. The spectacle of suffering is therefore the test individuals must face in order to prove their humanity. This test is described in the language of sensibility and of emotion in particular. It is the upsurge of emotion, and specifically of the emotion we have called *tender-heartedness*, which makes recognition possible – not in the sense of gratitude to an external benefactor, but as recognition of self by self, as access to what is best and specifically human in oneself.

   In this test of access to humanity there are a number of consequences of the importance given to sensibility and emotion provoked by the spectacle of someone else's suffering. The first is to arouse a passionate interest in the emotions and for the question of simulated emotions in particular. Given the role assigned to the emotions in moral life, it becomes crucial to be able to separate real emotions, the externalisation of the inner going back directly to the roots of the heart, from purely external, imitated or depicted emotions with no inner reference. Interest in this question increases the fascination exerted by the theatre, to which we have already referred in relation to the establishment of the impartial spectator. Now, however, and linking up again with the tradition of the *theatrum mundi*, fascination for the ability of actors to produce external signs of affliction and, for example, shed external tears without the corresponding feeling coming from the bottom of their heart, introduces uncertainty about the authenticity of sentimental expressions in real life. If actors can do this, why not ordinary people as well? It is above all the emptiness of the tears shed at the theatre which is a scandal for Rousseau. To the interpretation of emotion as the summum of presence to self[11] and, inseparably, of presence to others, is opposed the possibility of an interpretation of emotion as conventional sign, that is to say, for this topic, as superficial, as code and so consequently as the result of the distance taken by a strategic actor in relation to himself, since he manipulates emotion like a tool, clearly to deceive others for his own ends. For Rousseau, the disturbing possibility of a strategic use of tears, not only in the theatre but in real life, in women and particularly in children, leads him, as we see in *Emile*, to search for signs by which genuine tears can be distinguished from strategic tears, and to find arguments to resist these covert 'orders'.

A remarkable example of this anxiety is found in Ruth Yeazell's work on the question of feminine modesty in the sentimental novel of the eighteenth century,[12] in which we find subtle debates on the question of whether feminine modesty is natural or conventional and, in particular, an endless search for signs by which we can distinguish true from false modesty or, to take up the classic case of the blushing young girl discussed in the *Spectator* as well as in *The Fable of the Bees*,[13] between an upset rooted in natural virtue from a conventional upset, the fruit of education but without *deep* roots or, worse, a strategic upset simulated by coquetry in order to attract the very glances one seems to repel (we have seen that this contrast is always central in the modern treatment of emotion, particularly in sociology, where it intervenes in another canonical debate on the natural, that is biological, or cultural character of emotion).

The importance given to the emotions is therefore one of the weak points on which the topic of sentiment can be criticised from the point of view of a moral theory. Apart from giving rise, as we have seen, to a multiplicity of divergent interpretations, the emotions can be discredited as foundations and symptoms of a moral position due to their circumstantial character – bound up as they are with a particular situation in which they are tethered to the real or imaginary presence of a particular unfortunate – which does not enable one to construct a moral duty with general validity. Here again we encounter the essential tension of a politics of pity caught between the demand for generality and the need to present particular misfortunes in order to produce an effect of pity. This is the argument that Kant employs in his *Foundations of the Metaphysics of Morals* when he casts suspicion on impulsive, transient, and capricious emotions and compares them to the principles of a morality of duty, with a doggedness which is no doubt addressed less, as Robert Solomon remarks, to the philosophers of moral sentiments, than to their vulgarisation in sentimental literature and, in particular, in the feminine novel.[14] Beginning in 1740, and often in imitation of Richardson, there is a proliferation of novels written by women, particularly in England, to such an extent that the novel is progressively identified as a specifically feminine genre. Philippe Séjourné, who has gone through the *Monthly Review* and the *Monthly Magazine* from the 1770s until the end of the century, shows the extent to which novels were mostly subject to scornful criticism.[15] It is then also that the ability to have and to externalise feelings, which hitherto was not marked sexually or may even have been more frequently attributed to men than to women, is qualitatively transformed into a feminine defect. It is above all the feminisation of sentiment which entails its discredit and the accusation of sentimentalism.

6.3 The ambiguous pleasure of sensitive hearts

A second consequence of the importance given to *sensibility* in the Scottish moral tradition which inspired the novel plays a very important role in the scope of criticisms of the topic of sentiment. The emphasis on sensibility makes it possible to go beyond the accusation of indulgence to reveal a hidden motive: the search for pleasure. This denunciation rests on two elements which passed from moral philosophy to sentimental literature. The first concerns the difficulty of representing the moment at which the spectator fulfills his full humanity in the emotion aroused by the spectacle of suffering without giving way to happiness. 'A tear of sentiment, what sweeter reward', says the hero of François Vernes' *Voyageur sentimental*, which was modelled on Sterne.[16] For it is bliss to realise one's identity. But description of this happiness becomes problematic when it overlaps description of the unfortunate's suffering to such an extent that it completely covers it. Its display opens the way for the accusation of deliberately seeking out the spectacle of suffering, not in order to relieve it, but in order to obtain from it the precious moment of emotion and, on this logic, the happiness it arouses: in a letter which portrays the Parisian vogue for sensibility, Madame Riccoboni writes to Garrick from Paris in 1769: 'One would readily create unfortunates in order to taste the sweetness of feeling sorry for them.'[17]

The second element concerns the complex links between the register of sentiments, and specifically moral sentiments, and the register of sensibility; a sort of 'joker', as Stephen Cox puts it, which can enter into multiple connections.[18] The sentimental man is also sensitive. Neither one exists without the other, and sensibility, which in the seventeenth century had neutral or even negative connotations, in the eighteenth century becomes the expression of the highest moral values.[19] In particular, it is through this link that the moral question and aesthetic question are connected to each other, in Francis Hutcheson for example, before being separated by Burke with the concept of the sublime.[20] The morality of the man of sentiment is shown in his ability to discriminate, not in his actions. In the register of sentiments he is like the connoisseur in the register of taste. It is precisely the aesthetic tone of sensibility which introduces an ambiguity and tension into moral philosophy which is only overcome with the separation of the aesthetic and moral dimensions. In moral constructions, the sentiments, and especially the sentiment of commiseration, are rooted in a generic human capability so that potentially they are accessible to everyone. It is precisely the anthropological character of this capability which allows it to be introduced into the framework of the political city. However, inasmuch as sentiments are associated with sensibility they frequently appear as being distributed unequally between people with unequal sensory capabilities, in accordance with a principle which usually corresponds to a comparison between the educated elite and the uncultivated masses.

But the vocabulary of sensibility has more than just an aesthetic tone. It speaks also of the senses and through them of physiology, of the body and of sexuality. Sensitive persons especially liable to moral emotions like Pamela and Clarissa, are also sensitive, as Jean Hagstrum has clearly shown,[21] in a third sense of the word, closer to the sensual. Their sensibility, in the physical or medical sense of the word, is treated not just as a moral quality but as a property attached to the body and, in particular, to the 'nerves', to the length and finesse of innervation, and it is what conditions both their ability to suffer, or again, their ability to blush, but also and for the same reasons their ability to feel sexual pleasure, even, or especially, when they seek to shun it, and consequently their ability to arouse desire.[22] The multiple meanings associated with the idea of sensibility allows the toing and froing between moral discourse and sexual description in the sentimental novel. 'What is meant by virtue in this instance' writes Erich Auerbach with regard to *Manon Lescaut*, 'cannot be imagined detached from the whole apparatus of erotic sensations'.[23] But obviously it is this mixture which gives a hold, as we have seen with regard to *Shamela*, to the irony of contemporaries and which today is ever the object of the sarcasm of academic critics, [24] or to the denunciations of feminist literary history. Kristina Straub, for example, undertakes to unmask the unconscious involvement of the reader in the 'voyeurism' of Richardson's descriptions of the ill-treatment Belfart makes the poor Pamela suffer, which usually contain a sexual element, and with this example to expose the use of the gaze as an instrument for giving a subject-object type of structure to the relationship between the sexes.[25] We will see later how the introduction of considerations of pleasure in the topic of sentiment – the moral pleasure of sympathizing with someone else's suffering and then sensual pleasure – opens the way to new developments.

For the moment we note, as we have already had occasion to do concerning the Victorian novel, that the topic of sentiment is not defeated by these arguments. At least, in contrast with France, it has not been demolished by criticism in the moral theory of the Anglo-Saxon countries. The configuration which appears when pity becomes a political argument and the space of oppositions which is then installed between different ways of conveying suffering in discourse is firmly established. This is confirmed by a glance at current versions of the debate on sentiment which take up again, almost word for word, the arguments set out in the time of Sterne and Richardson. It is in these terms, that Robert Solomon for example,[26] in response to articles hostile to sentimentality by Michael Tanner,[27] Mary Midgley,[28] and Mark Jefferson,[29] deploys arguments directly derived from the Scottish philosophy of the first half of the eighteenth century against the main criticisms advanced against 'sentimentalism' which themselves revive, at least for the most part, themes developed in Mandeville: sentimentality hypocritically dissimulates cynicism; sentimental people indulge in narcissistic introspection and rather than taking action they seek emotion for itself, for their own pleasure (Tanner); sentimentalism gives an illusory picture of the world and dissimulates what is in fact a horrible reality (Jefferson); ostentatious sentimentality enables brutal practices to be dissimulated (Midgley); the appeal to sentimentality enables the spectator to be manipulated and dulls his critical sense, etc. A final criticism itemised by Solomon consists in reproaching sentimental representation for exerting a hold over the spectator which prevents his access to an 'aesthetic detachment' before the world. This criticism is based upon later arguments that will be taken up when we examine the *aesthetic topic*. But since this third way of confronting suffering as a spectator is established on the double rejection of denunciation and sentiment, we need first to remind ourselves of the extreme forms taken by criticism of sentimentalism in order to provide ourselves with the means to pick out its internal structure.

6.4 The amateur of suffering

It is actually possible to become amateur in suffering. I have heard of men who have travelled into countries where horrible executions were to be daily witnessed, for the sake of that excitement which the sight of suffering never fails to give, from the spectacle of tragedy, or an auto da fe, down to the writhings of the meanest reptile on whom you can inflict torture, and feel that torture is the result of your own power. It is a species of feeling of which we never can divest ourselves.'[30]

Taken from a work belonging to what could be called late gothic, *Melmoth the Wanderer* by Charles Robert Maturin, published in 1820, these lines sketch out a new figure of the spectator of suffering: the *amateur*, the *connoisseur*, words deriving from the French and normally designating the lover of fine things. There can be, then, amateurs or lovers of suffering as there are art lovers, who can extract an aesthetic delight from the spectacle given to them. A similar argument against the Gothic novel is already put forward in 1797 by a critic of the *Monthly Magazine* who considers attraction to the most horrible and bloody descriptions the result of a taste which has an addictive effect on a blasé public, at first through fictional excesses (descriptions of abductions are no longer enough for the reader) and also, in ironic tones, through real atrocities: Robespierre spread the taste for terror and blood.[31] In another passage of *Melmoth*, Maturin describes the feelings of a spectator – a mixture of indignation, horror and aesthetic jubilation – viewing tortures inflicted by Spanish monks on a young novice who is described to the reader as covered with blood but naked and of an 'exquisite perfection', insisting both on the horror of the scene and on its pictorial beauty which makes it 'worthy of Murillo'. In Maturin, and in the Gothic novel more generally, the aestheticisation of the spectacle of suffering extends and accentuates ironic criticism of the sentimental novel.

The moral criticism which in the second half of the eighteenth century raises suspicions about the literature of sentiment and unmasks its indulgent self-satisfaction hiding behind sympathetic tender-heartedness, actually opens the way to a more radical alternative: if the spectacle of suffering provides the possibility of pleasure – albeit the pleasure of feeling oneself the most human of men[32]– why not push the criticism in a utilitarian direction and consider the function of the spectacle to be precisely enjoyment and enjoyment to be the reason the spectacle of suffering is sought out? This is the route taken by Sade who was a reader of the English gothic novels (*The Monk* by Lewis in particular) introduced into France at the end of the eighteenth century where they were adapted and imitated in great numbers,[33] and more certainly of Richardson and the sentimental novel in its ironic version.[34] This can be seen in the extremely conventional character of the situations in which he places his unfortunate heroines and, for example, in the analogous structure – which perhaps cannot be explained by a direct influence – between *Justine*, published in 1791, and Jane Austen's first novel *Love and Friendship*, a parody of the novels of sensibility and gothic novels, which remained in manuscript until the twentieth century.[35] The question of the spectacle of suffering occupies a fundamental place in the works of Sade, as is indicated by the collective character of the scenes of cruelty which, in a complicated assemblage, almost always contain, in addition to the human objects made to suffer, subjects who inflict the suffering and others who enjoy observing them – not just spectators but, more precisely here, *voyeurs,* since the reason for the contemplation is an explicitly sexual interest. Furthermore, the qualities of the persecutor and voyeur are not applied to persons in Sade's narratives, but to places which can be successively occupied by the same character.[36]

The interest of this work for our study chiefly concerns two points. A first innovation consists in the complete identification of the spectator's pleasure with a sexual enjoyment, something which was only suggested in the ironic parodies. The particular effect of this is to reveal the wholly interested and perfectly selfish character of the spectator's motives and consequently, in the spirit of eighteenth century materialists like Hélvetius and La Mettrie, to radicalise criticism of Scottish moralism. Actually, beyond its physiological, instinctive character independent of the will, sexual pleasure offers this argument the inestimable advantage of not being shared. It profits only the one who enjoys it. This makes it the most difficult thing to be transformed into a common good. This property, which widely applied to political usages of sexuality, and which explains why pamphleteering denunciation, often with moralist and even puritan intentions, reverts with such intensity to forms inspired by pornography, is obviously especially prominent when the suffering of another person is treated as a stimulant for sexual enjoyment. In this case, criticism of moralism is not satisfied with reminding us – in the spirit of Mandeville, but also before him of Bayle and even La Rochefoucauld – of the all-powerful nature of selfish interest. It reverses the constructions which make altruism a faculty of human nature by completely identifying the satisfaction of personal interest with contemplation of another person's suffering.

But, as Jacques Domenech has shown in his book *L'éthique des Lumières,* in contrast with Enlightenment thinkers, in Sade interest lacks any 'capacity for founding a reasonable morality'. In this naturalism of the worst, the condition of the happiness of some is not just the misfortune of others, but the fact itself of seeking out and contemplating this misfortune. Domenech thus shows how the ground was laid for Sade's position by the novels of apologists like the abbé Gérard or the abbé Barruel who, intending to demonstrate against the philosophers that religion was the only bulwark of morality and consequently the impossibility of a morality of well-understood interest or, more generally, of a secular morality, portrayed libertines whose materialism easily led to immoralism. But in lending them speech in order to show their infamy, the apologists had them produce 'great dissertations' on the 'relativism of laws legitimising theft or crime' which 'prefigure the forms of Sadean rhetoric'. In fact, one only needs to alter the intention of arousing the reader's indignation for the discourse to switch from moralising criticism to the exposition of an immoral system. For Sade as for the apologists, 'interest betrays the fundamental vice of every individual'. To this end Domenech quotes this discourse, directed at Helvétius, which is taken from the *Helviennes ou Lettres provinciales philosophiques* of the abbé Barruel, which a modern reader could attribute to Sade without difficulty:

I dare not tell you, chevalier, all that my patient added on the virtues of so many other countries, of Matamba, Angola, Batimera, Babylon, Pekin, and Tonkin; on those strange virtues which consist sometimes in killing their children and the old, sometimes in strangling a sick person to relieve his pain, and sometimes even in cleansing themselves of their sins through sacrifices to the Goddess of pleasure.[37]

The second interesting innovation in Sade, particularly relevant for a political history, consists, as the foregoing example suggests, in the abandonment of the critical stance for a topical position which exhibits in wholly general terms, and in order to acknowledge its value, the manner of being that criticism seeks to bring to light by unmasking a secret. In itself there is nothing original in this movement. It functions whenever a form of qualification is set up in order to form the armature of a city. This is how the pursuit of fame, for example, which is regularly denounced from the Stoics[38] to the French moralists of the seventeenth century, who attach unprecedented importance to it by revealing that it contains the secret motive of men's actions, is identified as a positive anthropological quality by Hobbes, with a grandeur capable of providing a firm foundation for the construction of a harmonious city.[39] In the Sadean world, sexual interest is a valid, self-sufficient motive which supplants other motives for action. What is more, the desirability of sexual enjoyment aroused by the spectacle of suffering justifies one providing this spectacle and consequently justifies causing suffering to that end. We examine below whether a city founded on such a principle is possible.

6.5 Sadistic pity

The connection Brissenden makes between Sade and the novels which ridicule sentimentality should not lead us to confuse the two genres. Sade's work, especially in its political fragments, does not have the same kind of relationship to the topic of sentiment as Swift's ferocious pamphlets and, for example, his *Directions to servants* (published posthumously in 1745) or, above all, *A modest proposal for preventing the children of poor people becoming a burthen to their parents* (which proposal consists, as we know, in eating the children) do to the topic of indignation. Unlike Swift's denunciation of the cruelty of society, Sade does not employ irony to reveal the hypocritical character of the sentimental relationship to suffering. None the less, with Sade we are still within the framework of a politics of pity. This is what distinguishes *sadism,* the attitude to which his name is attached, from *cruelty,* which is immediately exhausted in the violence of the action, and, through the general aim adopted by the argumentative eloquence of Sade's characters, their inclination to description and the imperative of reflexivity as condition of possibility of sexual enjoyment, this distinction between sadism and cruelty also recalls the distinction we proposed earlier between *pity* and *compassion.*

Sadism establishes a new relationship to cruelty by leaning on the form of political pity set up in the eighteenth century. It is not the existence of great cruel aristocrats which is new here, nor even that their actions are recorded and related in writing. What is new is that cruelty is not just the object of a description, but also of a reflection and, as we will see, of attempts to justify it. Above all, this reflexive detour is undertaken from the perspective of a politics of pity. The least we can say is that Sadean heroes are not indifferent to suffering and misfortune, which moreover are often associated with poverty and so already with the people. The human object of cruelties presented as a spectacle never appears as a *misérable* being punished for his faults, nor even as an imprudent individual suffering the consequences of his lack of concern, but as indeed an innocent, as a *pure* unfortunate. Thus to begin with the reader is directed to *pity* specified either as *indignation* or, more often, as *tender-heartedness.* To employ once again the terms of the model we have extracted from Adam Smith, the reader is led to sympathise with a benefactor to whom the unfortunate would be grateful and so to adopt a topic of sentiment. But, and one of the main peculiarities of this kind of narrative is found here, this gesture is scarcely begun than a shift in perspective turns emotional tension in a different direction. The character on whom the sympathetic charge is fixed shifts from the position of a benefactor to that of a persecutor which entails a form of positive sympathy with the person being cruel. However, this has nothing in common with adherence to what we have called the communal figure in which the spectator is filled with joy by the suffering of some poor wretch with a negative status and who is viewed not from any position but precisely from the position of a spectator qualified by his membership of a

group. In fact, in a communal figure, the unfortunate is, we have said, a
wretch one punishes. The spectator develops the kind of attitude towards
him that Svend Ranulf, on the basis of material taken from Ancient Greece
and Nazi Germany, describes as *moral indignation*.[40] It is only from a contrary polemical position that this indignation can be denounced by showing
that it is not applied to the right target. In fact, what is at stake here is who,
what concrete characters, must fill the places of persecutor and victim.
From a different position, the person who arouses moral indignation and
is denounced as a *persecutor* turns out to be the *victim*. Those filled with
moral indignation are thus accused of *blaming the victim* and take up the
place of the persecutor. But things are different in Sade. The change of perspective does not change the occupant of the unfortunate's place who
remains an innocent. She affects the spectator's feelings which shift from
pity to delectation.

The reversal takes place on two levels (which are not in a chronological
relationship with each other): First that of *affirmation* and second that of
justification, and specifically political justification. The themes of these
two levels are different. The level of affirmation develops a theme of singularity and so of radical *difference*. Because it is political, the level of justification confronts the affirmation of difference with a problematic of
equality.

The affirmation of radical difference passes through the affirmation of
the particularity and irreducibility of tastes.[41] The most singular, uncommon tastes and the taste for sexual cruelty in particular, are associated with
a particular, innate *sensibility*. Here Sade adopts the terms of an affirmation, frequent among philosophers of sympathy and the novelists of sentiment, in which the tendency to sympathize with the suffering of
unfortunates is unequally distributed in accordance with the degree of
refinement and sensibility of different individuals. However, in adopting
these terms he inverts the affirmation since sensibility is no longer associated with pity but with cruelty. In Adam Smith there is a tension between
this assertion of an unequal distribution of sympathy, which recurs frequently but in an incidental manner, and his concern for the *symmetry*
required to derive a theory of social coordination from a balance of sympathy and so also the possibility of a harmonious society.

Sade's novels describe singular tastes in all their fanciful diversity, those
who have them, and how they satisfy them. Every Sadean hero has particular, individual tastes, each irreducible to the others. They do not exist in
total separation from each other however, and are able to *reach agreement*
amongst themselves. The fact of having uncommon tastes arising from a
particular sensibility, and the will to satisfy them, leads them to meet each

other, recognise each other and come together in micro-societies. But these societies are also secret societies. Although they recognise each other, these *amateurs* are separated from others. First of all they are separated by the refinement of their tastes, which are incomprehensible to the uninitiated. Also, or most of all, they are separated by their criminal character. They are in fact not only amateurs of those spectacles of suffering amply provided by everyday scenes of social life, but of more elaborate spectacles they provide each other by taking turns to cause suffering. By putting their tastes into action they fall outside the law. Their situation is therefore similar to that of the amateurs whose pleasures depend, as Sade says, on the satisfaction of 'frivolous tastes', except that the satisfaction of their tastes being prohibited, satisfaction must be clandestine, hidden away in isolated castles. Now, if it was a question only of 'frivolous tastes' rather than repressed tastes, justification would be pointless and in any case would not be *political*. In fact, we will see that the domain of tastes can be par excellence the domain of difference precisely when tastes are detached from politics, that is to say when their possession and exercise has no significance for the common good within a political system. Transition from the level of *affirmation* to that of *justification* is only necessary to the extent that these tastes are condemned to a clandestine existence. The aim of justification is to remove this clandestinity and to allow forbidden and dangerous practices to be performed in the full light of day.

6.6 The political justification of singular tastes

To justify the possession of cruel tastes, Sade adopts the argumentative language of political philosophy, although he does so in a fashion which makes it difficult to say when it is parody and when serious. This language would be utterly useless and even out of place if it was only a question of particular tastes for legitimate objects. But being forbidden, then to lift the ban on them their particularity must become a common good. This dilemma obliges Sade to introduce into the political philosophy of his time centred on the question of equality, a reflection on the singularity of tastes which is developed in the margins of the political question, parallel to it but, as we will see, from its residues.

Although Sade's demonstrations are often muddled and barely coherent, we can attempt to isolate several constructions from the scattered philosophical fragments in the fictional works. Inasmuch as these constructions are political and outline a utopian State, they cannot stop at the affirmation of the radical difference of particular tastes. They must confront the question of *difference* with that of *equality* within a perspective of harmonisation. Without trying to be exhaustive, three constructions will be identified in turn, each of which, as Pierre Favre has shown, leads to an acknowledgment of failure.[42] Actually, either these constructions allow the manifestation of sadistic tastes, but in a society which does not conform to a model of the political city; or they attempt to take into account the requirement of a common good but no longer allow the affirmation of particular tastes and thus depart from the Sadean ideal. The incoherence of Sade's political thought is often emphasised and is due at least in part to the way in which the author tries to satisfy different and incompatible requirements.

In accordance with the law of the genre, these different models are based upon a philosophical anthropology. In this pessimistic anthropology, the human faculty *par excellence* is the propensity for crime. This is a natural faculty inscribed, innately, in the form of a biological determinism which cannot be changed by education. There is something here which is like a principle of similarity. But this principle does not pick out a common humanity since it is not peculiar to human beings and applies to all natural beings. Alongside this principle of similarity two principles of dissimilarity are depicted, one weak and the other strong. According to the weak principle, the propensity for crime is realised in a multitude of different tastes. The principle can be said to be weak, firstly, inasmuch as the different tastes are not definitively attached to different persons (a single individual being able to exhibit different tastes) and, secondly, inasmuch as differences in taste are not put forward as a source of conflict.

According to the strong principle, if all human beings (like other natural beings) have an identical propensity for crime, they are radically distinguished from each other by their characteristic strength or weakness. This characteristic is definitive, attached once and for all to the individual, linked to *birth* and is sometimes treated as an innate biological property (although they are sisters, Justine is weak and Juliette is strong) and sometimes as a social property determining membership of the same class.[43] The *weak* are just as naturally inclined to crime as the *strong*, but their weakness encourages them to 'behave prudently' and therefore to prefer 'virtue and moderation'. If these arguments are not wholly new, in Sade they take on a systematic form which inaugurates the opposition between self-affirming strength and self-justifying weakness and the Nietzschean conception of morality as the disguised form of expression of *ressentiment*, invented by the weak in order to fetter the power of the strong and dominate them.[44] In real society, what must be transformed is precisely the way in which the weak oppress the strong by means of laws and prevent them from expressing their tastes.

6.7 The inconsistency of Sadean cities

The first construction proposed by Sade on the basis of this anthropology consists, as Pierre Favre has shown, in systemising the form of the secret society and extending it to the dimensions of the State. It appears in the first part of a narrative which adopts one of the classic forms used to demonstrate the possibility of constructing a harmonious society on a new principle: the form of a political utopia. This narrative of around 200 pages is inserted within a novel *Aline et Valcour ou le roman philosophique* which was published in 1793 but written in the Bastille between 1785 and 1788. A character, Sainville, narrates his stay in the kingdom of *Butua* dominated by a cannibal prince. The inhabitants of this State are distributed into two classes and they cannot change their class. The first class is that of the strong who are happy in this model kingdom. The other class is that of the weak, who are unhappy. The laws maintain the oppression of the weak by the strong. The strong are happy precisely because the weak are at their disposal and can be made to suffer at will. Nothing hinders the expression of the tastes of the strong.

Despite the particularity of individual tastes, harmony naturally reigns among the strong because they can fulfill all of their desires. In fact, Sade often considers the repression of desire to be the main cause of conflict, an idea which was taken up by Fourier[45] and which has played an important role in twentieth-century efforts to rehabilitate Sade. So something like a common good does exist among the strong, but at the price of the division of humanity into two radically distinct and unequal classes. The cohesion of the strong is only secured however insofar as they dispose of a class of unfortunates on whom they inflict cruelties and who, as it were by definition, never occupy the place of persecutor or of spectator. This class, or, in view of its wholly separate character, this caste, often appears as an anonymous, innumerable and almost inexhaustible mass. Given its total or partial destruction in the course of processes which secure enjoyment for the strong, this inexhaustibility is a necessary condition in order to avoid competition between pleasure seekers and so to maintain the latter's cohesion. It follows that the anthropological properties which define human nature and are formally accorded to all in this construction, can only be realised by some. If all are filled with the desire to affirm themselves by sexually oppressing their fellows, only some can put this into action and thereby fully realise what is written in their human nature.

This State would be perfect if consideration of the *future*, no doubt provoked by the *political* character of the utopia, did not introduce a constraint of scarcity. In effect, the exploitation of the weak by the strong is so great that this indispensable resource for the happiness of the strong is in danger of being exhausted and becoming unavailable for future generations. As Pierre Favre notes, this limitation does not apply to the secret societies of the novels because these are ensconced deep within wider societies from which inexhaustible supplies of unfortunates are provided. But in the closed island of Butua, with no outside world, unlimited exploitation of the human resources deprives the future generations of the strong of the necessary means for fulfilling their desires (an argument which is today taken up by ecology when it sets the class of strong humans as a whole against natural beings in a weak position).

We are given a second model in a remark made by Zamé, the prince of the model island *Tamoé,* the description of which takes up the second part of Sainville's narrative.

Let us accept for a moment, said Zamé, a State comprising four thousand subjects . . . let us call one half the Whites and the other half the Blacks; now let us suppose that the Whites unjustly identify their felicity in a sort of oppression of the Blacks. What will the normal legislator do? He will punish the Whites in order to deliver the Blacks from their oppression . . . Prior to the punishment imposed by this imbecile, the Whites were happiest; after his punishment, the Blacks are happiest. His action thus amounts to nothing since he leaves things as they were before. What he should do . . . is to make both equally happy and not some at the expense of the others . . . To achieve this he will agree with (the Blacks) on the kind of compensation which would give them some of the happiness taken from them by the Whites' oppression, in order to preserve a balance since unity of Blacks and Whites cannot take place; on this basis he will subject the Whites to the compensation demanded by the Blacks and from then on will only allow the former to oppress the latter when compensation has been given; then there are four thousand happy subjects, since the Whites are satisfied with their oppression of the Blacks, and the latter become happy through the compensation given for their oppression.'[46]

In this model there are always two radically distinct classes, the first comprising the strong who oppress the weak comprising the second. But a commercial relationship governed by law distributes happiness more equitably since the strong give financial compensation to the weak for the ill-treatment necessary for the satisfaction of their tastes. This solution, doubtless inspired by the example of brothels according to Favre, has the characteristics of a bastard arrangement that is neither the triumphant affirmation of force, nor a respect for common humanity which prohibits the equivalence on which this device of justice rests.

The third model, developed above all in '*Yet another effort, Frenchmen, if you would become Republicans*',[47] a short essay included in *Philosophy in the Bedroom,* published in 1795, permanently subordinates the fulfillment of human inclinations to the sexual oppression of a weak person by someone who is strong. However, in contrast with the previous constructions, the qualities of strength and weakness are no longer attached to classes given once and for all. But no more are they attributed to positions which could or should be occupied in turns by the same individuals, as Frank and Fritizie Manuel suggest, for example, in their attempt to bring Sade back into the fold of egalitarian utopianism.[48] Thus in this third construction if, for example, the law which allows men to subject any woman to their desires, grants the same right to women – a symmetry absent from the previous constructions – this is so that 'fiery temperaments' may be brought to light.[49] The possibility of fulfilling every desire and satisfying all tastes, which is formally granted to all and guaranteed by law, must permit the destruction of the social privileges which obstruct the manifestation of natural strengths and weaknesses. As in Pareto's later utopia, involving the movement of elites, or again in the reformist versions of the eugenic city,[50] the suppression of social conventions allows the strong to release and affirm their energy. We remain within an asymmetrical figure in which the unfortunate's place and the persecutor's place are not at all interchangeable. As such, and on the basis of pure sexual interest, the Sadean construction provides no lasting support for the formation of a moral position which could counterpose the sentimental position when faced with the spectacle of suffering. If it is not without a future, its operationalisation none the less requires profound reorganisation and the formation of new combinations.

7

The aesthetic topic

7.1 A third way

To summarise, on the one hand there is an unfortunate who suffers and on the other a spectator who views the suffering without undergoing the same fate and without being directly exposed to the same misfortune. To adopt an acceptable attitude, the spectator cannot remain indifferent nor draw a solitary enjoyment from the spectacle. However, he cannot always intervene directly; he cannot always go into action, that is to say, unify the framework within which he acts and the framework within which the unfortunate struggles in such a way as to bring together in a single situation the two originally different situations. The further the spectator is from the unfortunate the more the disjunction between their situations seems to be insurmountable and in consequence action becomes more problematic. We have seen that a politics of pity necessarily provokes this disjunction because, as a politics, it must rise above local miseries in order to form a general picture, although in order to keep the dimension of pity present it cannot be content with establishing equivalences, of an accounting kind for example, and must therefore compose this picture by assembling particular sufferings in such a way as to obtain an immense imaginary collection of all kinds of unfortunates.

Although forced to be inactive, if the spectator is to remain within a morally acceptable framework he is none the less encouraged to show an interest which takes account of the misery of the person he observes and if not to intervene directly in his life then at least to place himself in an active disposition of somone concerned for him. Pity consists in this. There is a route open to him: to pass on the spectacle, to communicate it to others. But his description cannot be realistic or factual. For reasons of symmetry he must depict in a single operation both the unfortunate's suffering and what he himself feels at the sight of it, how he is affected by it. This procedure frees a space in which emotion can be displayed within a discourse. Pity can be shown in the form of indignation. Emotion is then detached from the unfortunate and directed at a persecutor who is accused. Emotion can also be freed in tender-heartedness which ignores the persecutor and equally distances itself from the unfortunate, but in order to bring to the fore the presence of a benefactor. These two routes can be blocked by criticism: indignation is only a veiled persecution; tender-heartedness is no more than selfish enjoyment unaware of itself. But the unmasking of hypocrisy itself seems to be a dead end. The alternative it seems to propose at first – that of a concern out of cruelty – does no more than pass through pity in order to turn it into its opposite. Now if cruelty is possible, and even customary, in a communal figure, there can be no politics of cruelty which, also availing itself of two classes, the fortunate and unfortunate, could have the aim of using the pity the latter inspires for the happiness of the former.

However, the story is not over. A third possibility emerges from the criticism of the first two. It consists in considering the unfortunate's suffering as neither *unjust* (so as to become indignant about it), nor as *touching* (so as to be moved to tears by it), but as *sublime*. An initial movement of pity is contained and even repressed (in the way that indignation had to be contained to give room to proof), in such a way as to be taken up in the transformed form of *sublimation*. We will trace this third route through one of its topical modes of expression as it was constituted in France in the first half of the nineteenth century.

7.2 The painter of horror

Let us return again to the scheme taken from Adam Smith's *The Theory of Moral Sentiments*. A spectator looks at an unfortunate. This time he is not inclined to sympathise with the resentment of the suffering person and so follow him in accusation. He therefore checks that initial movement within himself which could have made him indignant. In effect, he has learned the lesson of the criticisms levelled at a topic of denunciation: in sympathizing with the resentment of the unfortunate and in accusing a third person, the spectator actually does no more than quench his own desire to persecute in revenge, to satisfy his envy, his taste for violence and destruction or, to take up Sade's terms again, to give vent to his natural propensity for crime.

But neither is the spectator inclined to sympathise with the unfortunate's gratitude to a benefactor and to follow him by shedding tender-hearted tears. He has listened to the criticisms which question the authenticity of a topic of sentiment: in hypocritical tender-heartedness the benefactor

actually seeks only to gain the kind of pleasure that the spectacle of suffering alone can give him.

Holding in check the emotion which rises within him to be released as
indignation or tender-heartedness, rejecting the masks of denunciation and
sentiment, this third spectator confronts the truth and looks it in the face.
What he sees is the horror. It is inasmuch as he is given up to naked suffering, imputable to no-one and with no hope of remission, that he sympathises with the unfortunate. His primary quality is courage: he dares to cast
his eyes on the unfortunate and look evil in the face without immediately
turning away towards imaginary benefactors or persecutors. He allows
himself to be taken over by the horrific.

Does this mean that the position of the actor we have called the *agent*
remains vacant in this form of the system? If this were the case the spectator would be hysterically confused with the unfortunate, given up to the
horror of a blind suffering but unable to say anything about it. In fact we
have seen that the possibility of a meta-describer who is able to weld
together the unfortunate's suffering and the spectator's sensibility in a
single statement can be generated from the other actor Smith calls the
'impartial spectator' whose basis is the desire for the approval of others.
Now the possibility of approval by someone else is conditional upon the
existence of an external reference point on which the internal movements
of separate spectators can converge. The existence of an agent is therefore
necessary in order to understand the possibility of sympathetic communication and the formation of a collectivity on this basis.

Who can we put in the position of an agent here? A painter or, more generally, an *exhibitor* who is able to get us to see suffering in its sublime aspect.
The painter sees the unfortunate suffer and depicts his suffering. But how,
it could be objected, can this character, who does nothing either for or
against the unfortunate and who oddly resembles the spectator himself, be
given the status of an *agent?* He can because by painting the unfortunate's
suffering, by revealing its horror and thereby revealing its truth, he confers
on this suffering the only form of dignity to which it can lay claim and
which it gets from its attachment to the world of the already painted, of
what has already been revealed within an aesthetic register.

But might it not be objected that it is always the satisfaction of a pleasure which the spectator seeks in the spectacle of suffering, and even in a
much more patent fashion in this than in the previous two cases? No, the
presentation of the unfortunate in his horrific aspect is the only one which
makes possible the communication of that unpresentable horror which
overcomes the spectator and which is none other than the horror residing
within him and which defines his condition.

Finally, a last objection, can the spectator and the agent really be distinguished from each other here, since it is now a case of an agent who observes? Yes, for the painter acts insofar as he paints. He is a creator and displays the horror in the materiality of a picture. The spectator does nothing. He sympathises with the painter; he is a painter who does not paint. It is at the cost of doing nothing that his contemplation of the horrific can be total.

Recognisable here is the portrait of the *dandy* as Baudelaire gives him to us in his theoretical and critical writings, particularly in the essay on Guy, *The Painter of Modern Life.*[1]

7.3 With neither indignation nor tender-heartedness

We will quickly examine the form in which the unfortunate's suffering is conveyed in this new topic, which we call the *aesthetic topic,* and how, inseparable from this, a crystallisation takes place of a collectivity formed by the trace left in those who communicate in this way. In the aesthetic topic, as in the topics of denunciation and sentiment we have already looked at, the spectator confronts the double demand of publicity of speech and symmetry in the statement. As in the two previous topics, the spectator must therefore blend within the same statement a recapitulation of the unfortunate's suffering and the specification of the observer's state. But this state cannot be described as *sentiment* since the refusal of sentiment, whether of indignation or tender-heartedness, is precisely what constitutes this topic's initial move: 'The distinguishing characteristic of the dandy's beauty consists above all in an air of coldness which comes from an unshakeable determination not to be moved' (*The Painter of Modern Life,* p. 29).

Unquestionably we find this double refusal in Baudelaire who takes up the criticisms of both indignation and tender-heartedness which were widely diffused at the end of the previous century. He places them next to each other in a way which might seem incoherent if, from the tension between them (and which can be connected with the opposition between 'social art' and 'bourgeois art' described by Cesar Grana[2] and Pierre Bourdieu[3]), a new position was not formed in which the spectacle of suffering is sublimated. In the era of revolutions, as Hannah Arendt emphasises, the unfortunate is either specified as '*enragé*' or as '*misérable*'.[4] But here the unfortunate does not appear in these two aspects which are connected to each other in the 'revolutionary speculations of Victor Hugo' or, as in the *Châtiments*, in the 'humanitarian idealism' of an indignant sounding social poetry.[5] Indignation, as *political* indignation or, more precisely, as *social* denunciation, for which the socialist discourse which accompanied the formation of the workers' movement was an essential medium, is unmasked by Baudelaire as the disguised manifestation of envy and as the pure desire to persecute.[6]

Beneath political indignation and the denunciation of a persecutor, the lucid gaze sees only selfish interest and, as in the passages of *Mon coeur mis à nu* devoted to the 1848 Revolution, the 'taste for vengeance' or again, according to a theme inspired by Sade (of whom Baudelaire was an admiring reader), the 'natural love of crime' (I, p. 679). 'We must always return to Sade, that is to say to *natural man*, to explain crime' (I, p. 595). As Pierre Pachet has shown, 'Baudelaire's politics' are 'close to Sade's' 'in the central role played by the idea of a criminal nature' and in the representation of a social bond immersed in a *cosmos* animated by 'the universal exercise of a limitless "tyrannical" or "despotic" violence'.[7] Thus, the chapter of *The Painter of Modern Life* devoted to the criticism of nature ('In Praise of Cosmetics', pp. 31–4) begins with an ironic reminder of the connection between nature and morality (Baudelaire is thinking here of Rousseau, but his remarks equally apply to the thinkers of the Scottish Enlightenment when they seek to make sympathy a natural faculty): 'The majority of errors in the field of aesthetics spring from the eighteenth century's false premiss in the field of ethics. At that time Nature was taken as ground, source and type of all possible Good and Beauty.' A portrait of nature taken directly from Sade is substituted for this false idea: 'it is she [nature] too who incites man to murder his brother, to eat him, to lock him up and to torture him.'

As for sentiment, as in the Gothic parodies of the previous century it is only hypocritical *sentimentality*. Either, when it is identified as a bourgeois attitude, it disguises self-satisfaction, complacency, hypocrisy (the 'guillotineurs have an *interest* in the abolition of the death penalty' (*Mon coeur,* I, p. 684)) and vanity or a form of 'eroticism' which is paradoxically qualified as '*holy*' (*Les Drames et les romans honnêtes,* II, p. 40). Or, when it is identified as an attitude of the weak, that is to say, in the first place of women and, in particular, of those 'people unhealthy from sentimental grisettes' *(ibid.),* it is attached, again as in Sade and, later, Nietzsche, to the instinct of self-preservation: the weak are *interested* in making pity a virtue in order to weaken the strong ('the woman Sand . . . has good reasons for wanting to suppress hell'(*Mon coeur,* II, p. 686). The truth of sentiment is revealed in the sentimentality which accompanies the 'philanthropic' intoxication of the hashish eater 'the product of pity rather than of love', 'the first germ of the satanic mind' freed by drug use which makes remorse the servant of pleasure: 'Remorse, that singular ingredient of pleasure, is soon drowned in the delicious contemplation of remorse, in a kind of voluptuous analysis.' In this way the principle of all 'beneficence' is unmasked and, for example, that 'nervous softening' which overcomes Rousseau with a 'sensual pleasure', filling 'his eyes with tears at the sight of a good deed': 'Jean-Jacques was intoxicated without hashish' (*Paradis . . .*, I, pp. 434–436). What is the nature of the dandy's 'heroism'? We see it in the dandy's ability to cast an impassive gaze on suffering, in his coldness and contempt for the sentimental.[8]

But once indignation and tender-heartedness have been repudiated, what position can the person speaking adopt within the statement in which the unfortunate and his suffering are confined? That of someone who looks. We have seen that the spectator is not the painter. The dandy, who precisely for this reason is higher than the painter in the scale of beings, does not paint, since he owes his greatness to the absence of utility, profession or occupation and creates nothing but himself.[9] His action is to do nothing. But sympathising with a painter, inasmuch as the painter looks, the meta-describer appears in the statement as the one who 'watches himself seeing'. This is the principle of Baudelairean 'reflexivity'[10] and of the closely related aesthetic project of 'containing at once the object and the subject, the world external to the artist and the artist himself' (*Philosophic Art*, p. 205). The aesthetic process (which, as we have seen with regard to the dandy, Baudelaire does not confuse with the fabrication of an artefact) thus consists in making the object enter the subject's interiority in order, by coming out from within, to reveal its unpresentable aspect. This process, and only this process, saves suffering from insignificance (from the absurd, from nihilism, etc.). Once the fictional characters of the persecutor and the benefactor have been dispensed with along with their illusory reflections, the *enragé* victim and the grateful *misérable*, suffering is looked at in the face and confronted in its truth, that is to say as pure *evil*. But it is by watching himself seeing evil that the spectator can unmask the truth of evil within himself and thus accomplish the fundamental aesthetic process which, in this topic, aims at the nondifferentiation of objective and subjective. The unfortunate's suffering is relevant insofar as it serves this process.

Take the brothel,[11] a typical site for viewing the suffering of the *misérables* in the person of the fallen and sickly prostitute, and consequently where the encounter between the dandy and evil takes place (the latter often personified by syphilis in French literature of the second half of the nineteenth century).[12] Baudelaire advises artists to frequent the brothel because sometimes, 'quite by chance, they [the prostitutes] achieve poses of a daring and nobility to enchant the most sensitive of sculptors, if the modern sculptors of today were sufficiently bold and imaginative to seize upon nobility wherever it was to be found, even in the mire' (*The Painter of Modern Life*, p. 37).

As this example suggests, a characteristic of this topic which distinguishes it from the previous ones is that, purposely detached from the political question, it is no longer subject to the constraints of a world conceived of in structural terms. In fact, as we have seen, one of the essential properties of the topic of denunciation as of the topic of sentiment, was to posit a *system of places* distinct from the human persons able to occupy them. Unfortunate, spectator, persecutor and benefactor, each could be by turns either one or the other. This constraint was actually necessary to secure a minimum compatibility between a politics of pity and the establishment of a political society which meets the requirement of common humanity within the framework of the political city.

7.4 The sublime and the picturesque

To understand this change we must briefly recall how the actor we have called the *painter* was constituted in the second half of the eighteenth century, an actor who cannot figure in Adam Smith's construction of the moral question because Smith posed it in political and social terms. Baudelaire takes this figure, as well as that of the dandy, (whose introduction into France by Barbey d'Aurevilly in particular is a feature of the wave of Anglophilia following reaction to the Napoleonic wars),[13] from the aesthetic debate of the previous century, particularly in the form it took in England. The constitution of aesthetics (traditionally dated from the appearance of Baumgarten's *Aesthetica* in 1750) immediately raised the question of its relationship with politics,[14] that is to say, in the terms of a contractualist political science, the question of the connection between *difference* and common humanity conceived of in the form of civic *equality*. Aesthetics is actually defined as a science of pleasure. Since like any science the constitution of its object is subject to a taxonomic imperative, it immediately carries out a radical distinction between two kinds of pleasure, elevated and low. Only some pleasures, the former, fall within the field of the aesthetic mode of knowledge.[15] The distinction is necessary if aesthetics is not to lose itself in a generalised hedonism. But in its train it brings two other kinds of distinction concerning the objects which can provide elevated pleasures on the one hand and the subjects capable of experiencing such pleasure on the other.

In fact aesthetic explanation remains contingent if any object whatever can provide elevated pleasures to no matter what kind of subject. To secure a distinctive aesthetic mode of knowledge we must either go in the direction of a specification of objects (the problem of the criterion of beauty) or in the direction of a specification of subjects (the identification of people of taste). The first route severely restricts the population of objects which are able to provide elevated pleasure. *Certain* pleasures correspond to *certain* objects. But, by the same token, this route can leave the specification of subjects relatively indefinite. Everyone is in a position to savour these pleasures on condition that they are presented with objects which can provide them. In this case, the addition of a theory of aesthetic *education* makes it possible to at least partially reabsorb the tension between the empirical matter of fact of an inequality of competence in matters of judgement of taste and the anthropological requirement of equality in the presence of the beautiful, which at the same time enables aesthetics to be hitched to politics. Socialising aesthetics are thus neoclassical.

The other route which, after their liberation from corporate restrictions, quickly finds favour with artists because it then opens up an almost unlimited field to their activity, is explored especially by English aesthetics. It consists in pushing back the limits on the list of objects which can give elevated pleasures. But a necessary result of this is that the restriction is shifted almost entirely on to the subjects who are capable of appreciating these pleasures.

This expansion of the range of objects of interest to the formation of an aesthetics extends from Burke's definition of an aesthetic of the *sublime* in 1757 to the debates at the turn of the century which signal the constitution of the *picturesque*, with the publication in 1794 of Uvedale Price's *Essays on the Picturesque*. The extension of the list of objects is carried out in the only direction open to it because it is a direction free from any prior investment, that of the *ugly,* that is to say, first of all, with the sublime – which implies a criticism of beauty,[16] – in the direction of the terrifying, dreadful, horrible and painful,[17] and then with the picturesque, in the direction of the trivial, exotic, popular, caricatural and carnivalesque. The process of pleasure is then defined by a double movement. In the case of the sublime, an initial movement of horror, which would be confused with fear if the spectator was not, as Burke notes, personally sheltered from danger,[18] or, in the case of the picturesque, of astonishment at the ugly, of disgust and rejection, is transformed by a second movement which appropriates and thereby appreciates and enhances what an ordinary perception would have rejected. The pleasure of the sublime is thus a delicious horror and a painful enjoyment.[19]

The category of the picturesque is constituted in order to classify and organise the objects which do not come into the categories defined by Burke: that of the beautiful – sweet and charming (founded on the passions 'which belong to generation') – and that of the sublime – terrible and obscure (founded on 'the Passions which belong to Self-preservation').[20]

Picturesque objects fall between these two categories as it were, and are characterised by irregularity, contrasts, and sudden variations, so that they may fall either on the side of the ugly or on that of the beautiful depending on the quality of the *gaze* brought to bear on them. The introduction of this new category presupposes a reorganisation of the previously established classes and, in particular, a devaluation of the beautiful which, detached from the Platonic ideal, is assimilated to those *average* forms that the greatest number of people are inclined to appreciate, out of habit as it were, to the detriment of the rare, extreme, eccentric forms – of deformities.[21]

But how should one look at an ordinary, ugly or trivial, object, a landscape with no apparent grandeur for example, or a cottage, a peasant, or a beggar, so as to isolate its aesthetic splendour? By seeing it, says, Joshua Reynolds in his *Discourse on Art* written between 1769 and 1790, in the way in which painters have portrayed it: when we have had 'continually before us the great works of Art to impregnate our minds with kindred ideas . . . We behold all about us with the eyes of those penetrating observers whose works we contemplate'.[22] The picturesque is thus the ability to see nature with the eyes of a painter.[23] This informed gaze is that of the man of taste who alone is able to contemplate the world with the eyes of the painter. By the power of a gaze which is able to frame it as it were, the object being contemplated is extracted both from the situation in which it is found and from the series of worldly objects to which it is attached by connections of use, in order to be connected to a different series which is that of objects already painted.

Only the man of taste can extract thus the power of a special enjoyment, of an elevated pleasure, from the ugly which is given to all. In a work written in 1801, *A Dialogue on the Distinct Characters of the Picturesque and the Beautiful,* analysed by Hussey,[24] Uvedal Price places three characters strolling in the English countryside who meet each other at an inn. One of them is ignorant in aesthetic matters while the other two are *connoisseurs* (who differ however in their aesthetic opinions, since one wants to maintain a distinction between the picturesque and the beautiful – closer to a standard of objectivity – whereas the other, more radical, subjects both categories to the power of the informed gaze). A first scene appears to them: a cottage, a hovel, near an old oak, next to which an old Gypsy and his emaciated donkey have halted. Mr. Seymour in his ignorance judges the scene ordinary, uninteresting and even ugly and Mr. Howard and Mr. Hamilton, the connoisseurs, endeavour to get him to understand what can be seen with the eyes of an amateur; the status conferred on them by the powers of a vision capable of seizing, and so of creating, the picture in the imagination by detaching objects from the ordinary connections in which they are as it were stuck: natural objects like waterfalls, animals or trees, artefacts – huts and carts etc., – or human figures constituted by the gaze as *figurines*. Not everyone has the same aptitude to become a character. The obtuse Mr. Seymour must also be got to understand how the parson's coarse daughter, foolishly judged by him to be ugly, is picturesque if one knows how to compare her with the house she both inhabits and resembles – like her, full of contrasts and irregular, with the appearance of poverty and, at the same time, neat and tidy.

To start with the picturesque belongs to nature in the aesthetic literature of the end of the eighteenth century. But the introduction of human figurines and the connection between the picturesque and the tour[25] open the way to a human picturesque and, as a result, to an urban picturesque of the *misérables*: gypsies, bandits, prostitutes, ragged children and, above all, beggars. They are no longer only an opportunity for the spectator to reveal his interiority, for a representation of his own feelings and his tender-heartedness in the face of suffering – as in the scenes of *A Sentimental Journey* in which Sterne describes his many encounters with the poor – but become the subject of a description which focuses upon their external appearance in order to paint them, to pick out the character, to make them seen as painters would see them., We come across this picturesque again, but now sublimated, in Baudelaire's *Paris Spleen*, with its painters: 'By my profession as a painter I am impelled to scrutinize attentively every face, every physiognomy that comes my way, and you know what delight we painters take in that faculty which gives more zest and significance to life for us than for other men' ('The Rope', *Paris Spleen,* p. 64); or again with its ragged, wild or begging children:

On the other side of the gate on the highway, standing in the midst of nettles and thistles, was another child, pitifully black and grimy, one of those urchin pariahs whose beauty an impartial eye would discover if, as the eye of a connoisseur detects an authentic master under the coachmaker's varnish, it peeled off the disgusting patina of poverty. ('The Poor Child's Toy', *Paris Spleen,* pp. 35–6)

7.5 Aesthetic difference

Inclusion of the horrible and the ugly, of the sublime and then the picturesque, and finally, at the start of the nineteenth century, especially in Goya,[26] of the grotesque, considerably extends the list of objects capable of being apprehended as they would be by a painter and thereby opens up an almost unlimited domain to the aesthetic. But, as Luc Ferry comments, the price to be paid for the development of this mode of knowledge is an

increasing subjectification of the aesthetic gaze. If subjectification really is
an accompaniment of the individualisation which characterises the artist's
condition and, more generally, the relationship to art in the democratic age,
which is the substance of Ferry's thesis, nonetheless, parodoxically it has
also, at least in the most consistent and radical forms expressed in the aesthetic of the *connoisseur*, precursor of the *dandy*, lead to the abandonment
of the project of maintaining contact between thought and pleasure, be it
only elevated pleasures, and of the requirement of common humanity
developed by eighteenth century political science, by the science that
inspired Rousseau when he became *politiste*[27] and in which the topic of
indignation found an essential resource on which to base a discourse of
denunciation in the form of a fundamental equality by birth and of rights.
For if, as Ferry insists, it is true that reflection on taste as the faculty providing access to elevated pleasures was for a long time accompanied by a
dogged refusal to abandon all idea of the objectivity of the beautiful, nonetheless the extension of the objects offered to aesthetic appreciation necessarily led at least to the marginalisation, if not the total abandonment, of
the idea of criteria of beauty.

Now what maintained contact or, to use an anachronistic term, an inter-
face between aesthetics and politics, was nothing other than the idea of
objectivity in the sense of perception without a particular perspective, the
origin of which is found not in experimental science but, as we have seen,
in the moral enterprise of the eighteenth century, from which science took
it fifty years later, and especially in Smith's attempt to reconstruct both
morality and the bases of a morally acceptable politics around the double
figure of an unfortunate and an impartial spectator who observes him from
a distance.[28] For if any or almost any object can provide elevated pleasures
and consequently any or almost any subject can be exposed to such objects,
how do we explain the fact that *some* can and others cannot savour these
pleasures other than by pointing towards properties inherent in the person,
like aristocratic qualities? The paradox of good taste as both a faculty of
human nature in general and the prerogative of elite minds runs through
the aesthetics of the eighteenth century and, in the aesthetic theory of the
abbé Du Bos for example, inhabits the debate on how the word 'public' – as
a general term subject to a restricted use [29] – should be understood.

The aim of Kant's aesthetics is precisely to untangle this thorny question.
Its destiny was, as usual, purely philosophical and consequently it had no
effect on the conceptions of connoisseurs and artists.[30] It is the last attempt
to combine together within an intelligible whole, and by means of the
machinery of reflective judgement, the subjectivity of taste which accompanies the expansion of the field of objects relevant to aesthetics on the one

hand and, on the other, the retention of a quasi-political requirement of common humanity, constituted here as intersubjectivity, by reference to a 'possible universal community', to a 'transcendental sociability', rather than to an interactionism of sympathetic relationships.[31] In contrast to what happens in simple subjective appreciation (I like this wine), the claim to universality and its communication to another person who is free to contradict it takes precedence here over pleasure. The appeal to a common faculty of judgement precedes the singular pleasure which thus owes its existence to the possibility of it being based on something that can be presumed to exist in anyone else, so that 'the feeling of aesthetic pleasure is nothing other than the feeling of this communicability of judgement'.[32]

But the project of integrating political and aesthetic legitimacy, the public space and the circle of connoisseurs, in a single general form, a project which to a large degree was foreign to English aesthetics as Shapiro has shown,[33] is no longer relevant at the end of the century, and even less so after the French Revolution, for those whose judgement is henceforth authoritative in this area: artists, critics and amateurs. For what authorises the shift of aesthetic limitations from objects to subjects is, in a circular manner, precisely the detachment from politics that this shift makes possible. Certainly, the man of taste is an 'aristocrat of the mind' – not of birth (as Beau Brummell, the model of the dandy, boasts when claiming lowly origins in order to make the freely chosen aristocratic character of his tastes and manners more prominent).[34] But ideas like these do not conflict with the political constructions in which the democratic idea is worked out because this kind of aristocracy only manifests itself with regard to objects which henceforth are radically apolitical and, at the same time, marginal at the level of the rights of man, even if they may be essential in the sphere of definitions of human excellence.

Taste applies to objects which give secret pleasures whose existence is unsuspected by the common run of men (a commonplace found both in Hume and D'Alembert),[35] but because these pleasures have no political relevance they can therefore be defined as *frivolous* in relation to people's rights (as we saw Sade say when calling for the extension of aesthetic liberalism to sexual tastes, the secret society of those with such tastes perhaps being understandable as a metaphor of the nascent aesthetics). The constitution of the aesthetic as such, and its break with politics, thus accompanies the development of a democratic political project, sometimes in the same authors. Politics takes responsibility for almost everything in this division of labour: the construction of the State, the social bond, public morality and, again in Smith, the economy. The aesthetic is constructed as the thought of pleasure, of the secret, of the rest. In this its realisation is a manifestation of that 'art of separations' which according to Michael Walzer is a characteristic of liberalism[36] and which continues the series of great divisions (between the natural and the supernatural, nature and society) which accompany the formation at the same time of an autonomous science of nature and a conception of the political as a contractual bond between human beings separated from the world of objects.[37]

But it is precisely in this apolitical space thus separated out and held in reserve that a theory of *difference*, of difference in the pure state, can be developed at the same time as the modern conception of political *equality* is being constructed. Difference constituted in this way, withdrawn from the jurisdiction of the public space to be confined within the order of pleasures, is *pure* difference in the sense that it is satisfied with its self-proclaimed existence. It is distinguished from the social differences with which politics is concerned inasmuch as it is not subject to an imperative of *justification* to the same extent and as a result it does not have to submit to a public test of its general validity. Its mode of manifestation is to be *affirmative*. But, as Reinhart Kosellek has shown for the establishment of the critical apparatus in the Enlightenment, withdrawal from politics may only be provisional.[38] In the way that criticism, which to start with sought to gain acceptance on the grounds that it was confined within the limited space of the Republic of Letters (Bayle's distinction between defamatory libel and legitimate criticism), then seizes hold of the entire political space at the end of the century, it is difference affirmed in matters of pleasures – that is to say in a domain outside of the public good and of no concern to the common run of people – which will constitute one of the most reliable bases of political anti-liberalism in the second half of the nineteenth century.

7.6 The passivity of the object

A spectator who sympathises with an unfortunate through a painter or, more generally, an *exhibitor*, thus finds himself freed, or, as we shall see, freed at least to a considerable extent, from the requirements of symmetry which were imposed on sympathy when it was conceived of as a political mechanism. For it is not claimed that the positions occupied by the painter and his object are reversible. In an aesthetic topic, the painter alone can see and show what is relevant about the unfortunate in his misery. There is not a great deal to be said about the relationship of the *misérable* to the painter however. Let us take again the example from *The Painter of Modern Life*. To be sure, if artists were to go more frequently, or more shrewdly, to brothels, they could 'find in the mire' a 'nobility' which is moreover everywhere for those able to see it and be 'enchanted' by it. But those 'poses of a daring and nobility to enchant the most sensitive of sculptors' which are sometimes taken by prostitutes, are achieved 'quite by chance', without being intentionally sought. The beauty extracted from the horrific through this process of sublimation of the gaze, which is 'able to transform any object whatever into a work of art',[39] owes nothing therefore to the object. Being natural, within the tradition of the picturesque it only has worth in the eyes of a spectator who can constitute it as something worth looking at.[40] In the aesthetic of the *Salon de 1846* the natural world is a world stripped of the things that fill it, a world of pure subjects.[41] As a human object, this world is similarly radically without will. It is in this sense that fashion and caricature, which Baudelaire introduces into the field of aesthetic objects, are constituents of the modern conception of art. They share, as G. Froidevaux has shown, a 'shifting of beauty's site of origin from the object to the subject'. Actually, for Baudelaire, who in his essay 'On the Essence of Laughter' (*The Painter of Modern Life and Other Essays,* pp. 147–65) takes the previous century's view of laughter (laughter is explained by the feeling of superiority man experiences with regard to another man or to nature), the caricaturist who aims to represent the ugly has 'the power to deform virtually all the objects of his observation and to create a representation whose comic effect is not due to the nature of what is represented, but to the nature of the contemplator'.[42]

What constitutes the painter's specificity and determines his disymmetry with regard to the object? It is his mobility. The painter in this topic, and the spectator when he sympathises with him, are able to change their positions in relation to objects which remain in their place. The *flâneur* who loses himself in the crowd of big cities[43] goes from the café to the street, from the brothel to the salon. In each of these places he sees wretched objects; he contemplates them and moves on. The same property is never conferred on the objects who, even when they are human objects, and even when they are granted the power to see (here, consequently, power par excellence), can only gaze on a single scene, the one before their eyes here and now (like the poor child gazing at the rich child of 'The Poor Child's Toy' in *Paris Spleen*). How is the Baudelairean *flâneur* distinguished from the hidden spectator – *Mr. Spectator* – who also constantly moves about, and whose metaphorical importance for setting up a public space defined by an aperspectival objectivity we have already noted? He is distinguished from him by the fact that the latter goes everywhere in order to join up networks. Each day he puts back into the common space what he has seen and, more importantly, heard in local places, so that he feeds a 'generalised conversation'. Lacking interiority he holds nothing back and so lets things go.

While similarly passing from one object to another, the *flâneur* devotes himself to a completely different process. In the first place he himself circulates so that when he is faced with different kinds of suffering different aspects of a limitless interiority well up. The *flâneur* is each time the same and different, becoming each of the unfortunates who appear before him.

Jerrold Seigel is right to situate the origin of the 'death of the subject' in the literary tradition in which the aesthetic topic is set out, the tradition which, from Sade to Bataille, passes through Baudelaire, Barbey or Huysmans.[44] None the less, we should be clear about what qualities of the subject disappear here. Death is the instance responsible. Actually, a subject which can be grasped in its unity can appear in terms of a retrospective and cumulative test, a final judgement. The subject really is 'dismissed', but only as a defendant. The 'radical liberation' Seigel speaks of – the destruction of the subject after that of the object, the concept of which he attributes to Sade as read by Bataille – is therefore solely a liberation from responsibility, which in any case logically follows from the setting up of a world without proper objects. It does not go so far as to give up the feeling of self in the experience of the moment, that is to say, it does not renounce enjoyment. In this topic it is by enjoying (or, what amounts to the same thing, simply by inverting the terms, by suffering), as an instance of enjoyment, that the 'exploded subject' of the *flâneur* lost in the crowd, drifting, given up to the impressions of the moment, exists, that is to say, can present the unpresentable in its essentials through the multiple facets of a fragmentary writing.

7.7 The operation of the sublime on pity

A question cannot be avoided. What remains of sympathy in this topic? If the positive sympathy of the spectator is only addressed to the agent we have called the painter, and if there is nothing in his intentions which is directed towards the unfortunate as such, can we still speak of sympathy in the sense we take it to have in Adam Smith's arguments? To deal with this objection we must bring a relationship into play which we have neglected until now. An aesthetic topic does not dismiss the spectator's sympathy for the unfortunate, even if this relationship is weaker than the one he has with the painter (but likewise, does not Smith say that the spectator sympathises more intensely with the benevolence of the benefactor than with the gratitude of the sufferer?). This is what distinguishes it from the non-reversibility of a Sadean model. In fact, in this topic the spectator sympathises with the unfortunate inasmuch as the latter is *put on view*. He is 'subjected to the gaze', 'feels penetrated and *possessed* by the other' with the 'passivity of an object being looked at' and 'becomes a thing in the eyes of others and in his own', as Sartre says with regard to Baudelaire.[45] But if he is put on view, it is in his suffering and by being inserted within an arrangement which, in the absence of a persecutor and benefactor, reveals the horror of this suffering and identifies it with evil – an evil irreducible to any scientific or religious kind of understanding and which can only be apprehended in an aesthetic grasp of the world.[46] It is because in the unfortunate evil is a suffering, because he is radically a suffering being, that the spectator here is distinguished from the Sadean hero immersed in the joys of debauchery. And in Baudelaire this sympathetic relationship may go so far as a quasi-identification with, for example, the ragpicker, who like the *flâneur* feeds from the refuse he gleans in the big city, or even more so with the streetwalker, who he 'nonchalantly includes . . . in the brotherhood of the *bohème*'.[47]

But this sympathy is not redemptive,[48] and if it sometimes promises compassion it is in order to shatter an expectation which is first aroused only in order to be deceived. Now the aesthetic topic rarely functions on its own. To produce its specific effect it must rapidly pass through other topics on which it briefly touches. Besides, the same could be said of the previous topics. Authentic indignation, for example, must pass through a pity which must be checked so that attention can be concentrated entirely on the identification and denunciation of a persecutor. Likewise, sentiment touches on indignation and keeps hold of it at the moment it turns into accusation in order to turn it around in the direction of the benefactor.

For examples we can take some of the pictures in *Paris Spleen* in which unfortunates, and specifically poor children, appear ('Cake', 'The Poor Child's Toy', 'The Eyes of the Poor' and 'Counterfeit'). The unfortunates at first seem to be described in terms taken from sentimental literature (to which Baudelaire directly refers in 'Cake': 'I was beginning to think the newspapers might not be so ridiculous, after all, in wanting to make us believe that man is born good' (*Paris Spleen,* p. 28)), which not only provoke pity for the being whose poverty they illustrate, but also open the way to tender-heartedness by arousing expectation of the arrival of a benefactor. But in these short sketches the expectation is immediately cut short by an outcome which radically departs from a topic of sentiment and seeks to plunge the reader into horror and disgust. The child who receives a piece of white bread from the narrator, for one short moment close to being a benefactor, which he sees as a cake, is savagely attacked by another equally poor child who could be his brother ('Cake'). In 'The Poor Child's Toy', the child with 'magnificent' toys looks enviously at the toy of a poor child beyond the gate on the highway. Is this a parable on the vanity of the goods of this world? No, the poor child's toy is a living rat in a box covered with wire. Or, a 'dear love' one evening on the terrace in front of a dazzling café on the one hand, and, on the other, a *misérable* on the street accompanied by two children in rags. The picture is set for a scene of tender-heartedness (women are sentimental). But the woman demands that the narrator get the proprietor to send them away. A kind man, before going out, gets money ready to distribute to the poor on his journey. In the right trouser pocket he places a two-franc piece intended for a particularly generous offering. But it is counterfeit. The beneficence is only a secret enjoyment: 'there is no sweeter pleasure than to surprise a man by giving him more than he expects' (*Paris Spleen,* p. 59).

8

Heroes and the accursed

8.1 Aesthetics and politics

To what extent does the aesthetic topic lend itself to political use? While the topics of denunciation and sentiment are orientated towards collective action, the former by making speech an instrument of mobilisation against those responsible for misfortune, the latter by making it a means for bringing together men of good will for beneficent assistance, and are thereby open to political investments, the aesthetic topic seems to renounce action and seems only to inspire a purely individual relationship to distant suffering. Besides, is it not mistaken to associate with a politics of pity with an attitude whose salient features are precisely not to be interested in politics and to reject pity? We will argue that the aesthetic topic was politicised in essentially two ways which, while being at the opposite poles of the political Right and Left, have enough in common to support swings from one to the other and to justify a connection in spite of their antagonisms and polemics.

We have seen that the novelty of an aesthetic view of the world is due to the possibility it offers, by the very fact of it not being political, of allowing a space for radical difference outside political constructions directed towards an egalitarian conception of the social bond. The models which attach distant suffering to political theory strive to distinguish the system of places from the empirical persons able to occupy them, which allows, as we have seen with regard to Adam Smith, a symmetrical apprehension of the relationship between the unfortunate and the spectator (the same being the case for the other places of persecutor and benefactor). But this requirement does not have the same force in an aesthetic topic which can therefore insert different persons firmly and durably in the different places. Through the eyes of the painter or exhibitor the spectator contemplates the unfortunate who is put on view, but this does not mean that the unfortunate, confined within his destiny and thereby having the status of an object, has the ability to do likewise.

Renouncing the reciprocity of perspectives, the aesthetic topic equally renounces justification in terms of a common good. Strictly speaking, there is no good common to the unfortunate subjected to his suffering and the spectator who, instructed in the aesthetic dimension this suffering can assume by the person who points it out to him, must nonetheless possess in himself, in the form of a gift or inherent sense, the faculty required to make something of this suffering, that is to say to examine it, take it into himself and get it to work like an operator so as to apprehend and display an internal evil. Moral capacity is assigned solely to the person who, in amazement, takes the other person's suffering by surprise and grasps hold of it.

This basic inequality suppresses the need of justification, at least in its universal definitions. What the spectator may say about the unfortunate is not intended for him. What he may write is not designed to fall into his hands. Thus he does not have to adapt his words so as to allow room for the possibility of the unfortunate taking them up himself or at least of a dialogue (for example, by censoring what, from the unfortunate's point of view, might be judged contrary to his dignity and consequently unacceptable). Like every modern artistic expression, his speech can therefore be essentially *affirmative*. It has nothing to do with an attitude seeking democratic legitimacy which intends speech to circulate in a debate. Consequently it can not only dispense with justification but discredit it as a desire to get the approval of the masses and so as weakness. Finally, the aesthetic topic has nothing to do with the persecutor and even less with the benefactor. It rejects both denunciation and sentiment and, appealing to the control of any emotion other than aesthetic, refuses to be either indignant or tender-hearted. This double refusal contains the possibility of a radical rejection of pity.

8.2 Resentment = denunciation + sentiment

The primacy of affirmation linked to an aesthetic vision of the world and the rejection of pity undoubtedly find their most vigorous expression in the work of Nietzsche. The perspectivist method, which relativizes values which at first sight seem to be opposites by turning them round against each other, confers a particularly striking form on the double rejection of denunciation and sentiment we first identified in Baudelaire.[1] Nietzsche develops the criticism of sentiment with the greatest virulence, rediscovering arguments and tones already encountered in the previous century, in the polemic against Schopenhauer (to which the first part of *Daybreak* is dedicated)[2] who, in *The Foundations of Morality* had, unlike Kant, emphasised the ethical dimension of the sympathetic emotions, of suffering faced with the suffering of someone else. Where Schopenhauer thinks he can discern altruistic sentiments, there is in reality only hidden egoism. All disinterestedness is only the dressing up of an interest: 'We follow our *tastes*, and this is what we give noble terms to and call duty, virtue and sacrifice.'[3] And how are these interests to be revealed? By replacing the question 'which one?' with the question 'what does he want?'[4] First argument: it is our own frailty which disturbs us at the sight of the misfortune of someone else. Second argument: we have pity so that we can feel ourselves superior to the unfortunate.[5] Third argument, that of pleasure: 'The condition of sentimental soft-heartedness' is a pleasure which is experienced in bad faith.[6]

A weakness for pity and justificatory aims (which is opposed to affirmative and pitiless power) are the two inseparable components of nihilism whose conjectural history is given in *On the Genealogy of Morality* in the manner of the fictional geneses of eighteenth-century political philosophy.[7] The interest for us of this history is that it makes pity the manifestation of *resentment* and consequently links criticism to the unmasking of an *accusation*, not only in denunciation, where it is quite visible as we have seen, but more importantly in the feeling which claims to eschew it. Nihilism, and we can follow Gilles Deleuze in his interpretation here, is nothing else but that 'deplorable mania for accusing' which expresses the 'spirit of revenge'.[8] But resentment assumes different forms depending on the position within the structure of domination occupied by the groups which embody it.

Consider to begin with the totally dominated, not only the slaves, Jews and Christians of the past, but also all those of our time who are reduced to total powerlessness, and women for example. We will call these the *dominated-dominated*. Reduced to impotence, they cannot act but cannot forget. Their consciousness is invaded by 'mnemonic traces' and this 'memory of traces is full of hatred in itself and by itself'.[9] But their resentment is creative: 'The beginning of the slaves' revolt in morality occurs when *ressentiment* itself turns creative and gives birth to values: the *ressentiment* of those beings who, being denied the proper response of action, compensate for it only with imaginary revenge.'[10] What they create is 'bad conscience', that is to say the 'internalisation of pain' which leads to the '[i]nstinctive exclusion of all aversion, all enmity, all feeling for limitation and distancing', to love as 'the state in which man sees things most of all as they are *not*'[11] and, as Gilles Deleuze says, to the 'God of the poor, the sick and the sinners'.[12] Christianity is reinterpreted in terms of the politics of pity, and the topic of sentiment is in the first instance attributed to the dominated-dominated. In the modern era Rousseau is their spokesman:

'*Feminine sensibility*: Rousseau, rule of feeling, testimony of the sovereignty of the senses, mendacious.'[13] As in Sadean anthropology, with
something like bad faith, the dominated preach pity to the dominant so as
to evade their blows.

In the next stage of this history the dominated acquire a relative power.
The will to power then manifests itself in the demand for justice: 'The will
to power appears . . . among a stronger kind of man, getting ready for
power, as will to overpower; if it is at first unsuccessful, then it limits itself
to the will to '*justice*', i.e., to the *same measure of rights* as the ruling type
possesses'.[14] Neither wholly dominated nor wholly dominant, these clai-
mants are *dominant-dominated*. Stronger now, they can give way to that
form of resentment which not only says 'it's my fault', but 'it's your fault',[15]
that is to say, to the demon of accusation. The topic of denunciation is
transferred to the workers' movement and to socialism. But this is so as to
reveal its antagonism with sentiment as illusory. For it is the same difference. Not only is 'the *democratic* movement . . . the heir of the Christian
movement' but 'apparently in contrast to the peacefully industrious democrats . . . the foolish philosophasters and enthusiasts of fraternity who call
themselves socialists . . . are actually at one with them'. What they have in
common is preference for the '*autonomous* herd' and above all 'the religion
of pity'. They are 'at one in the belief in a morality of *communal* pitying,
as though this were morality as such, as the height, the *attained* height of
man'.[16]

But do the dominant escape resentment? No, since under the pressure of
the dominant-dominated they too come to subscribe to the morality of pity
out of fear and hypocrisy. Dominants under constraint, they are only the
dominated-dominant. Like the most deprived, they seek protection by slip-
ping into the topic of sentiment which is thereby distributed at both
extremes of the scale of domination. 'The degeneration of the rulers and
the ruling classes has been the cause of the greatest mischief in history! . . .
For ultimately, the higher men measured themselves according to the standard of virtue of slaves.'[17] The result: 'the moral hypocrisy of those who
command. They know no other method of protecting themselves from
their bad conscience than passing themselves off as the executors of older
or higher commands'.[18]

Nevertheless, it is not enough to attach denunciation or sentiment to the
will to power of groups in confrontation. To set not only values against
values but groups against groups is to remain for ever within critical perspectivism. To move towards a politics we must leave perspectivism, that is
to say we must attach criticism to a principle of equivalence which has a
more general validity. This principle is force. Force is different from domi-

nation, for the history of domination has been and will be, at least until the return of the origin, that of domination of the strong by the weak: 'One of the finest remarks in *The Will to Power* is: "The strong always have to be defended against the weak."'[19] And again: 'The slave does not stop being a slave by being triumphant; when the weak triumph it is not by forming a greater force but by separating force from what it can do.'[20] All of the many collectivities who are the actors in Nietzsche's text are driven by the same will to power, by the state of their force when applied to other forces ('the will (will to power) is the differential element of force'[21]). This goes for all of them, dominant or dominated: slaves, ruling classes, Christians, men of power, superior and inferior races, socialists, the sick, women, chiefs, democrats, degenerates, higher castes, and so on.[22] 'What all of them want is to preserve their feeling of power, even if this requires constant attention and innumerable sacrifices in favour of their subordinates; or, in other cases, we subordinate ourselves to the powerful when it is the only way of affirming our existence.'[23] All the collectivities of past or present history are weak: the strong, the heros belong to the origin and the future. How will we recognise them? In the first place they will be pitiless; they will not suffer from the suffering of others: 'they load that condition [being soft-hearted] with deprecations and believe it to threaten their manliness and the coldness of their valour'.[24] The hero of the origin has a clearly predatory character: 'the blond beast of prey, the magnificent *blond beast* avidly prowling round for spoil and victory'.[25] This physical, racial hero, bracketed off by commentators for the last thirty years, yet clearly present in a multitude of prophetic aphorisms,[26] will inspire the fascist use of Nietzsche which we shall shortly give an example of.

But what do we know of the future hero? Gilles Deleuze tells us something. First of all, 'the hero is joyful'.[27] His force manifests itself joyfully because it is not reactive but active. He does not justify himself but is *affirmative*, since justification is a reaction. Compared with Socrates, Dionysus is 'the *affirmative* and *affirming* god'.[28] But if he is active, in what does his action consist? It is not defined in opposition to the inactivity of someone who contemplates the suffering unfortunate without helping him. This would be to fall back into the bad faith of pity, into responsibility, that is to say into the memory of the trace and so, necessarily, into the spirit of revenge and resentment. His action is therefore irresponsible: 'Irresponsibility – Nietzsche's most noble and beautiful secret.'[29] His action consists in being, that is to say in becoming, that is to say in making 'an affirmation of becoming': 'the affirmation of being'.[30] This joy manifests itself in the *tragic* which 'is the aesthetic form of joy'.[31] The hero suffers, but not in the manner of the complaining unfortunate or sympathetic spectator. For there are different qualities of suffering: 'there are two kinds of suffering and sufferers. "Those who suffer from the superabundance of life" make suffering an affirmation in the same way as they make intoxication an activity.'[32] 'It is joy that is tragic. But this means that tragedy is immediately joyful, that it only calls forth the fear and pity of the obtuse spectator, the pathological and moralising listener who counts on it to ensure the proper functioning of his moral sublimations and medical purgings.'[33] Against these bad spectators who give 'a mediocre sense born of bad conscience' to the spectacle of suffering, we need an 'artistic listener' and 'a logic of pure affirmation and a corresponding ethic of joy' for this spectator.[34] Such, for Gilles Deleuze, is the 'anti-dialectical and anti-religious dream which runs through the whole of Nietzsche's philosophy'.[35] By revealing and realising the will to power, the hero 'makes existence an aesthetic phenomenon'.[36] Since, in Nietzsche, 'it is in Art that the will to power is embodied in its absolute transparency', but because the 'mode of being of the work of art is the mode of being of the universe . . . Life itself is "the fundamental artistic phenomenon"'.[37]

8.3 First use: Nietzsche against humanism

By drawing on the extensive repertory of more or less faithful and more or less explicit re-readings in which the subject is resentment, we can identify an initial political embodiment of the Nietzschean version of the aesthetic topic. By holding on to the aristocratic heroism of the aesthetic topic, it consists in the rejection of weak, democratic justification to which the power of affirmation is counterposed and, the two movements being intrinsically linked, in the disqualification of pity in the nineteenth-century form of a would-be universal humanitarianism. To start with the aesthetic posture was able to acquire a political dimension insofar as it provided a point of support against political positions which sought humanitarian legitimacy. But in this first case, the emphasis is placed inseparably both on the criticism of pity, considered as the main symptom of the degeneracy inherent in democratic conceptions, and on egalitarian social aims. Nietzsche is employed first of all to combat the forms of humanitarianism which get their emotional and discursive resources from denunciation.

We can get a fair idea of this use by reading Pierre-André Taguieff's work on Nietzsche's reception in the French nationalist Right at the beginning of the twentieth century.[38] Although the founders of *Action française*, and Maurras first of all, were hardly sympathetic and even hostile to Nietzsche, due to anti-German prejudice,[39] the authors cited by Taguieff, such as A. Bertrand-Mistral, Edouard Berth, Henri Massis or Georges Valois, who join the initiators of doctrinal nationalism (P. Bourget, M. Barrès, E. Drumont, C. Maurras), praise Nietzsche for having 'fortified their energy' by freeing them from the 'democratic and humanitarian quagmire'.[40] The power of affirmation is emphasised in contrast with the spirit of discussion which is associated with the spirit of tolerance and pity, with universal sympathy portrayed as the revenge of the weak and mediocre. Reading Nietzsche in a traditionalist spirit (the germ of which, according to Taguieff, can already be found in Nietzsche) these nationalists saw tolerance, discussion and pity as different expressions of one and the same *irresolution,* that 'dialectical poison' which by refusing to cut through and choose, eternalises and clogs up debates, substituting chaos for the revelation of an order in voluntary affirmation, and being as such the striking sign of modern *decadence*.[41]

There is a form of reference to suffering in this theme, but it claims to be radically asymmetrical. The only suffering which matters is that of the hero. Now the hero, that is to say, the one who affirms his will in accordance with his own forces and relinquishes the disguised manifestation of the will to power in the expression of altruistic sentiments, is recognised in that being pitiless he no longer demands pity for himself. The hero cannot be identified with an unfortunate. Those who suffer without recognising any heroic dimension are the common run of humanity whose unimportant suffering gives them no status or distinction.

Vaunting the hero's suffering may itself propose a form of sympathetic relationship which may manifest itself in, for example, a willingness to make sacrifices in the hero's image. In the nationalist imagination which aestheticises the figure of the communal hero this relationship is found in the sacrifice made for someone who is the historical incarnation of a people's sublimity. Through the same process it can give rise to descriptions which are strongly aestheticised because they vaunt the grandeur of suffering. Many examples of this invested with political meanings could be given, from Wagnerian inspired vignettes to the self-portraits of Mishima as the tortured St Sebastian. However, by virtue of the radical asymmetry between the suffering of the weak and the suffering of the strong this involves a departure from the framework we have adopted. For although he suffers, the hero's status does not derive from this suffering. He does not come under consideration insofar as he suffers but due to the fact that he is strong and heroic. If he was weak his suffering would have no relevance or value. Deserted by the sublime, his suffering would sink into insignificance or abjection.

8.4 Second use: Nietzsche with the rebels

We now consider another way of referring to Nietzsche and of displaying an aestheticising relationship to suffering. Less radically hostile to pity than the previous use, it is interesting for having thrown a bridge between the aesthetic topic and the topic of denunciation, and in having thereby provided resources for the spectator of distant suffering. We find it especially developed in the work of Georges Bataille, but also in other authors such as Pierre Klossowski or Maurice Blanchot who were close to him from the end of the 1930s to the middle of the 1950s.

It possesses features we have already come across: the asymmetry of the aestheticising position; the attraction of a heroism which takes its distance and stands out from the crowd; the criticism of modernity and also, on the other hand, the unmasking of resentment within pity which only simulates commiseration with unfortunates the better to make an accusation. It is always the desire of the weak for revenge which is disguised beneath good sentiments. These different themes are quite explicitly associated with Nietzsche who is an obligatory reference here. However, it is distinguished from the previous version by, on the one hand, a complete lack of any reference to nationalism and, on the other, a different treatment of the criticism of modernity and of the relationship to Christianity. The critique of modernity is here, as in traditionalism, bolstered by an idealised past. But, especially in Bataille, this aristocratic, feudal or primitive past – the 'old world' – (with its features taken from medieval history and, in particular, ethnography) is not identified with *order* but, on the contrary, with *disorder*. It is contrasted with modern, industrial and democratic order, with the order of production and consumption, as expenditure is opposed to consumption, heroic excess to calculative reason, sovereigns and conquerors to the contemporary 'domesticated and docile' crowds.[42] Thus, it is in its disorder, excess, release, and chaos that the heroic grandeur of the 'old world' must be sought.

The Nietzschean reference equally sustains a virulent criticism of Christianity which is not found in the writers of the nationalist Right, mindful of maintaining an alliance with Catholic traditionalism. But as can be clearly seen in Georges Bataille, for example, who was formed in the Catholic tradition before opposing it, Christianity is, as it were, turned against itself and many features, like the criticism of calculation, the eulogy to *spending,* and the themes of *excess* or of *abjection,* lean on the Christian theme of the gratuitous gift or on monastic traditions of ascetic feats,[43] except that the supersession of Christianity is directed here towards the display of 'sovereign man' and subordinated to the unmasking of Evil, always hypostasized with a capital E. Finally, whereas the nationalist Right directed their attacks on humanitarianism at liberalism and socialism, the target here is sentimental humanitarianism insofar as it is the final avatar of Christian miserabilism.

What is the secret of sentimental pity? Precisely its hidden alliance with the social order; its ability to unite the dominated-dominated, who seek in a cowardly way to soften the hearts of their masters, and the dominated-dominant, who feign tender-heartedness in order to get support. And how is this secret to be disclosed? By once again revealing the partiality of a deceptive universalism and the secret it disguises. Sentimental pity, beneath its apparent consideration of every misfortune whatever it may be, actually holds on to just one figure of misfortune: that of the unfortunate who does not accuse, who fails to acknowledge his own violence, who preserved in gratitude as it were, cuts himself off from evil, and whose resentment and hidden violence is expressed precisely in a preference for benevolence insofar as it contains a tacit accusation directed against those unfortunates who denounce and accuse. This orientation thus offers the possibility of a connection with the topic of denunciation. But this connection must be constantly controlled so as to maintain the maximum difference from the social humanitarianism behind which Christian miserabilism hides.

What are the favoured figures of the unfortunate in this theme? As in the topic of denunciation, they are those who are accused. Only the accused are relevant since the humanitarianism unmasked here is no more than the medium for a hidden accusation. But denunciation takes it upon itself to exonerate those accused who are innocent. Now the postulate of innocence is still a concession to sentimental humanitarianism. To take it upon oneself to exonerate the accused who are innocent is still to play the game of morality and thereby to involve oneself in the resentment which is supported by morality in its choices and accusations. Thus the emphasis will fall on other types of accused: on the *guilty accused;* on those accused who through crime affirm their base action without repentance and who openly and publicly lay claim to the evil which is in them (as it is in everyone). The *Accursed* also offer the possibility of aesthetic heroisation. They are heroic in their detachment from the crowd anaesthetised by its belief in good, and more importantly because by not begging forgiveness they do not try to justify themselves but affirm themselves as they are. Through their violence, through everything they are, they unmask the secret violence of resentment buried deep within benevolence and they constantly question everything. They risk everything, they are excessive in evil, and their excess gives them sublime beauty. It is precisely this dazzling beauty which is unbearable to the common run of humanity and can only be contemplated by those already lost, in themselves, in the depths of their inner experience.

8.5 Sade in the Bastille

A paradigmatic figure stands out in France in the years following the Second World War, the synthesis of the Accursed's features: *Sade in the Bastille.* It is the figure, then, of someone who is accused and even persecuted, since Sade is in prison; but it is the figure of an accused who far from being an innocent, lays claim to the evil he is charged with, at least in his writings, and who consequently cannot be cleared (which would presuppose that we wanted to exonerate him of his crimes) and who can only be restored in his exemplarity by casting light in his person on the evil that he himself puts on view. A good way of unravelling this version of the aesthetic topic thus consists in following the trace of Sade in the writings published in Paris during the post-war years. With the help of the excellent bibliography published by E. Chanover in 1973, with its 588 references, we can make a rapid and schematic periodisation of writings on Sade.[44] Primarily of interest to doctors up until the 1930s, or to the inquisitive lovers of literary or erotic oddities, at the end of the period between the world wars Sade begins to be taken seriously, and even venerated, by the Surrealists (Breton, Desnos, Eluard, Char and Peret who devote texts to him[45]) who are bolstered by the enormous work of erudition undertaken first by Maurice Heine and then by Gilbert Lély. But it is during the war and especially in the immediate post-war period that Sade is referred to in major theoretical works.[46] If we follow Pierre Klossowski, Georges Bataille, who sailed very close to surrealism according to Sartre,[47] was particularly important in fixing the partly mythical genealogy going from Sade to Nietzsche through Baudelaire.[48] To give substance to the figure of the Accursed, we turn then to two studies of Sade written by Georges Bataille, the first republished in *Literature and Evil*[49] and the second in *Eroticism.*[50] We will also make use of two works extensively quoted and discussed by Bataille, *Sade mon prochain* by Pierre Klossowski[51] and *Lautréamont et Sade* by Maurice Blanchot.[52] Finally, we will also refer to the chapter of *Literature and Evil* on Jean Genet and, more precisely (once again it is the reprint of an article published in *Critique* in October 1952) on Jean-Paul Sartre's work on Genet: *Saint Genet, comédien et martyr.*

Sade, the Accursed, is solitary ('the solitude of his prison' – *L*, p. 98[53]), 'unrecognised' (his manuscripts are lost, stolen – *L*, p. 86), and 'in chains' (*L*, p. 87). But this chained man is 'a monster' (*ibid.*), 'one of the most rebellious and furious men' (*ibid.*). He is 'the very essence of release' (*L*, p. 86) and his book *The 120 Days of Sodom*, which belongs not to writing but to action, since Sade is not at all a 'man of letters' (*L*, p. 91),[54] is 'the first book to express the true fury which man holds . . . the book that can be said to dominate all books' (*L*, p. 88). What makes him a hero? The fact that he gave himself up to 'excess' to a degree which goes beyond 'common possibilities' (*L*, p. 97). The fact that he accepted the sacrifice of reason (of calculation, work, production, etc.), since 'by definition, excess stands outside reason' (*E*, p. 168). The fact that he is, precisely, this release in chains, who 'loved' Evil (*L*, p. 90), but so that he could achieve a 'clear consciousness of what can only be attained by release' (*L*, p. 94), to gain access to 'the vision of the "whole man"' (*E*, p. 165). He attained this release through a 'passion that he may sometimes have cursed [which] meant that the sight of other people suffering excited him to the point of insanity' (*L*, p. 97). But if he could attain this release through eroticism, it is because the erotic drive is in itself a release and because 'revelation' already 'breaks these limitations' (*L*, p. 99). 'Erotic conduct' is opposed to 'normal conduct' as 'spending' is to 'getting' (excess to reason, disorder to order, etc) (*E*, p. 170): 'There is in [sexual desire] an element of disorder and excess which goes as far as to endanger the life of whoever indulges in it' (*L*, p. 99). Sade is thus a hero for bringing man's limitations to self-consciousness: 'he experienced states of release and ecstasy which seemed to him of great significance with regard to common possibilities. He did not think that he could, or should, cut out of his life these dangerous states to which his insurmountable desires led him' (*L*, p. 97). *Lucidity* here is the supreme quality of the hero: he asked himself 'that unfathomable question which they [these excessive states] raise for all men'. In this way he reconciles 'violence, which is blind, and the lucidity of consciousness' (*L*, p. 98). This man in chains is thus the most *free*, that is to say at the same time the most modern and the most antimodern since he is 'remote from the world where thrift is the rule' (*E*, p. 170). He proposes the 'need for an existence freed from all limits' (*E*, p. 166) and 'a sovereign type of humanity whose privilege would not have to be agreed upon by the masses' (*E*, p. 166). But because 'solidarity with everybody else prevents a man from having the sovereign attitude' (*E*, p. 171), Sadean freedom, this 'unfettered freedom', requires 'a sort of heroic cynicism' which 'cuts the ties of consideration and tenderness for others without which we cannot bear ourselves in the normal way' (*E*, p. 171).

At this point in the picture Georges Bataille inserts a long quotation from Maurice Blanchot which advances an interpretation of the way in which 'De Sade seems to reason somewhat' and which uses the terms of a forceful Nietzschean kind of scientism or biologism.[55] The 'demands of sovereignty' are asserted through 'an enormous denial' (*E*, p. 171). But this negation is total because it is also negation of oneself: 'Denying others becomes in the end denying oneself' (*E*, p. 175). It is by this negation that Bataille recognises Sade as the first to not only suppress the object (a process already found in the Baudelairean aesthetic) but, through the absence of distinction between object and subject, to fragment or destroy the subject.[56] How does this negation of the self manifest itself? In a 'will for self-destruction', a 'demand for nothingness' (*L*, p. 89). Georges Bataille here takes up a theme developed at length by Maurice Blanchot. The Sadean hero knows that it is incoherent to take power as a principle without exposing himself to suffering at the hands of someone stronger the same treatment he himself inflicts on someone weaker. But it matters little to him: 'For if indeed luck does reverse itself and turn into misfortune, the latter will actually be no more than another facet of fortune itself'.[57] For he demands for himself the tortures he makes others suffer: 'from these ills, these agonies, she derives pleasure; these tortures delight her'.[58] This is the price we must pay to 'found man's sovereignty on a transcendent power of negation'.[59] Bataille pursues this argument which shifts Sade from the side of the unfortunate, or rather which puts him in a place in which the opposition of victim and torturer is transcended. The torturer's violence is silent, it does not justify itself, but only ever says that it exists, never that it has a right to exist. By speaking from this place Sade lends a voice to the victim: 'In complete contrast with the torturer's hypocritical utterances, de Sade's language is that of a victim. He invented it in the Bastille when he wrote the *Cent vingt Journées*' (*E*, p. 190). From his prison he conducts a trial which is not directed at his judges and which does not seek to clear his name, but which accuses men, God and nature in their totality. He thereby reveals that 'those things which repel us most violently are part of our own nature' (*E*, p. 196).

8.6 The sovereign gutter-snipe

In spite of numerous references to the sovereign, the conqueror, the old aristocracy, etc., the exceptional nature of the Sadean hero, that which puts him outside the common run of humanity, has nothing to do with social class. This is Maurice Blanchot's argument at the beginning of his book. To be sure, Sadean libertines 'generally belong to a privileged class'. But 'power . . . is not merely a state but a choice and a conquest'; 'Actually, Sade's heroes are recruited from two opposing milieux: from among the highest and the lowest, from among the mighty of the world and, at the opposite pole, fished up from the sewers and cesspools of the lower depths'.[60] Blanchot takes the example of La Dubois: 'for the poor, crime alone can open the doors to life; villainy is the recompense for injustice, just as theft is the revenge of the dispossessed':

> Now, what happens? A few men have become powerful. Some were bequeathed power by birth, but they have also demonstrated that they deserve it by the way in which they have accrued it and enjoyed it. Others have risen to power, and the sign of their success is that, once having resorted to crime to acquire power, they use it to acquire the freedom to commit any crime whatsoever. Such then is Sade's world: a few people who have reached the pinnacle, and around them an infinite, nameless dust, an anonymous mass of creatures which has neither rights nor power.'[61]

The chapter of *Literature and Evil* on Jean Genet, the 'sovereign gutter-snipe' (*L*, p. 156), allows us to clarify and connect with our own times the figure of the Accursed as Georges Bataille conceives of him. The 'modern man who rebels against, and rejects, everything outside himself', admires in Jean Genet the 'passion for "nullity", for the negation of the most attractive values, which reaches a form of perfection owing to the continuous expression of abjection' (*L*, p. 148). From the start, what is fascinating in the monstrous books of Genet, who 'has chosen to explore Evil as others have chosen to explore Good', is the form of 'the revolt of a man banished from society' (*L*, p. 149). This excluded person is, George Bataille says, a potential saint: 'Genet wants abjection even if it only brings suffering' (*L*, p. 150). Such is how his 'fundamental aspiration towards sanctity' for which 'abjection is the only path' (*L*, pp. 150 and 151) manifests itself. But this surpassing to sanctity is the form taken by the aspiration to 'sovereignty' when it is fulfilled in the punishment desired and sought after: 'Genet can only be sovereign in Evil: sovereignty itself may be Evil, and Evil is never surer of being Evil than when it is punished' for the 'true royalty of crime is that of the executed murderer' (*L*, p. 152). Sanctity and sovereignty are equivalents: 'Sovereignty is the power to rise, indifferent to death, above the laws which ensure the maintenance of life. It only differs from sanctity in appearance' (*L*, p. 155). They come together in an aesthetic: 'The beauty which inspires lyricism is an infraction of the law – of that which is forbidden and which is also the essence of sovereignty' (*L*, p. 155). Seeking 'that perfect Evil which is perfect beauty' (*L*, p. 157), Genet 'knows that he is sovereign' (*L*, p. 155).

How is this sovereignty recognised? By its absolute freedom of aesthetic choice, free from all moral or political restrictions. Thus Bataille dwells on this passage taken from *The Thief's Journal*: 'he . . . spoke about morals. Simply from an aesthetic point of view, I could not listen to him. The good will of moralists clashes with what they call my bad faith. If they can prove that an act is detestable because of the evil it causes, I alone can judge its beauty and elegance from the lyricism it arouses in me. I alone can refuse or accept it' (quoted in *L*, p. 155). Bataille applies the Christian language of grace to this sudden revelation of the beauty of Evil (it is 'something resembling a state of grace', *L*, p. 156) and, more precisely, traditional kinds of analyses (probably reminiscent of readings of Kierkegaard) which emphasise the nonreflexive character of love in the sense of *agape*. Take the character of Armand, for example, the 'most detestable figure who may have interested Genet more than any other' (*L*, p. 156). Genet can reveal his aesthetic grandeur on condition that it is absolutely foreign to Armand's intentions: 'Is Armand's cowardice a hidden form of aesthetics? Does he have a disinterested preference for cowardice? He would then be at fault before himself. Genet, who sees into him, is the only one able to envisage his cowardice from an aesthetic point of view: he goes into raptures before him, as one might before a magnificent work of art' (*L*, p. 157). We return here to our starting point: to those Baudelairean prostitutes who, from the 'mire' where they wallowed, achieve 'quite by chance' without having willed it 'poses of a daring and nobility to enchant the most sensitive of sculptors'.

8.7 The liberating release

How can the figure of the Accursed find a place within a political picture? By way of freedom. Even in chains, through his essential release the Accursed offers proof of freedom. For release, like sanctity, beauty and sovereignty are on the side of 'infractions' of the 'rule', of transgression of the 'forbidden'. 'Liberty is always open to revolt' (*L*, p. 169). It is always possible to effectuate transitions from revolt to revolution, although it must be done with prudence. Sade in the Bastille still serves as someone to get us through. Sade in chains is freed by a riot in which 'popular sovereignty, which is both turbulent and rebellious' expresses itself and consequently by a 'release' which has the characteristics of 'festivity', 'the very essence of release' (*L*, p. 86). Certainly, we must beware of exhausting the exemplary character of Sade in revolutionary banality: 'The sense of the revolution is not 'given' in his ideas' (*L*, p. 86). It may be only a matter of a 'misunderstanding', but this misunderstanding has the character, as a note points out, 'of what André Breton designates speaking of *objective chance*'. The man 'obsessed by the idea of an impossible liberty' (*L*, p. 87), this 'unfortunate', 'in chains for ten years', was delivered from his cell by a liberating riot.

The connection between revolt and revolution and the emphasis put on exclusion make it possible to supersede the distinction between social categories which the workers' movement of the nineteenth century, in its desire for organisation, respectability and political recognition, and Marx himself as well, strove to keep apart: they make it possible to overcome the opposition between the working classes and the dangerous classes, between the proletariat and the lumpen proletariat, between the poor and the underworld, the masses and the mob, the representative of a collectivity and the solitary rebel, political violence and individual delinquency, etc. These transitions privilege an encounter and alliance between the aesthetic topic and the topic of denunciation. Nevertheless, the need to remain distinct from denunciation imposes an exacting demand on the properties that candidates for the place of the unfortunate must possess in order to be relevant for an aesthetic gaze. One kind of unfortunate is immediately excluded: those who recognise the topic of sentiment, who are attached to the Good and are inclined to gratitude in the expectation of a benefit. These unfortunates, these weak accomplices of the strong who torment or exploit them are abandoned by the aesthetic topic to their fate for 'submission and obedience . . . are on the side of the Good . . . Good is as closed as a rule' (*L*, p. 169).

But the alliance with denunciation also has its limits. In common with denunciation, the aesthetic position recognises that the unfortunate passes himself off as someone accused and even persecuted. All the texts examined insist thus on Sade's suffering, on the stupidity and malice of those who were responsible for his incarceration (and especially his mother-in-law). For only someone persecuted gets to the heart of Evil from where he reveals the Evil in all of us. However, the Accursed can only be identified with difficulty as an unfortunate who a denouncer would exonerate by revealing a persecutor. For we have seen that this would again assume an asymmetrical distribution of Good and Evil; a division between Evil, assigned entirely to the persecutor, and Good which would then be the share of the unfortunate and the person who assumes responsibility, on his behalf, for denunciation and accusation and who would still be something of a benefactor, in spite of the violence with which he is inspired. This restriction especially excludes unreserved adherence to any position on the basis of which a claim to exercise political power could be made.[62] Sade, freed by the riot and a 'fervent republican' (*L*, p. 91), has nothing in common with a revolutionary in the usual sense of the term, because he can never be on the side of the State, of power. It follows that if the Accursed can devote himself without regret to Evil, under no circumstances can he be, for example, a political torturer serving the State. In all the writings on Sade published in the 1950s this prohibition is expressed in a ritual reminder of Sade's horror for the guillotine and guillotiners which at times gives rise to somewhat surprising comments on Sade's humanity. Thus, this 'monstrous man' is 'resolutely set against the judge' (*L*, p. 91, translation modified) and resolutely opposed to 'punishment' and 'repression' (*ibid.*); as soon as the Revolution is in power he was 'boundlessly generous' and 'we know that he saved the Montreuils from the scaffold and that Madam de Montreuil, his mother-in-law, had had a *lettre de cachet* issued against him' (*ibid.*).

Forbidden to the torturer – who is on the side of violence and Evil but also on the side of power and so, on this account, on the side of silent violence or of justified and consequently hypocritical violence – the unfortunate's place is not one that is easily available for an ordinary victim (a political victim of torture for example) who in thinking to act well does not provide the necessary guarantees of monstrosity. By the same token these exacting constraints limit the possible uses of the aesthetic topic as a political resource by the spectator of suffering. While it is effective for integrating in a political problematic those who, from the point of view of denunciation as well as sentiment, find themselves excluded – gangsters, bandits, marginals or lunatics – it leaves us disarmed in the face of suffering which is explictly political unless it includes dimensions of horror and solitude, as in the case of great terrorists acting on their own without the support of a popular movement for example. Its political value, however, is due to the pity it arouses – reluctantly since it displays a certain contempt for this feeling – for the unfortunates without hope of redemption from either of the other two topics whose pictures we have sketched. It is difficult to call upon the aesthetic topic for dealing with the suffering of real weak, anonymous unfortunates – the massacred or starved, the poor of the shanty-towns etc. – and ultimately it is most effective in the domain in which it was born – that of fiction.[63]

PART III

The crisis of pity

9

What reality has misfortune?

9.1 The proposals of commitment

In relation to the media, the spectator occupies the position (described at the end of chapter 3) of someone to whom a *proposal of commitment* is made. A different spectator, who recounts a story to him, and who may be a reporter, that is to say an eye-witness, or who may have gathered information supposed to have come from an eye-witness (as in the case of press agency reports), conveys statements and images to a spectator who may take them up and, through his words, pass on in turn what he has taken from these statements and images and the emotions they aroused in him. These are not just any kind of statements and images. Informed by one or other of the topics whose broad features we have sketched out, and as such mixing a description of suffering and the expression of a particular way of being affected by it, they propose to the spectator a definite mode of linguistic and conative emotional commitment. The spectator can accept the proposal made to him, be indignant at the sight of children in tears being herded by armed soldiers; be moved by the efforts of this nurse whose hands are held out to someone who is starving; or feel the black beauty of despair at the execution of the absolute rebel proudly draped in his crime. He can also reject the proposal or return it.

As many works published in the last fifteen years have shown, and particularly those of David Morley and the *Glasgow Media Group* on the viewers of *Nationwide* (a popular British television news magazine), those of S. Livingstone and P. Lunt on *Kilroy* (a British television programme presenting debates between members of the public and experts) and above all the work of T. Liebes and E. Katz on the reception and interpretation of *Dallas* by six different publics, far from passively absorbing the spectacle put before them, television viewers put to work important critical capabilities.[1] According to Liebes and Katz, these critical abilities, present to an unequal extent in different publics, essentially depend upon familiarity with the media, that is to say both on the competence acquired through the use of television and on the information given by commentaries in the general or specialised television press on programme makers, producers or presenters, conditions of filming and so on. By *critical abilities* Liebes and Katz refer to the ability to distance oneself from the spectacle itself in order to make inferences concerning the film-makers' *intentions* and usually in order to impute intentions to the film-makers other than those manifestly presented by the programme.[2]

The critical spectator must then assume responsibility for unmasking the *manipulation* of which he thinks he is the target and endeavour to establish a different way of being concerned by what happens, by what the presenter passes on to him for him to pass on to someone else in turn. But as soon as this posture is adopted, bringing the critical investigation to a halt becomes problematic. Contrary to what takes place in a face to face relationship, here the inherent uncertainty of communication, which presupposes a decisive halt to the exploration of the other person's intentions, cannot be alleviated either by interpretation of external signs sometimes unwittingly given by the interlocutor and which may be thought to betray him, or by relying on prior information concerning the sensibility and beliefs we attribute to him. One of the consequences of the increasing distance between the unfortunate and the spectator and of the interposition of a presenter by the media, is actually to make the 'transcendental limitations' of communication patent by suppressing the possibility of reliance upon contextual indicators.[3] The 'requirements of communication' – concerning 'checking the other person's intentions' – which come up against 'basic limitations' in the case of individual communication in a face to face situation, thus have 'empirical corollaries' in the case of communication at a distance. Take, for example, the fourth limitation of communication (the 'requirement of truth, authenticity and appropriateness' which is undecidable because subject to the other person's criticism which I am not obliged to accept). Pierre Livet, from whom these comments are taken, illustrates this by what he calls 'collective charity' in the case of communication at a distance.[4] The latent undecidability of the authenticity of a gift in face to face situations (since the donor's intentions may be hypocritical), is nonetheless mastered practically by taking into account contextual indicators, but in charity at a distance this undecidability is made manifest as it were since the 'donor' who is 'only ever in contact with an administration', 'cannot even hope to see his benefit acknowledged by the beneficiary' and because it is 'accepted from the start that part of the donor's intentions can be diverted'.

The media situation, by not only distancing the spectator from the unfortunate but also from the person who presents the unfortunate's suffering to him (without himself necessarily having witnessed them), makes more exacting the necessary conditions of trust which, as many experimental studies have shown, are broadly dependent upon an effect of presence.[5] The media situation thereby considerably increases the uncertainty inherent in communication which, when it is a question of communicating misfortune, is made fragile by the existence of a conflicting number of ways of being affected when faced with suffering. In fact, the critical relationship maintained by the different topics (some of the figures of which we have identified) already introduces suspicion, sometimes latent and at other times explicit, about the emotions, desires, and intentions which accompany representations of suffering and, more radically, about the very existence of the unfortunates whose misery is shown.

We will argue that this uncertainty has increased over the last twenty years along with an increase, following a partly independent logic, in the quantity and intensity of the spectacles of suffering put before spectators and committed to appearing affected by the suffering they show (since we have seen that such a spectacle cannot find its justification in itself but must be directed towards eliciting action in the world). In this chapter and the following one we examine some of these uncertainties (each of which weighs unequally on the different topics) and the anxieties they generate. To identify them we start with a schema used to analyse the relationship between real and fictional emotions taken from Bijoy Boruah's *Fiction and Emotion*.[6]

9.2 Real emotions and fictional emotions

Bijoy Boruah's work is produced within the framework of theories which aim to link emotional states to cognitive processes and, more particularly here, to *eliciting situations* including a judgement, which consequently presupposes the mobilisation of a belief and orientation towards a formal object, that is to say towards an evaluative framework allowing identification of particular objects falling under a certain description to which this belief corresponds. To take up a contrast we have already used in chapter 3, emotions are associated with declarative thoughts (*thinking that*) and not *entertained thoughts,* corresponding to states in which one is *thinking of.*

But how can we explain the fact that emotions like fear or tears can be displayed in a situation we know to be real as well as in relation to objects we know to be fictional (as, Boruah says, when I cry when reading *Anna Karenina,* for example)? Boruah's solution distinguishes between general

evaluative beliefs which support judgements on objects falling under a
certain description (lions are dangerous) and *existential beliefs* which
support judgements on the very existence of the object (the lion is in the
courtyard). These two types of belief are linked by the imagination which,
on the one hand, nourishes evaluative beliefs (as we have seen with regard
to suffering in the previous chapters) and, on the other, can stand in for existential beliefs. In fictional emotions, evaluative beliefs are activated normally, but the imagination makes up for the want of existential beliefs. This
allows Boruah to affirm (against Kendal Walton's theory of the *fictionalised self* [8] which supposes that the spectator descends, as it were, into the
fiction and makes himself believe that he himself exists in this mode) that
fictional emotions are not the result of bad faith but can be considered
genuine emotions.

However, the absence of existential beliefs is far from being negligible.
Let us extend the schema of emotions on which Boruah relies. Informed on
one side by evaluative beliefs (nourished by the imagination) and by existential beliefs (for which the imagination can substitute itself), emotions are
also connected on the one hand with *desires* and on the other with *intentions* committing one to *action*. The evaluative belief in the nastiness of
lions and the existential belief in the presence of a lion are connected with
the *desire* for survival so as to arouse the *intention* to flee which is fulfilled,
in leading to *action*, by taking to one's heels. According to Bijoy Boruah,
emotions charged with an intention to act are orientated towards action,
that is to say towards a change of situation. Thus, he says, anger supported
by belief in an injustice contains at the same time the desire to punish the
guilty. But we have seen that in the presence of fictions, absent existential
beliefs are replaced by the imagination with which evaluative beliefs are
combined. In the cases of both fiction and reality, retention of the same
evaluative beliefs accounts for the continuity between real and fictional
emotions. But to define reality it is the criterion of action which predomi-
nates. What is put forward as something on which one can act or attempt
to act (even if the lion's strength makes action uncertain) appears as real.
Fictional emotion can then be defined as an 'emotion without action'.

9.3 Four uncertainties

We start from the hypothesis that emotion staged by the media occupies an
unstable position between real emotion and fictional emotion. It is attached
to real emotions inasmuch as the suffering of unfortunates put on view is
given as real, assigned to a form of support arising from existential belief,
its authenticity capable of being the subject of argument. It is precisely to

the extent that the suffering reported is real that the spectator's emotion must equally have the characteristics of a real emotion for it to be morally acceptable. But the spectator is sheltered. He is not in the same situation as the unfortunate; he is not by his side during his agony or torture. The inaccessibility of action may bring media-staged emotions close to fictional emotions. To prevent the unacceptable drift of emotions towards the fictional we must maintain an orientation towards action, a disposition to act, even if this is only by speaking out in support of the unfortunate. But also there must not be too much doubt about the real existence of the unfortunates represented, or about the intentions or desires of the presenters and spectators.

Basing ourselves on the schema of emotions used by Boruah, we can identify four forms of uncertainty which may give rise to a worry about the well-foundedness of a media-staged emotion and thereby loosen its relation to reality. The first uncertainty concerns evaluative beliefs; the second, existential beliefs; the third, desires; and the fourth, the intentions which commit one to action.

To begin with we will examine the uncertainty concerning evaluative beliefs by focussing on the element which seems to us to play a central role in the critical relationships between the different topics and which concerns the presence in each of them of a principle of *accusation* and a mode of *selection* of the unfortunates who matter. We will then consider a particularly striking example of increasing uncertainty concerning existential beliefs. Actually, existential beliefs do not bear only on belief in the existence of the world of suffering and of the unfortunates who endure it. For this very general belief would not be enough to support the introduction of pity into political argument. Existential beliefs then must bear on unfortunates who are ascribed a particular status in some way. Specifically, the object of existential beliefs is the occupation of the system of places we defined on the basis of Adam Smith's *The Theory of Moral Sentiments.* To be sure there are unfortunates who have been offended, but who are they and who are their persecutors? How can we identify them without too great a risk of deceiving ourselves in the tangle of actions, arrangements and social roles? And we know as well that benefactors exist; but how do we recognise them and distinguish them from hypocrites who, on the pretext of doing good, only follow their appetites and disguise their interests? And so on.

The topics as we have portrayed them so far are not enough to answer these questions. They must be extended into more specific and tighter descriptions which note the features which permit us to identify the occupants of the different places and which allocate characteristics to the pre-established system of roles and firmly fix them there. We will use the term

ideologies to refer to these descriptions which make it possible to give substance to the actors of misfortune and we will consider cases arising from
what has often been called the crisis of ideology, inasmuch as they introduce an uncertainty about the *reference* of statements concerning suffering.

In the next chapter we will examine the last two uncertainties on our list,
which may equally be thought to have grown considerably in recent times.
The third uncertainty brings suspicion to bear on our desires. To be licit,
our emotion in the face of suffering must be underpinned by the desire to
see the unfortunate's suffering diminish or cease. At different points in this
work we have seen that a questioning of the altuistic character of our
desires has been a constant feature of debate on the reality of moral sentiments since the eighteenth century. However, we will attempt to show how
the unmasking of the obscure depths of desire we have witnessed in the
recent past, and based in particular upon psychoanalysis, has taken such a
radical turn that henceforth nothing has seemed able to escape it.

Finally, the fourth uncertainty, essential for our purposes, concerns the
intention to act which we have seen plays a determinant role in the judgement
brought to bear on the acceptable character, on the moral or on the contrary
illicit, even perverse character, of a media-staged emotion. To be able to
presume an intention to act without too many questions, action must not
appear to be entirely out of reach, even when its object is far away. Action
being essentially carried by speech in this case, there must in particular be a
reasonable adherence to the belief that *speaking is acting*. One of the conditions of this belief is the existence of a clear distinction between the world of
representation and the world of action. Informed by representation, words
must really be deployed in the world of action in order to be effective. We will
attempt to show how the radicalisation of deconstructionist criticisms and
their diffusion in a broad public (particularly of specialists of the media
themselves, journalists, television commentators, etc.), has helped to blur this
distinction and thereby hold the order of action at arm's length and even to
render it illusory. To take an example we will encounter shortly, if the demonstration, in the political sense of a street demonstration, is staged entirely
for the purpose of its representation and mediatisation; if we have left the
order of representation for a 'hyperreal' world in which images and reality
are one and the same, then the criterion of action disappears and we can no
longer distinguish between the real and the fictional.

9.4 First uncertainty: the conflict of beliefs

To start with let us rapidly clarify the way in which doubt spreads in the
sphere of evaluative beliefs. To do this it will be enough to bring together

and order comments scattered throughout our descriptions of the different topics. Our argument will be that the critical relationship between the topics has the effect of revealing in each of them a disguised mode of *accusation* and a disguised form of *exclusion* which as a result is in conflict with their claim to universality and the good. This critical unmasking has been a feature of the political use of the different topics and specifically of their immersion in a space polarised in terms of the opposition between *Left* and *Right*. But how could the different ways of apprehending suffering have avoided this in a political order which places the argument of pity at its centre? More precisely, the tension between the different topics of suffering is politicised in the sense that it has been possible to connect all of them to different ways of selecting and retaining from the ocean of the world's unfortunates those unfortunates who really matter, that is to say, in the final analysis, those to whom it is appropriate to give aid. Within the realm of political struggles the conflict of beliefs supporting pity thus corresponds to a conflict over the identification of the unfortunates whose cause is judged to be politically worthy. This conflict takes on a primordial importance. The central problem confronted by a politics of pity is actually the *excess* of unfortunates. There are too many of them. Not only self-evidently within the domain of action (which requires a ranking and the definition of priorities), but also in the domain of representation: media space is not unlimited[9] and cannot be entirely given over to showing misfortune.

To reveal the partiality of visions of misfortune, and the veiled accusations levelled against the unfortunates left on one's hands, the conflict of the topics has taken the form of a reduction to interests and relations of force. Their universalist aim is questioned and the different topics are thrown back to the communal bond against which they were albeit constituted. It is in fact a characteristic of the communal bond that it is not afraid to accuse and does not claim to be impartial. Moral indignation accuses and excludes. Being on the side of closely related unfortunates ('the French first of all') and especially of those whose conduct is deemed to conform, then those it accuses of being responsible for misfortune, those it persecutes and excludes, must be foreigners or members of ethnic minorities (Jews, Muslims, etc.), marginals (homosexuals, prostitutes, etc.[10]), or those tainted with pollution and regarded as impure (like the '*caqueux*' who were victims of social segregation in Brittany until the eighteenth century[11]). Their suffering is not given any consideration because they are held to be responsible for their ills and thought to be dangerous to the community.

With regard to the chevalier de La Barre affair analysed by Elisabeth Claverie, we saw how the topic of denunciation was constructed precisely against the communal bond by taking sides with someone who has been accused and whom one exonerates. Claiming universality, the topic of denunciation disregards the allegiance of the unfortunates for whom responsibility is taken. As the bearer of humanitarianism it is as opposed to communitarianism as the political Left is to the Right. To be sure, it does not eschew accusation, but it only accuses *accusers* and in order to exonerate stigmatised innocents. However, as we saw when considering the criticisms of denunciation, coming precisely from the Right, this humanitarian and universalistic aim can be undermined in two ways: on the one hand by showing that the only reason for the defence is to disguise an accusation. What the denouncer really wants is not to exonerate an innocent but, under cover of doing good, to accuse and in so doing to exact vengeance. On the other hand it can be undermined by revealing partiality in the choice of unfortunate. Far from being open to all suffering, denunciating prefers unfortunates who protest, who appeal or even, in a kind of persecution mania or 'paranoia' (often imputed to critics on the Left by those on the Right),[12] who invent false accusations and persecutions so that they can in turn, and with good conscience, accuse and persecute innocents.

The topic of sentiment also lays claim to universality. It is open to every kind of distress. However, its rejection of accusation, since it ignores the persecutor in order to concentrate on the benefactor, seems to protect it from the accusation of being accusatory. But it is precisely on the basis of this option that it can be accused of partiality, especially by the Left, and in the same gesture its disguised accusation can be revealed. Actually it is easy to bring out the preference of sentiment for a particular category of unfortunate: those unfortunates who *do not accuse* and who, even before receiving any benefit, are already predisposed to gratitude. By showing how this preference goes together with an accusation levelled against the unfortunates who protest, appeal and accuse, the topic of sentiment and the communal bond can be connected with each other in the same rejection. The sentimental position is only a hypocritical way of dissimulating communal exclusion and of putting the very ones who persecute and exclude in the benefactor's position.

It will have been noted that we can recognise here one of the main thrusts of criticism directed against nineteenth century philanthropy by the Left (more vigorously in France than in the Anglo-Saxon countries). Philanthropy is accused on the one hand of picking out the *deserving poor* – that is to say those who do not protest – the better to exclude the bad poor – protestors and revolutionaries etc. – and, on the other hand, of covering exploiters with the benefactor's mask.[13] Mostly developed in social history studies published over the last thirty years, this criticism has revealed a will to social control and the domination of the popular classes by the bourgeoisie underlying the actions and professions of philanthropical or human-itarian faith.[14] As it is a question of evaluating philanthropic action, the enterprise of moralisation which is a feature of it, frequently expressed in sentimental terms, can be stressed. The 'moral reading of poverty' writes Giovanna Procacci in a recent work which focuses on the treatment of the social question in France in the first half of the nineteenth century, '... above all spread the idea that the poor were responsible for their poverty, which notwithstanding was wonderfully in accord with the sentiment of charity'. However, with the secularisation of the 'conception of poverty', 'a distinction is made between, on one side, the beggars and vagrants who dis-organise a rural economy and so deserved nothing, and, on the other, the "submissive" poor who had to be reintegrated within the social mechanisms of production and consumption'.[15] In this way the theory of domination extends into a social critique the arguments which we have seen have been made since the eighteenth century against benevolent sentiments and which are here now revealed to be the expression of class interests.

As for the aesthetic topic, we have already had occasion to suggest, in chapter 8, how it found suitable unfortunates, particularly in its recent forms. The principle of selection is deduced from the double criticism from which this topic issues. In contrast with sentiment, it keeps its distance from denunciation. On the one hand, it points towards the rebel by dwelling, as in denunciation, on an unfortunate who is *accused*, excluded and put under a social ban, and on the same grounds it rejects the communal bond as well. But the person accused cannot be an innocent that one is content to exon-erate, for the presumption of innocence would close down the revolt and open the way to the return of sentiment. The solution we identified by fol-lowing the figure of Sade in the Bastille in post-war literature, and espe-cially in Georges Bataille, consists in taking sides with a *guilty accused* or, more precisely, with an accused who proclaims aloud and from on high his responsibility for the crimes of which he is accused. But, how can this con-figuration, often associated with libertarian formulae, be said to be an accu-sation? Here the trace left by the reading of Nietzsche in his commentators enlightens us. For the accusation which drives the aesthetic topic wishes to be no less radical than its will to look at evil in the face in suffering: it is *an accusation against accusation*. Thus all accusation, be it explicit as in denun-ciation or decoded as in the revelation of resentment beneath sentiment, can have the finger of shame put on it and be cast back into oppression, in a radical supersession towards an absolute liberation.

Does the aesthetic topic belong to the Left or the Right? While leaning to the Right in its elitist component, in its preference for affirmation (in opposition to justification and debate) and in its taste for the strong (oppressed by the weak) and for solitary and tragic heroes, it leans to the Left when, stressing the defence of someone accused (rejected by society), it is linked to denunciation and takes the sentimental view of misfortune as its principal adversary (the 'good sentiments'), as was the case in the version we took as our model. But this compromise always has a tactical character (as in the way the surrealist aesthetic allied itself with the 'revolution', for example). The aesthetic topic is of the Left, but in a critical way, so as to subvert and supersede it. It grants itself the *lucidity* of an avant-garde.

To pursue the description of the uncertainties we have picked out from the model used by Boruah to analyse relationships between fictional and real emotions, we start with three groups of texts. The first deal with the question of the camps in the Soviet Union and this will serve to illustrate the increasing uncertainty with regard to the identification of unfortunates. The second, which reveals the unconcious drives underlying two kinds of altruistic actions – social work and political militancy – will provide us with a fair idea of the way in which desire becomes prey to suspicion. Finally, the third, which questions the distinction between reality and its representation, particularly televisual representation, and plunges the universe into the postmodern beyond of the spectacle – since denunciation of the society of the spectacle still assumes the possibility of something not belonging to appearance – will enable us to note how it has been possible to reduce the very intention to act to a naive illusion. Each of these three groups of texts is addressed to one or other of the three topics we have identified. While the first deprives denunciation of its defences and removes all assurance from it, the second ends by discrediting good sentiments. As for the third, it extends the topic of the sublime to the extreme point at which the negation of all externality renders the question of suffering, and of its representation, simple-minded or outmoded. In this analysis we have deliberately chosen to mix together works and documents of unequal importance and theoretical scope in order to stress the collective character of the questioning thus produced and in order to bring out the way they oscillate, to unequal degrees depending on the case, between the constative and the performative. As well as portraying anxieties, in the manner of a self-fulfilling prophecy they have also helped to reinforce and to disseminate them and, in particular, to sow doubts about the truth of discourses and images transmitted by the media either by revealing, as in the case of the Soviet camps, the stubborn blindness of the major means of information (especially those of the Left), or again by arguing from the fact, not in itself very debatable, that all representation is the result of a construction, in order to extend considerably the empire of manipulation and illusion[16] and, as a result, of suspicion. Finally, through the description of a current debate, we will see how these uncertainties, which have become *platitudes*, now serve to bolster, if not the renewal, at least the reinforcement of antihumanitarian arguments (which have otherwise shown a remarkable stability since the eighteenth century). By examining the counter-arguments opposed to them we will seek to identify how the spectators' anxiety might be reduced without averting their gaze from misfortune or abandoning the project inherent in the modern definition of politics of facing up to unnecessary suffering and relieving it.

9.5 Second uncertainty: the avoidance of reference

This second uncertainty does not focus on evaluative beliefs but on what Boruah calls 'existential beliefs'. No doubt is raised about the existence of victims and persecutors, unfortunates and benefactors, accursed beings and artists who reveal their sombre beauty; but there is uncertainty about the occupants of the different places. The general framework is accepted without question, but doubt arises when this framework has to be filled in with a more detailed description allowing one to pass from a character drawn with broad brush strokes to the precise identification of real persons. Such an uncertainty may be attached to the proposal of commitment itself which then has an ambiguous character, or the spectator may introduce uncertainty and thereby withhold his commitment and fail to go along with the proposal put to him.

This uncertainty is rarely the result of a perceptible inadequacy, as would be the case if, for example, the reported scene was confused or obscure or if the gestures of the different actors were too ambiguous to be determined (which could be the result when a video film is used as evidence in a trial for example: is that man preventing the other one from drowning or is he pushing his head under the water?). Rather the uncertainty bears on the ability of different candidates to occupy the available places. This or that person suffers; someone shows it, someone sees it; he is a victim; but then this or that other person must be responsible; this or that person gives his support; but it could be otherwise; one could give miserable representations of the persecutor also. And does not the benefactor actually produce the misfortune of the person he claims to help? And the exhibitor, does he not have his own interests: to use the suffering of others to demonstrate his own representational skills? As for the victim, who knows whether or not behind the great presence of his suffering on the screen he conceals reserves of violence even worse than the violence from which he seems presently to suffer, ready to be unleashed, or perhaps already at work, far from witnesses and out of sight etc.

One of the principal ways of reducing referential uncertainty is to fix *systems of accusation* by constructing stable chains so that the places in a particular situation can be filled by connecting different actors to large entities, to collective persons, States, classes, ethnic groups, etc., whose determination includes allocation to one or other position of the system of places and its stabilisation. By following this chain we can then distribute the actors of the represented situation, allocate them to their places and provide them with a description including their status arising from the place to which they have been allocated. Whereas the topics, whose portrait we have drawn in the previous chapters, are relatively open in the sense that they can accommodate a fairly wide range of actors in each of the places (which we could put in another way by emphasising their structural character) without however including a tight description of these actors, the existence of such and such a chain enables us to give a detailed description of the occupants and consequently to refine the selection of candidates. It is then, only when these chains are established and stabilised, that we can properly speak of *ideologies*.

One example of such a chain immediately stands out: the one that, in the France of the 1950s, connects States, treated as actors on the international stage (acting through diplomacy or war) and thereby on the stage of history (the United States, the USSR, Europe, East and West, the colonies, etc.); political regimes (communism, democracies, imperialism, socialism, etc.); the kind of collective persons we call parties, the best representative of which, the one whose existence seems the least debatable during this period, is the Communist Party, which also acts by calling for demonstrations and mobilising, for example; classes, particularly the two antagonistic classes, the bourgeoisie and the proletariat, themselves having an immanent and historical capacity for action; groups, which can be given an empirical description (and therefore be the subject of debate on whether and how they can be connected to classes), such as workers, intellectuals, bosses, executives etc.; individuals with a status in the terms of the topics of suffering, like political prisoners, the unemployed, the oppressed, exploiters, criminals, etc.; and finally human persons given individuating properties such as their name, sex, age and so forth.

Faced with reference to a real situation, a demonstration for example, with both injured police and protesters, an arrest, etc., to fill the places the entire network of the chains must be called upon, the different links of which are interdependent (which is what is meant when one claims to determine the 'historical meaning' of the situation). It follows that if there is uncertainty about just one of the links there is every chance that this will have repercussions on the others. Although chains can be followed in both directions, even so they are developmentally orientated or hierarchised so that the degree of certainty with regard to the allocation of places in the picture of a real situation depends on the confidence one has in the stability of the positions allocated to the large entities. A crisis of ideology is characterised precisely by the dissemination of an uncertainty of this type throughout the network.

9.6 1950: the Soviet camps and the identification of the victims

Consider the example of the debate on communism which, from 1947, the year of the publication of *Humanisme et Terreur*,[17] to 1955, when *Les aventures de la dialectique*[18] appeared, set Maurice Merleau-Ponty and Jean-Paul Sartre against each other,[19] the latter's version of the conflict appearing in 1961 in a text devoted to the story of his friendship with Merleau-Ponty and of their break.[20] Almost forty years afterwards this debate is still astonishing for its bitterness and for the Byzantine and frequently obscure character of the arguments conducted by the most famous philosophers of the post-war period over hundreds of pages for more than ten years. As in the case of the polemic between Jean-Paul Sartre and Albert Camus which followed the publication of *L'homme révolté* in 1951, and which Raymond Aron comments upon in *L'opium des intellectuels*,[21] the vigour of the dispute seems all the more surprising for making adversaries out of individuals whose political agreement broadly prevails over their differences (at least until the years 1953 to 1956 during which Jean-Paul Sartre aligned himself with the Communist Party). This led many commentators to look for extrinsic motives like, for example, an opposition resulting from different careers or from the effects of competition in the Parisian intellectual world,[22] or even a French peculiarity, especially marked since surrealism by the connection between moral non-conformity, aesthetic modernism and revolutionary exaltation.[23]

Now it seems to us that one of the stakes in this debate is precisely the identification within local contexts of actors who are able to occupy the places of victim, persecutor or benefactor. If, as Raymond Aron writes with regard to Sartre and Camus, the protagonists in these polemics share the fact of being 'humanitarians' and of wishing to 'reduce suffering and liberate the oppressed',[24] they should be able to make their judgements converge on the tricky question of the selection and ranking of the unfortunates who matter. One albeit distant advantage of adherence to Marxism was its ability to orientate denunciation. In effect it provided benchmarks for picking out the suffering which was relevant within the immense tide of human misery and for overcoming temporal or spatial distance by connecting the suffering of human persons here or there to the large entities occupying the global stage on which humanity's historical destiny is played out. In the debate which set Jean-Paul Sartre and Maurice Merleau-Ponty against each other this is how all the entities whose list we have rapidly drawn up are referred to; the biggest and smallest appear, often in the body of a single page, or in a single sentence.

How is uncertainty introduced? Through the more insistent appearance on the public stage than hitherto of victims of the Soviet communist regime following publication of testimonies on repression in the Soviet Union, and in particular of Arthur Koestler's novel *Darkness at Noon* devoted to the Moscow trials, which was immensely successful in the immediate post-war period. The Moscow trials fundamentally called into question the Marxist form of denunciation because its accusation cannot claim to exonerate innocents but rather, as in a communitarian figure, quite clearly aims to charge them and eliminate them. Now if communism is the persecutor in the Soviet Union, how can it be invoked to defend the oppressed against exploitation in France and elsewhere in the world? In *Humanisme et Terreur* Maurice Merleau-Ponty acknowledged the existence of repression in the Soviet Union, even if in retrospect he seems to have underestimated its importance. But essentially he tries to find arguments which will prevent this uncertainty from spreading throughout the whole network to take in everyday situations like a strike by workers belonging to the CGT. Without going into the details of a particularly honest and subtle argument which especially has the 'incomparable advantage', as Lefort notes in his Introduction, 'of making visible a mechanism of justification which is usually hidden',[25] we note that the defence mounted by Maurice Merleau-Ponty loosens the links between communism in France and communism in the USSR[26] and distinguishes an autonomous Marxism relative to the actions realised in its name by emphasising its critical capacity and ability to unmask the mystification of liberal humanism: liberal humanism 'puts up with the violence in the reality of the Western democracies and con-demns it where it is raised to the status of a principle and plays a role in the emancipation of the oppressed'; 'Marxism, understood as critique of the existing world . . . remains valid and as such cannot be surpassed'.[27] The demonstration is supported by evoking the victims of imperialism (Vietnamese or Palestinian peasants, p. 51; the bodies of mutineers shot by Pétain in 1917, p. 53; the regime endured by Dreyfus on Devil's Island, p. 300, etc.) which *balance* acts of violence committed in the East and West: what is denounced when it is a question of the USSR is no worse than what is hidden when it is a question of the West. The possibility of a choice is suspended.[28] The balance is then tilted in favour of the Soviet Union by a second set of arguments which consolidate the unbridgeable gulf between communism and fascism on the one hand (so as to 'ward off the idea of a preventative war' which is justifiable when confronting fascism), and which require judgement to submit to considerations of situations and contexts on the other.[29]

The argument is underpinned by a use of the temporal dimension that it is worth spelling out. In effect, while human victims are situated within time, because what human beings are victims of (a trial, a repression, a massacre, a famine, etc.) belongs to the order of events, large entities are famous survivors. Not only must we take the present into account when judging them, but also the past and the future. But like human beings, they can only be judged by their actions, that is to say by the positive or negative events which have affected, presently affect and will affect the life of persons. Their trial thus leads to a mixture of current victims (of a repression taking place for example), past victims (of a massacre which took place in a period now over, for example), and future victims (whose persecution we can foresee and attempt to prevent), without clear distinctions always being made between them. The collection of victims will clearly be more problematic the longer the stretch of time involved. But in certain political circumstances a considerable temporal span does not prevent past victims from being evoked alongside present victims and envisaged future victims. In the case here in question, 'the USSR is bathed in the glory of its victory over Nazi Germany';[30] the past victims of Nazism and those of the struggle against fascism therefore undoubtedly lend all their weight to the trial. But the future also figures here, and if it is by nature uncertain, if 'there is no science of the future' (p. 63), it is invoked none the less so as to leave open the possibility that the USSR may again be 'on the side of the brave', of 'the primacy of the future', and of 'the will to create humanity'.[31] As for the present, it offers a portion of contingency, of the unpredictable, a 'fundamental chance', which must relativise political judgement, that is to say judgement concerning actions undertaken by those holding political power.[32]

A clear conclusion is drawn from this series of arguments: acknowledgement of the fact that injustice and victims exist in the USSR should not cast any serious doubt on the identity of those who occupy the place of victims and persecutors in capitalist societies and, in particular, in France, nor should it lead to any systematic suspicion about the intentions of communists when, in multiple concrete situations of political struggle, strikes, demonstrations, legal actions, etc., they denounce the exploitation of the victims of capitalism and when they charge imperialism with responsibility for this.

In January 1950, three years after the appearance of *Humanisme et Terreur*, Maurice Merleau-Ponty published an article in *Les Temps modernes* on 'L'URSS et les camps' which is a response to the publication, with a commentary by David Rousset, of the *corrective labour code of the RFSSR* in *Le Figaro*. Nourished by new information, criticism of the USSR now goes much further than it did in *Humanisme et Terreur*: 'Short of receiving illumination, we accept that these facts call the meaning of the Russian system entirely into question.'[33] The main arguments used in *Humanisme et Terreur* are none the less retained. On the one hand, 'in the balance of forces the USSR finds itself *grosso modo* on the side of those who struggle against the forms of exploitation familiar to us' (p. 338). On the other hand, even if the Soviet concentration camp system and the Nazi concentration camp system share common features, communism and fascism cannot be equated because communists accept the camps and oppression in the name of humanist values rejected by the fascists: 'This means that we have nothing in common with a Nazi and that we share the values of a communist'; a communist 'has values *in spite of himself*. We may think that he compromises them by embodying them in the communism of today. Still, they are our values and, in comparison, we have nothing in common with a good number of the adversaries of communism' (p. 337). These arguments seek always to prevent the ten to fifteen millions of Soviet internees (according to the estimate accepted by Merleau-Ponty), and their communist persecutors, from spreading into the critical networks in such a way as to make it impossible to identify victims and executioners here in France and everywhere else except the Soviet Union.

The argument used is one of geographical and political distance. When we are far from the USSR we find communists who are 'men like us' and a 'healthy communism'.[34] Distance, which metaphorically increases the length of the networks, prevents the USSR from spreading into the system of accusation. The evidence of victims there creates no uncertainty about the identity of victims here or elsewhere.[35] The camps in the USSR must be denounced and, without singling out their inmates in particular (p. 343), all oppression everywhere must be criticised ('forced labour in the colonies', 'colonial wars', 'the conditions of black Americans', 'Spanish detainees', 'Greek prisoners who at this moment are dying on the islands'). Besides, the support of Marxism remains indispensable to introduce order, by means of equivalence, into the procession of unfortunates increased and potentially destabilised by the millions of Soviet internees. How otherwise can we avoid the pragmatism of those 'American intellectuals' for whom: 'The facts of exploitation across the world pose . . . only dispersed problems to be examined and resolved one by one. They no longer have any political idea' (p. 339).

In his text devoted to Maurice Merleau-Ponty in 1961, Jean-Paul Sartre tells the story of how in the rift between them his friend came to abandon a line of defence that he, Sartre, will take it upon himself to maintain and even consolidate. Maurice Merleau-Ponty saw the entry of North Korean troops into South Korea as proof that Stalin thought world war to be inevitable and the socialist countries were preparing a preventative war. This new world conjuncture, which made the USSR a 'preying power' like the others,[36] threw the identity of victims, those who persecute them and those who bring them assistance into confusion; as Jean-Paul Sartre says, it was no longer possible 'to distribute the roles': 'Everywhere on earth we exploit, massacre and pillage'.[37] According to Sartre, the conclusion Merleau-Ponty drew was silence: 'Words could only lie: there remained this refusal of complicity, silence.'[38]

For his part, Jean-Paul Sartre congratulates himself for having escaped such a withdrawal into silence. How did this come about? In the first place by abandoning the whole picture in order to focus on one part of it; by concentrating, he tells us, on the suffering of the Koreans: 'I did not reflect so far and this is what saved me from melancholy. Merleau did not notice the Koreans, I saw only them. He moved too quickly to world strategy and I was stuck on the blood.'[39] And, in the same gesture, he escapes by committing himself in an *affaire*: the Henri Martin affair. It is by participating in the Henri Martin affair that he switches: 'My vision was transformed: an anticommunist is a dog, I was not part of that, I will no longer ever be a part of that. You will find me truly naive and in fact I had seen others without being moved. But after ten years of ruminations I had reached breaking point and only needed a nudge. In the language of the Church, it was a conversion' (pp. 248–9).[40]

Commitment in the Henri Martin affair (defended until then primarily by the communist press), to which Sartre devoted a book in 1953 including, besides his commentaries, documents and testimonies of the non-communist left (J.-M. Domenach, M. Leiris, Vercors, J. Madaule, F. Jeanson, etc.),[41] allowed uncertainty to be reduced by redirecting indignation in an unquestionably just cause. It was truly a question of an *affaire* in the sense we defined in chapter 4. There is a constant implicit or explicit reference to the Dreyfus affair (for example, p. 206, with regard to the question of a pardon for Henri Martin).[42] Henri Martin is a nobody whose biography can be given (in the first pages of the work): a worker, son of a worker, hero of the FTP when seventeen years old, committed volunteer in the navy immediately after the war. Sent to Indochina he gradually realised, as the letters to his family published in the same volume testify, that he was not being used against the Japanese and fascists as he had been led to believe, but against Indochinese who were demanding their freedom. Henri Martin is indeed an *innocent* unjustly *accused* for political reasons. First of all he is accused of an act of sabotage in which he had not taken any part. Then, after refusal of three separate requests for termination of his enlistment, he is accused of being guilty of undertaking the demoralisation of the army by distributing leaflets in favour of peace. Arrested, judged for the first time in October 1950 by the Toulon maritime tribunal (which acquitted him of the charge of sabotage), he is condemned to five years imprisonment with a dishonourable discharge. Having signed an appeal and the Appeal Court having annulled the judgement on the grounds of a drafting error, he is judged a second time in July 1951 by the Brest maritime tribunal. Unanimously found guilty of demoralisation of the army, he is sentenced to five years imprisonment despite supporting testimonies from naval officers, old resistance fighters, notably those of the Vice Admiral Muselier and Louis de Villefosse.

It is by starting from below, leaning on the case of this particular person unjustly condemned, and by rising back to the top, that is to say to the political causes of this injustice, that the facilitating paths connecting the misfortunes of ordinary people with the conflict between large entities can be restored. In this plea, Jean-Paul Sartre does not in fact exploit the link between Henri Martin's action and the objectives of the proletariat, communism and the USSR. Henri Martin, who does not belong to the Communist Party, is simply someone who acted according to his conscience. On the other hand, taking apart the motives of his adversaries is an opportunity to reveal the hidden bases of the fury of which he was the object: it is the Korean war which allowed a 'police operation' undertaken within the framework of a colonialist war to be transformed into a 'crusade' against the USSR.[43] It is indeed then a question of the USSR in this affair, but solely in the heads of reactionary governments and consequently without the identification of the victims of the Right directly affecting what takes place within the USSR.

How is the uncertainty, if not completely reduced, then at least contained? By disconnecting the revelation of victims in the USSR and criticism of the Communist Party from the fate of the unfortunates, the victims of capitalism and imperialism. The USSR and the Communist Party can be criticised without breaking with Marxism, the revolutionary will, the proletariat, or the denunciation of capitalism and imperialism. At the cost of a realignment of the system of large entities (China opposed to the USSR, Lenin to Stalin, etc.) it is possible to maintain the facilitating paths which allow one to pass from the denunciation of daily injustices to political analyses which give them a global and macro-historical meaning.[44]

9.7 1975: The Soviet camps and the crisis of denunciation

To continue this examination of *referential uncertainty* we transport ourselves twenty-five years on and open André Glucksmann's book published in 1975: *La cuisinière et le mangeur d'hommes. Essai sur l'Etat, le marxisme, les camps de concentration.*[45] This is in part a self-criticism (the book written by Glucksmann about May 1968 was still strictly Leninist) and marks an important date in the history of the leftist movement.

Here we find again the tension which was at the heart of the debates of the 1950s: on one side repression in the USSR and the Soviet camps, and on the other the future of the Revolution and the critique of capitalism and imperialism. Behind these different questions there always looms the tricky problem of the identification of the unfortunates who matter. Like those of the 1950s, the book aims to hold together the facts, now more firmly established and better known, concerning repression in the USSR on the one hand, (Glucksmann leans on the work of Solzenitzin), and the denunciation of injustice, oppression and misfortune in the non-communist world on the other.

There are, however, considerable differences with respect to the state of the debate in the 1950s. The first essential difference is that equivalence can now be established between the Nazi camps and Soviet camps and, by the same token, between the Nazis and the leaders of the USSR.[46] The Soviet Union is no longer protected by its participation in the war against the Nazis. To compare victims of Nazism and victims of communism no longer poses the difficult ideological problems it did when communism was qualified in the first instance by its opposition to Nazism. Secondly, and as a result of this, the disqualification of the USSR spreads to other entities, not only to the Communist Party but also to Marxism inasmuch as it participates in totalitarianism (with the abandonment of the frontier separating Stalin from Lenin and Marx), or to the proletariat inasmuch as it is identified with the militant workers of oppressive communist parties. The critical position is not abandoned notwithstanding, it is generalised instead.

The first result of this deconstruction is an enormous proliferation of unfortunates. In the debates of the 1950s the unfortunates who mattered were somewhat stereotypical: they were emblematic figures of the struggles taking place against imperialism (Indochinese peasants, Black Americans etc.). They were invoked, but usually without their suffering being described in detail. On the other hand, the desire to maintain a strategic kind of discourse, to emphasise action, struggles and how to conduct them, as well as the very high level of abstraction at which debates were pitched, often applying to large entities such as parties or States and figures drawn from metaphysics, tended to limit detailed description of the suffering even though it was reference to this suffering which supported the indignation and denunciation which inspired these passionate debates. The same comments can be made with regard to the book Glucksmann published in the Autumn of 1968: *Stratégie de la révolution*,[47] which is a Marxist analysis of the May-June events and puts forward a plan of revolutionary action for the future. In this work, where opposition to the Communist Party goes together with a strict Leninism, emphasis is placed on struggles, action and strategy. This discourse of revolutionary strategy gives little space to the description of suffering and, especially favourable to the multiplication of large entities (nations, political entities, social classes, etc.), only knows individualised human persons in the form of the militant identified with the proletariat. If the people or even the peasantry or the working class can enter into descriptions of misfortune, the proletariat, the state of the class when it is conscious and mobilised 'pure action', does not lend itself to misery.[48]

In André Glucksmann it is precisely the collapse of the proletariat on to the side of the persecutor and its replacement by the *plebs* – a term he takes from Michel Foucault[49] – which opens up the possibility of a rich description of suffering. In the first place it is suffering which, along with exclusion, imprisonment and a form of stubborn resistance to oppression in all of its forms ('barrack discipline, factory despotism, racist containment in the shanty-towns, prison terrorism, and hierarchy wherever it reigns supreme'[50]), establishes an equivalence between all those 'Marxism refers to as rabble (the "lumpen"), proletarians in rags, common law, reactionary or backward (the Christians of the Lip parish or peasants), as *déclassé* (vagrant intellectuals, hippies), as unstable and dubious ("marginal" young workers), as foreigners (OS émigrés), as unnatural ("queers"). All of this has the makings of concentration camps.'[51] To these accursed ones close to us – they belong to our society – will be added the most distant suffering of all those Third World peoples in revolt (the Chinese realising the Cultural Revolution, for example) no longer hidden or picked out by belief in 'the unity of the communist movement' (p. 40), but also victims from the past henceforth lumped together, of fascism, of the Nazi and Communist camps and, finally, future victims of 'fascistic 'final solutions' looming on the horizon' (p. 10). These unheard of sufferings are the hidden truth of our time ('the twentieth century, the century of the concentration camps'), of 'our policed world' which can no longer consider itself innocent and without connection to 'that universe of horror which henceforth haunts it' (p. 16).

Here one is truly in the presence of that sort of universalism, provoked in the second half of the twentieth century by reflection on the horror of the camps, that Joseph Amato calls the universalism of genocide and that he contrasts with the optimistic universalism of the Enlightenment. But as Joseph Amato comments,[52] the multiplication of victims, their distance in time and space, the difficulty of counting them and above all of bringing them together under the same rubric (as victims of imperialism for example) and ranking them,[53] tends to exhaust the reserves of indignation and give way to 'indifference and apathy'.[54] Amato's emphasis on the need to rank victims in order to give a political meaning to pity is not solely due to the scarcity of the technical means which can be deployed to come to their aid but also, or perhaps especially, to the scarcity of media space which cannot be filled by the representation of every case of suffering all at the same time and finally, as he explicitly suggests, to the relative scarcity of emotional resources which can be mobilised to cope with it.

But the difficulty the spectator confronts may be even more embarrassing than that described by Joseph Amato. For uncertainty does not only bear upon the ranking of unfortunates. It bears more radically on the allocation of the status of unfortunate or victim to the candidates. We have seen that for the allocation to be valid we must be able to give each of the actors a description which establishes their place in the system. In the terms of the denunciation which prevails here, the identification of unfortunates presupposes the identification of their persecutors and of those who, by sharing their resentment and indignation, display solidarity with them. Now the state of uncertainty into which the system of accusation is plunged does not permit the different actors to be stabilised in the different places. Is the unfortunate who appears on the screen really the victim presented to us? Is it even a case of a genuine unfortunate? Is he not a persecutor in disguise or at least a potential persecutor? And is the benefactor a real benefactor? Is he not the secret ally or alibi of the persecutor? But the candidate for the persecutor's place, is he not himself a benefactor unjustly slandered, or even an ignored unfortunate? Who knows![55]

How realistic is action?

10.1 Third uncertainty: the opacity of desire

We now broach the third kind of uncertainty deriving from suspicion cast on the authenticity of the altruistic and disinterested desire to help someone else which is supposedly translated into body language by emotion. This uncertainty is central to our subject. The unmasking of a hidden motive to fire a desire in television viewers to see suffering on the screen, for example, is a recurring theme of media criticism, especially of the criticism frequently made by journalists.[1] To be sure, since the end of the nineteenth century criticism of 'sensationalism' has been a feature of the development of newspaper reporting which, when it claims to expose a reality the journalist has encountered first hand, is accused of pandering to the 'unhealthy curiosity' of the public 'through the most detailed account of the most horrifying crimes'.[2] Essentially this criticism is directed at the treatment of crime and sexual scandals. But over the last twenty years the diffusion of psychoanalysis, and of suspicious interpretations more generally, has made this uncertainty more extensive and given it an ability to appear plausible and resist denial which is clearly unprecedented. In this section we give some examples of how a recent insistence on desire and, at the same time, on its opacity, have bolstered the suspicions of impurity which have fallen on altruistic desire for two centuries.

We have already met with the expression of such a suspicion on many occasions: in writings inspired by Hobbes or Mandeville seeking to ridicule sentiment and sentimentality; in Baudelaire when he ironises in a Sadean vein on the the hypocrisy of good sentiments; in Nietzsche assimilating pity to an illness; and finally in constructions which call upon Bataille's reinterpretation of Nietzsche showing the will to power and resentment always at work in the mystified expression of altruistic values. Equally we have seen how this use of suspicion leans sometimes on the topic of denunciation, in order to question the validity of sentimental attitudes and mostly consisting in attacks which unmask the economic or symbolic class interests of the philanthropic bourgeoisie, and sometimes, with a more radical aim, on the aesthetic topic, in a total rejection of morality and its 'Judeo-Christian' roots.

However, until the mid-1970s these attacks primarily came from political or artistic avant-gardes and were essentially directed against the bourgeoisie, order, Catholicism, etc., that is to say they were launched from the *Left* against the *Right*. Similarly, when this theme was introduced into sociological or historical academic criticism at the beginning of the 1960s for the most part it was used to link philanthropic or hygienist charitable action to the demands of capitalist exploitation.[3] Such an orientation reserved the possibility, at least implicitly, of there being an emotion authentically sustained by the desire to see an end to someone else's suffering, as in the case of revolutionary indignation at poverty or of protests against imperialist wars for example.

This reserve possibility falls in turn when, in addition to the denunciation of the motives of political opponents, the motives inspiring denunciation itself are themselves unmasked. Basically this challenge was carried out with the help of a psychoanalytic vocabulary. First of all *desire* is made the motive of every emotion and every would-be altruistic action and then, by means of a rhetoric of suspicion, behind altruistic desire either egoistic desires are revealed, which enables a bridge to be established to the theme of hidden interests, or frustrations and repressions.

We will consider two examples of this. The first, which concerns social workers, shows how external criticism is turned into internal criticism. Unmasking the hidden interests which sustain the benevolent action of social workers extends the criticism of good sentiments and charitable action as instruments of soft domination which usually involved an analysis of how the sexual repression of social workers from a Catholic bourgeois background was used to repress the lower classes.[4] But these analyses have not only an historical use. At the end of the 1970s they were reappropriated by social workers involved in avante-garde politics who made desire fundamental to their professional and political actions and subjected it to criticism. For example, in a selection of texts collected by the review *Champ social* in 1976, we read that ' to be sound, a charitable and altruistic desire must refer to its own desire'.[5] Now the analysis of this desire shows that it is far from being beyond reproach. The chapter devoted to 'The sexuality of the social worker' shows, for example, how the social worker 'will find a

libidinal satisfaction in taking responsibility for the problems of his clients':
'Some social workers do not deceive themselves and are well aware of the
ambiguity of being tuned in to the other's desire (to borrow a famous
phrase of our profession)'.[6]

Repression of sexual desire is transformed into an appetite for power
mystified as altruistic desire. The same argument is found in the radical criticism of the motives of militantism from which we take our second
example. Take, for example, a pamphlet published in 1972 by the
Organisation of Young Revolutionary Workers.[7] What are the reasons that
lead a militant to militate? 'No question is more embarrassing for a militant. At worst they will launch into interminable spiels on the horror of
capitalism, the poor children of the Third World, fragmentation bombs,
rising prices, repression . . .'. The 'militant is incapable of acknowledging
and confronting his desires'. He is motivated: (a) by a disclaimed religious
attitude ('spirit of sacrifice, intransigence, desire to convert, spirit of submission');[8] (b) by 'a desire for promotion' ('they rediscover in militancy a
personal importance that the degradation of their social position denies
them'); (c) by repressed sexual desire (the militant rejects 'what is subver-
sive in love and positive in the rejection of limits').[10]

A particularly exemplary expression of the criticism of the desire which
leads militants to commit themselves to causes, developed out of and
staying close to its Deleuzian original, can be found in a volume of the
review *Recherches* published by F. Fourquet in 1974:[9] (a) 'There is no man,
there is no praxis – there are only drives and intensities. There is no world,
there are no productive forces, there is only desire and power' (p. 106); (b)
the militant is inhabited by the 'venom of resentment' (p. 56); (c) *denunciation*, the militant's mania, is the manifestation of this resentment (p. 62);[11]
(d) desire is desire for power: 'We start from this empirical observation:
there is a strange and intimate correlation between desire and power'
(p. 110); (e) we must acknowledge our own desire and look it in the face
(p. 113).[12]

10.2 Fourth uncertainty: the vanity of intentions to act

Let us now consider the fourth uncertainty which concerns the intention to
act in favour of the unfortunate. In the first chapters we saw that orientation towards an action intended to bring the suffering of the unfortunate
to an end, or to relieve it, is one of the principal conditions which has to be
met in order to justify the contemplation of distant suffering and make it
acceptable. Equally we saw that when it is impossible to act directly the
distant spectator must rely on the powers of effective public speech. In the

isolated situation of reading, hearing or viewing media addressed to everyone only in their dispersion, he must at least make himself available as someone who will give public display to his emotion and who will pass it on in words to someone else. But for such a disposition to constitute a commitment to action and so be recognised as containing an *intention* to act, he must reasonably believe that his words are effective, that is to say, that they are capable of acting on reality and of transforming it. Now this belief itself presupposes a clear distinction between the real world in which action is deployed and the world of representation which provides the information needed about reality to guide action.

The classical theories of political communication are inserted within this kind of framework.[13] Take a situation of governors who have the monopoly on direct action on the political reality of the world, and governed who lack the capability of direct action. The latter can nonetheless act on the world by making their voice heard, by using speech to exert pressure on those who govern. They have some control over reality mediated by the power they exercise over the decisions of those who govern them by representing them. The further away the reality to which action is directed the stronger is the insistence on the effectiveness of these mediations so that it will be stronger in a case of, for example, interventions to save unfortunates in a distant country than in that of help for an evicted family next door or fellow workmates who have been laid off. But these differences do not affect the reality of the action deployed in the world. Thus the street *demonstration* which, along with the vote, petitions and the expression of an opinion in answer to an opinion poll, is one of the ways in which the speech of the governed can become effective by exerting pressure on the governors, is no less authentically directed towards action when it brings together citizens in a protest to make demands which affect them personally (against redundancies, for example), than when it is in support of other people (against the expulsion of political refugees for example), or in support of a distant cause (peace in a Third World country for example).

In this schema, representation by the media provides information about the world which is needed more to guide action when the reality is distant and to which therefore one has less access through direct observation or through the verbal testimony of people one knows personally or of those who have first-hand knowledge of the facts. The principal question then is that of the quality of the information, that is to say, basically of its objectivity inasmuch as this can be guaranteed by the independence, especially financial independence, of those who transmit it. Now this conception of political communication has been fundamentally challenged by analyses which, taking over from the critique of ideology developed by the

Frankfurt School, have undertaken to *deconstruct* the confection of media-staged facts.

The enterprise can be schematised into three stages. Starting from the denunciation of the false neutrality of the media, or of those media which convey a dominant and manipulated ideology – which corrected the classical conception of political communication without putting it in question since objectivity remained the underlying normative position – it strove to reveal the multiple complicities between politics and communications technology which reach the point of identification within a single sphere: that of the spectacle. Whereas in the first case the world of action and the world of representation remain distinct (even though representations may be subject to the manipulations denounced by criticism), in the second case they tend to interpenetrate each other with the idea of staging action with, from the start, a view to its media representation. However, although criticism reveals an almost absolute domination of the empire of the spectacle, normative support for the point of the criticism still comes from the possibility of a world which would not be falsified, where action would not be a simulacrum and where words would be really effective, because critique presupposes precisely recognition, albeit implicit, of a possible state of the world which is the opposite of the reality criticised. It is just this possibility which in the final analysis is ruled out by constructions which aim to dismantle the distinction between the world and what simulates it. But then the purpose of criticising representation in order to know the world and, more importantly, the intention to act through words on a world external to the representation through which we know it, become illusory. The intention to act cannot be fulfilled because nothing escapes the spectacle. When the spectator thinks he is acting he is in fact no more than an actor in the theatrical sense. He maintains the simulacrum.

Open Patrick Champagne's recent book, *Faire l'opinion*, which is a good example of the second type of analysis.[14] Starting from a study of peasant demonstrations Champagne pursues wider ambitions since he makes a global challenge to the political game which creates the illusion of democracy. The general argument is that the externality of public opinion, on the basis of which political men pretend to base the legitimacy of their actions, does not in fact exist. His principal image is that of the circle.

Politicians act as if they were attentive to a public opinion whose voice weighed on their decisions. Now the objects and persons – opinion polls, newspapers, communications advisors, television, political scientists, Minitel [domestic viewdata service], journalists, Audimat, spokesmen, computers, demonstrators, etc. – who claim to reveal this public opinion as a supposedly external force which they merely bring to light, in reality mutually support each other in order to construct this public opinion and produce belief in its existence. It is then this illusory belief that the sociologist undertakes to deconstruct.[15] Deconstruction is carried out on different terrains. First of all, opinion polls are deconstructed by taking up the major themes of methodological criticism produced by Pierre Bourdieu in the 1970s: the formulation of questions producing an effect of closure and imposition, the verbal character of responses which tell us nothing about practices, the exclusion of non-responses, etc. These criticisms of method, which are hard to dispute, are utilised here to bolster denunciation of 'opinion poll peddlers' who create 'a simple artefact' but who, with the support of political scientists, succeed in making public opinion exist by creating a belief in its existence.[16] The second terrain is that of the politician's self-representation. What seems to be natural to the politician is 'in reality manufactured' by communication advisers.[17] Finally, the same enterprise of deconstruction is carried out on the terrain of journalism and information: events are constructed; there is a 'field of production of media events' and 'it is not by chance that the press is regularly accused of artificially fabricating events or of giving too much publicity to certain groups or causes' (pp. 243 and 260). The illusion that something called public opinion exists is due to the support given by these different instances of the construction of an artefact (what the author calls a 'generalised domination' alluding to generalised exchange in theories of kinship). Politicians profess opinions in order to please a public opinion which is itself the result of the artefact of polls and of the imposition of politicians' categories by political scientists and journalists.

Does the demonstration, the traditional means for giving political expression to public opinion, not introduce an externality into this 'circle of belief'? No, because nowadays at least, it is also constructed by spokesmen who do not represent 'real groups' but 'collectivities manufactured by and for politics' with a view to their media existence: they tailor '*demonstrations for journalists*' and create 'specific productions to move or amuse those who watch it before putting it on view for their readers or television viewers' (p. 235).[18] It is also impossible now 'to dissociate facts and the account given of them, the street demonstration and the demonstration seen and shown by the media' (ibid.). Those who believe they are being active by demonstrating are in fact only theatre actors: 'While intending to act on the public opinion grasped by the pollsters, the demonstrators at these gatherings are often not so much fully fledged actors as simple involuntary extras of a spectacle whose script they do not always know' (p. 259). Thinking they act, they merely make their contribution to the empire of the spectacle: these 'false groups' are 'not so much action groups as representation groups whose only function is basically to give approval to their organisers' (as an example of a 'false group' the author refers to *SOS Racisme,* pp. 260–2[19]).

While denouncing the empire of the spectacle and the illusion of public speech which thinks it escapes the spectacle and lays claim to genuine action, Patrick Champagne preserves, at least in the form of nostalgia and wish, the requirement of a speech which would become action by being applied to reality. Commenting that formerly demonstrations 'were more real forms of expression' (p. 201), the author ends his book with a plea for a politics capable of 'breaking the circle' and giving back speech to the base or the people (p. 281). It is just this demand which is abandoned in the reflections which seek to surpass criticism of the 'panopticon' or even of the 'society of the spectacle'. Let us leaf through some of Jean Baudrillard's books and, in particular, *Simulacra and Simulation*[20] which, published in France in 1981, provides the theoretical basis for the more recent developments of his views in his analysis of the treatment of the Gulf War[21] by the media or on the false mass grave of Timisoara.[22] Why are we no longer in the society of the spectacle? Because as a criticism of false representation, criticism of the society of the spectacle still remains within the logic of representation and thereby assumes the existence of an externality in the form of a reality which could be represented, or distorted, by signs. Now in 'the era of simulacra and simulation' which we have now entered, the sign is 'reversion of all reference'. The 'system' in which we are submerged 'is no longer itself anything but a gigantic simulacrum', which is 'never exchanged for the real, but exchanged for itself, in an uninterrupted circuit without reference or circumference' (pp. 5–6). In the absence of the possibility of reference to the real, the criticism of illusion also disappears.[23] There is thus 'dissolution of TV in life, dissolution of life in TV – indiscernible chemical solution' (p. 30). At a stroke, we can no longer distinguish 'cause and effect', 'subject and object', the end from the means or, of course, particularly relevant for our purposes, active and passive (p. 31). Communication takes place 'in a closed circuit, as a *lure*' (p. 81). We remain within the image of a circle, but it is a circle absolutely closed on itself and which excludes any possibility of an externality: 'the medium is the message – the sender is the receiver – the circularity of all poles – the end of panoptic and perspectival space – such is the alpha and omega of our modernity' (p. 82): 'The absorption of one pole into another . . . thus the impossibility of any mediation, of any dialectical intervention between the two or from one to the other. Circularity of all media effects' (p. 83).[24] Take the Gulf War: 'In this war forum which is the Gulf, everything is hidden . . . only the telly functions as a medium without message, finally giving the image of pure television': 'information "in real time" moves in a completely irreal space, finally giving the image of pure, useless, instantaneous television, in which its primordial function bursts out, which is to fill the void, to fill in the hole of the screen through which descriptive substance vanishes' (pp. 66 and 22). In the 'hyper-real' universe of 'virtual images' 'which only refer to themselves' in which the media immerses us, we are only 'ever acting-out – cnly acting: action!' (p. 45). Belief in the possibility of an action, or of speech which in being externalised in the world would be the mediation of an action, is thus a meaningless naivety.[25]

Misfortune is good for something, however. The inaccessibility of action, its *irreality*, would give a desperate character to the spectacle of distant suffering if the effect of impotence was not lessened by the reality of this suffering being weakened by uncertainty about the status of representation: objective or tendentious? Real or fictional? Factual or constructed? Authentic or faked? One effect of the 'crisis of confidence' affecting the media that J.-L. Missika connects, probably correctly, with the 'disenchantment and doubt' produced by the discovery that the televised image is 'an intellectual construction',[26] is that it also relieves the anxiety, loss of self-esteem[27] and sense of indignity which is often said to be provoked by seeing wounded, imprisoned, tortured, starving or even dead people, without being able to do anything.

The form of defection which consists in turning off one's set – which can always be denounced as selfish indifference as we have seen – is actually not the only way of relieving the spectator's inactive anxiety. There is another possibility, corresponding to the attitude described by Missika, which consists in shifting attention from the scene viewed from afar to the medium by means of which it has been conveyed and, as a result, in disengaging oneself from the proposal of commitment which appears in the image in order to redirect the emotions and discourse in which it is displayed on to the channel itself. Criticism of representation can then, if not prevail over concern about what is represented, at least encourage a suffering to be bracketed off and a doubt to be raised about its reality which, blurred by the acknowledged opacity of the medium, no longer appeals to a demand for action with the same force.[28] If, as two of the editors of the *Dictionnaire de la communication* write, 'the false deaths of Timisoara will eclipse the several thousands of genuine victims of the bombings of popular quarters in Panama',[29] then indignation, horror and shame at the massacre of innocents can always be suspended to the benefit of doubt.

10.3 Humanitarian society and its enemies

In order to clarify how the uncertainties we have referred to have come into contact with the question of pity, we can join the polemic which recently took place around 'humanitarian action' and which is itself situated within a project denouncing the 'return of moralism' which has wider objectives. We note straightaway that the term humanitarian action lends itself to confusion. In fact, the criticisms which interest us focus not so much on actions on the ground accomplished by members of the many Non-Governmental Organisations (NGOs) providing aid to populations in difficulty in different parts of the world, nor yet, for the most part, do they focus on the problems of diplomacy and international politics posed by the development of these activities,[30] but essentially they address the question of media representation and, in particular, televisual representation of the suffering endured by those to whom the members of humanitarian organisations wish to draw the public's attention. It is the revival of humanitarianism and the spectacle of distant suffering together that are really on trial here. Let us add that this trial has taken place above all in France where humanitarian organisations are much less powerful however than in Anglo-Saxon countries, or even than in Germany or Switzerland.[31] The trial has been conducted around the figure of Dr Bernard Kouchner in particular, both a practitioner (he was a founder of Médecins sans frontières and then of Médecins du monde) and a theorist of urgent humanitarian intervention who has written a number of books on the subject. The polarisation around Bernard Kouchner is the direct result of two major innovations he introduced into this domain. The first innovation was to make the greatest possible use of the media to show the suffering of populations in distress and to lift the veil of indifference which covered them. The second was to bring humanitarian action and politics together, to join private initiatives with State interventions or interventions by international organisations, with, in particular, a number of attempts to get the United Nations to recognise a 'right to humanitarian intervention'[32] which would legalise a limit to national sovereignty and, when a population is threatened by its own government, legitimise intervention on the territory where it takes place (Bernard Kouchner was a minister in successive socialist governments from 1986 to 1993). These really were innovations. Until recently the practice of humanitarian organisation was governed in effect by two fundamental rules inherited from the way in which Henri Dunant established the Red Cross: a rule of political neutrality and a rule of confidentiality. These were conceived in order to overcome reluctance on the part of States and to encourage their collaboration, but they came into question after what was acknowledged to be the complete failure of the Red Cross in the face of the Nazi State. But in spite of everything they remained in force (doctors practising within the framework of the CICR undertaking, for example, not to reveal anything they might have seen).

Recent criticisms of humanitarianism can be summarised fairly rapidly since essentially they take up arguments whose recurring nature since the start of the debate on pity more than two centuries ago has already been noted. Open the November 1991 issue of the review *Le Débat,* for example, part of which is devoted to humanitarian action and the right of intervention, and consider the questions put to Bernard Kouchner by the editors.[33] Emphasis is immediately placed on the media and on television in particular (humanitarian action steps in '"on terrible, unbearable images", the leitmotif of television'). The first question, referring to an article by Olivier Roy in *Esprit*, concerns uncertainty of reference. Actually it bears on the relationship between media representations of suffering and identification of the unfortunate. ('When there are no images, what do you do? And when there are too many, what genocide do you choose? And what do you do when the images are fake? Or when, for the sake of some fine images, one perpetuates conflicts, hatreds and misunderstandings?') And what if those shown to us as unfortunates are in fact persecutors, at least potentially?[34]

The next question is connected to our second uncertainty. It questions the validity of a sensitization which plays on the spectator's *emotions* ('the Gulf crisis and its sequels have clearly demonstrated that the real trigger is a media phenomenon, with the moral emotion aroused by unbearable images and the pressure of public opinion which results from it'). Finally, the third objection starts from deception or media error ('the same recent events, from Timisoara to Kurdistan, have succeeded in making one wary about the havoc wreaked by on the spot news and the rigging it allows'), in order to foresee a generalised scepticism making intentions to act collapse into indifference (what if 'stardom in the North prevails over the victims of the South? Beyond the emotion of the initial moment, are you not afraid that these strategies of the image will not end up feeding skepticism and indifference?'[35]).

Note that in a remarkably concise form these question call to mind objections and criticisms which have been too numerous and repetitive over the last three years for us reasonably to summarise them all. We cite some taken either from articles in reviews or from press interviews (especially interviews with intellectuals regularly published by *Le Monde*) or from several recent pamphlets which denounce the return of the 'moral order' or the 'tyranny of ethics'. To a question from *Le Monde* about 'Somalian babies', Debray answers with the arguments of apathy and selfish desires.[36] In a work aiming to reveal the birth of a 'post-moralist society' in the return of 'the moral order', Gilles Lipovetsky devotes a chapter to what he calls 'media charity'.[37] Above all it is the ambiguity of desire which is involved here. 'Media charity' is 'post-moralist' in the sense that it reconciles 'pleasure and good intentions': 'No more must anything spoil the consumer happiness of the citizen-television viewer, distress itself has become an opportunity for *entertainment* [English in original]. Mass hedonistic culture is affirmed once more in the revival of charity.' In another recent work entirely devoted to the critique of 'the moral order', the third argument, that of impotence, is invoked instead: '"human rights" and the "duty to intervene" are no more than incantations intended to serve as an alibi for our inability to act'.[38] We end this brief series of examples with an article by Georges Sebbag which was also published in *Le Monde* in 1993 and entitled: 'On ethical cleansing'[39] (as far as the joke is concerned the title doubtless refers to the massacres which were a feature of ethnic cleansing in former Yugoslavia). Here we have a violent pamphlet directed against 'antiracism, the duty to intervene and the protection of populations in danger' all at the same time.[40] But the article sets about the 'bluff of humanitarian health' and its mediatisation most of all. It repeats most of the themes we have already come across: facile emotion (the spectator 'is offered the spectacle of desolation so he can give vent to his melancholy'); impotence ('a coterie of singers, a medical lobby, a fraternity of comedians and some patented moralisers, obsessively or even hysterically brandish the universals of humanitarian health and ethical cleansing in the media . . . whether on their own or together in numbers, one of the main constituent features of these individuals is their force of inertia'). But he extends criticism to the 'conformism', the loss of autonomy, in short, the 'alienation' that the 'spectacular return of human rights' would disguise,[41] by ironising on the use of the word 'genocide'[42] and by exposing to ridicule or hatred all those who carry the burden of inequality of whatever kind and however near or far away they may be.[43]

Criticism is easy, but art is difficult. It is therefore fitting to ask the critics what they want and what they propose. Those to whom we have referred do not tell us clearly. We can only conjecture. Thus, the criticism which uses all the resources of the pamphleteering style against humanitarian action – irony, 'black' humour, abuse, etc. – suggests a connection with the assault on pity and humanitarianism we encountered in Nietzsche's reception among the young members of *Action française* at the beginning of this century. Since spectators are manipulated and deceived by the evocation of unfortunates and by the images of suffering they are shown, one solution immediately comes to mind: stop giving your attention to misfortune; no longer concern yourself about it, say nothing about suffering; throw a veil over those that Georges Sebbag, in the article quoted, calls the sick, the wounded, the junkies, the drop-outs, the starving babies, the dying terrorists, etc., all those that the Nietzschean nationalists of the beginning of the century called the weak in comparison with the hero's strength. A less radical solution which seems to underly some of these criticisms might be to vary the attention given to suffering in accordance with a scale of appropriateness determined by distance from the spectator.[44] But then how can we avoid the possibility of this criterion falling back on the immediacy of the communal bond, nostalgia for which seems not to be absent from this new offensive against 'moralism'.[45]

10.4 Justification of the humanitarian

The humanitarian question and its mediatisation has come under attack not only from outside the humanitarian movement. There have also been internal reflections and an internal debate. We will refer to these in our attempt to identify the major lines of justification for humanitarian interventions and their media representation. The main target for the accusations of recent polemics, Bernard Kouchner, has also been the main advocate of the humanitarian movement. We will therefore give considerable space to his writings. We will continue to stick to the spirit of the uncertainties which has served as our guide by particularly stressing the problem of action.

First observation: justification of humanitarianism cannot disregard the relative discredit of the different topics we have identified. The response to this sometimes anticipates, in order to refute them, interpretations which reduce the humanitarian movement to one or other of the topics, and sometimes presents the movement as the result of an encounter between dispositions associated with different topics which fuse together and surpass them. On a number of occasions Bernard Kouchner marks his distance not only from an aesthetising exoticism,[46] but also from the forms of denunciation which prevailed until the 1970s (especially in the leftist circles to which he then belonged),[47] as also from sentimental pity and good sentiments (as, for example, the ironic title of one of his books indicates, *Charity Business*, which contains many warnings against 'the great orchestra of world charity', 'tearful blindness' or the 'blackmail of charity'[48]). In other cases he presents his action as resulting from a desire 'to establish a bridge between two ways of thinking, two hitherto antinomic comportments. On one side traditional Christian thought, the hand held out to the poor, one by one. On the other, a political practice inspired by the Left, the exact opposite . . . charity for a "man of the Left" was a refusal to change life, to give up on revolution, not to seek to seize power in the name of justice'.[49]

The second uncertainty we have disclosed is also taken into account in Kouchner's writings, that is uncertainty about the occupants of the system of places and particularly about the identification of the victims who, as we have seen, can easily change places with the persecutor when the system is unstable. The French humanitarian movement precedes and heralds the crisis of Marxism in the middle of the 1970s (in fact it was to escape from the dilemmas of a revolutionary action which seemed to have no effect that in 1968 Bernard Kouchner joined a mission of the CICR to war-torn Biafra[50]). Its solution leans on medical ethics in order to support the cause of any victim in mortal danger.[51] More precisely, it involves a particular treatment of time which isolates the *present*[52] from the past and the future. It is thus particularly opposed to forms of denunciation which, on the basis of a theory of history, treat groups as persons whose future intentions can be probed by taking account of their past actions. It thereby allows the identification of *actual* victims without being too worried about whether they are on the side of the good, not only by relieving them of the weight of an accusation which, as F. Tricaud comments, 'seizes on an irremediably past action and takes it to task as if there was still time to do what was never done',[53] but also by not seeking to anticipate their future conduct and consequently putting aside the 'invasive fear of consequences'.[54] How then are victims identified? By placing oneself 'always on the side of those being bombed and not of those sending the bombs. A single rule: to stay at the bedside of the minorities', but 'without illusions, since the minorities may themselves become oppressive'.[55] This focus on the present moment maintains the distinction between pity and justice evoked at the beginning of this book. In fact, the exercise of justice, which always follows an accusation or at least a criticism, is retrospective: one can only judge accomplished actions. On the other hand, even when put to work outside the judicial institution, the logic of justice involves a trial in which adversaries confront each other by advancing arguments and proofs. Now the demands of the present moment do not allow for 'careful weighing up, handling, interrogating and doubting . . . In contrast with justice, humanitarian action is not an adversarial procedure'.[56]

We will quickly pass over the third uncertainty concerning desires – because its undeveloped treatment swings between belief in the obsure depths of the unconscious and adherence to a morality of duty[57] – and move on directly to the problem of the relationship between action and the representation of distant suffering by the media.

Reference to action is central in the justification of humanitarianism. It is from the standpoint of a demand for action that criticism can be made of the topics in which a discourse on distant suffering takes place. Thus, for example, the humanitarian is opposed to political denunciation as understood by the post-war French Left as action by words: the form of speech that is derided as merely 'verbal' in order to emphasise its ineffectiveness, that is to say, precisely its inability to change reality. Bernard Kouchner cannot find words hard enough for the 'armchair warriors',[58] the 'great indignations of the generation of petitioners',[59] the 'meetings of little groups' where it is appropriate to 'bewail . . .the fate of the world, regret the disorder of things, to aspire to change the course of society'.[60] Action itself however, when it is exercised from a long way off, still belongs to the order of the useless, of illusion, even of mystification.[61] Ultimately what justifies the humanitarian movement is that its members are on the spot. Presence on the ground is the only guarantee of effectiveness and even of truth.[62]

10.5 Media action

If the capacity for action is shifted entirely on to the *actors* of the humanitarian movement, are not spectators then allocated a purely passive role (and the same question can be asked about those receiving aid)? But if the spectators are passive, are not those who wax indignant at the mediatisation of humanitarianism justified? We have seen that the justification of the spectator of distant suffering rests on them having an orientation towards action. Now if this orientation is illusory, does not the spectator fall back on the illicit consumption of distressing spectacles which, like fictional representations, are intended to arouse disturbing and deep inner emotions? This is indeed the reproach most frequently addressed to Bernard Kouchner, also by members of the humanitarian movement belonging to competing organisations,[63] and at times it does not seem far removed from what he himself acknowledges when he deplores the 'drift' of news in search of the 'sensational at any price', the 'perversity of images' or when he apologises for the 'cynicism' with which the media is used.[64]

But then why not dispense with it? We know that the need for mediatisation, the need for publicity and to kick up a fuss, has been a leitmotif of Kouchner's discourse that is strongly reaffirmed in his last two books. 'The best causes vegetate in indifference, the just struggles go on without the intervention of cameras'.[65] 'There is less risk of dying in front of the camera.'[66] By recording images of poverty or oppression and diffusing them in the media, journalists ensure a degree of protection to suffering or oppressed populations, as also to those who come to their aid since it becomes more difficult to get rid of them by expelling or killing them. Against whom are these populations protected? Bernard Kouchner repeats many times: against their own rulers. Thus publicity given to their violent acts has its effect on the rulers of States who martyr the populations, often ethnic minorities, under their control, at best moderating their violence and at worst encouraging them to act with prudence and dissimulation. But these violent acts are obviously not publicised in the countries where they are committed. The effects of publicity thus presuppose the existence of an international public space. They are produced by means of diplomatic interventions, that is to say by means of pressure that may be exerted by other countries on the leaders of those States where the suffering and atrocities shown by the media are taking place. The effects of media publicity given to the suffering of oppressed minorities are produced on other leaders therefore. But why then is diffusion in a wide public necessary? Do not the leaders of States have specialised and sophisticated means of information at their disposal? The argument usually invoked here is that State leaders would dare to intervene only if under pressure from their own national public opinion or, at least, only if they conclude that this public opinion will support them. A consequence of this reasoning is that spectators are given a completely preponderant role, at least in democratic States, in the series of mediations which have to be activated in order to end or reduce distant suffering. But how then can we, as is often the case, both accord such importance to public opinion[67] and emphasise the passivity of spectators or deplore their 'voyeurism'?

It seems to us that an answer to this question is to be found in the ambiguity of the expression *action of public opinion* in which *action* is understood both in the sense of *efficient cause* and in the sense of *intentional action*. There is an extreme situation, no doubt never completely realised, in which an absolutely passive public opinion could nevertheless exert a causal action. This would be when leaders, who almost have a monopoly of the ability to act on the international stage, in relying upon the representations they have of the emotions, desires and intentions of the spectators, or in anticipation of their future votes, take the initiative of intervening. This situation is similar to the quite real case we find when, as often happens, leaders take decisions in the light of opinion poll results. Now the action of giving an answer to an opinion poll only very approximately and very weakly corresponds to what we usually mean by the fact of accomplishing something or of acting and to the *usual experience of action.* In the case of the opinion poll, the speaker in effect falls on the side of *merely verbal speech*, so-called precisely because it does not commit, rather than of *effective speech,* whatever, we will argue, the causal effect of this speech and even if it is possible that in some cases giving an answer to an opinion poll would be more efficient than other forms of speech.

We will recall these forms in order to clarify how the action of opinion can be connected with the usual sense of action. It is actually in this case that speech, which we have seen was the spectator's main resort for coping with the moral demands raised by the representation of distant suffering, can be understood as effective speech and so be an adequate response to the demand for action.

10.6 The manifestation of speech

There is speech and there is speech or, as Maurice Merleau-Ponty says, 'authentic speech' and 'second order speech'.[68] To clarify the conditions under which speech can be tested as an effective form of expression, we recall some of the properties associated with the natural semantics of action by going: (a) from intentionality to; (b) its incorporation in bodily gestures and movements set out in the world of things, which consequently presupposes; (c) the sacrifice of other possible actions and which; (d) by manifesting itself in the presence of someone else; (e) testifies to and seals a commitment, realising, to use the expression of Maurice Merleau-Ponty again, a 'confirmation of the other by myself and of myself by the other'.[69]

To move towards action the spectator's speech on the suffering he has been shown must first of all be intentional in the sense that it is not just part of the flow of chatter about everything and nothing in which, consequently, nothing particularly matters, but is the object of a justification using expressions of 'intentional attitudes' (such as 'I will', 'I believe', 'I think'), and by referring to intentional states of desire and belief. Intentionality concerns not only the fact of saying something but of *meaning to say*. Intentionality in the 'weak' sense leads in that case to the 'strong sense' which involves a 'practical intentionality, conscious and voluntary movement' of the speaker towards the world.[70] The reason invoked for acting is thus in a non-contingent relationship to the action; it is not external to it (in the manner of a cause) but is orientated towards an end which it implies. And similarly, the emotional or affective dimension of this speech manifests a dispositional force, as Charles Taylor says, which expresses the commitment (Charles Taylor says 'partiality') towards the object echoed by the speech.[71] Linked in a non-contingent way to action, intention in the strong sense, which is what interests us here, is no longer necessarily antecedent to it (as in conceptions of intention which rest on a dualism of mental states and bodily movements). We take up Charles Taylor's analyses here[72] and the sociological application of these analyses suggested by Louis Quéré.[73] Action and intention are connected to each other in effective action realised in the world. Intention incorporated in action is 'expression'. This expression is 'authentic' when it is made manifest in the action which incarnates it without requiring an inference from the other person (of the type: he is at the office because his car is in the car park); when , by incorporating it in the action, the person who communicates expresses a tendency which is not only observable, (as would be, for example, looking distraught minutes after the announcement of a massacre on the television or radio).

The expressive conception of an incorporated intention which manifests itself in the tendency to act links the strong intention to gestures and movements of the body. It is first of all connected with gestures, with shifts and movements, that speech manifests its intentionality and tries out its effectiveness. Consider the simple fact of being asked for money for a good cause. The intention to respond favourably to the request, which one has announced to one's wife for example, only becomes real in the act of filling out a cheque, sealing the envelope and posting it. This material implication imposes a constraint involving a sacrifice (minimal in this case; but how many letters remain to be written and posted?). It follows that the more the movements which accompany speech are significant, the greater the sacrifice of other possible actions and other uses of the time in which they are performed, and the greater the chance of speech being experienced in the mode of action.

However, the expressive conception of the relationship between intention and action is realised above all in the public space (which is why giving money, as we suggested at the start of this book, which requires hardly any movement and is performed in the isolation of the domestic household, on its own is ultimately more detached from action and a weaker form of reaction to the spectacle of suffering than public speech). In a public performance, the actors 'make their intentions, dispositions, motivations, sentiments, etc., mutually manifest to each other'.[74] They commit themselves through speech whose fleetingness is abrogated by the memory of those in whose presence it is produced and who may later remind the speaker of it in order to challenge him to justify the reality of his intentions and the consistency of his actions over time.

In what C. Tilly calls the repertoire of collective action[75] there is a particularly appropriate social form for making the intentional, gestural and effective character of speech clear: the *demonstration*. In order to isolate some of the features which characterise the effective forms of public speech let us look at the collective work edited by Pierre Favre recently devoted to the demonstration.[76] We note first of all the continuum going from street meetings, to sites where speech takes place and passes from person to person spreading rumours, to the passing crowd around a testifying speaker, to the riot,[77] and finally to the organised march. As M. Offerlé comments, the street demonstration is born of the street.[78] The coordination of speakers, their coming together in a precise aim, and their formation into a march led in a preestablished direction according to a plan of

action, has required a know-how which was built up during the second half
of the nineteenth century with, in particular, the creation of stewards (an
innovation taken from forms of protest in Great Britain which, according
to D. Cardon and J.-P. Heurtin, was imported into France with the 'Ferrer
demonstration' of 17 October 1909[79]). The coordination of speakers and
marchers is ensured by the existence of a *manifesto*, of a call to *demonstrate*
coming from an individual or collective person (organisation, temporary
committee, journal, group of individuals, etc.). The function of a call to
demonstrate is not only to say what must be said on the march, so as to pre-
determine and fix it in a way that might easily be considered 'authoritarian'. It objectivises the *meaning [vouloir dire]* of a speech which at every
moment risks being deformed in the hubbub of the street, or being diluted
in a multiplicity of aims. Similarly, the techniques of group speech (the
scansion of slogans taken up by everyone in succession) demonstrates
the *intention to do [vouloir faire]* of a speech orientated towards action,
of a speech which wants to achieve something and which is addressed to a
ruling authority in a confrontational relationship which, as Pierre Favre
underlines, always presupposes the possibility of a transition to violence:
'unpredictable by nature' in its unfolding, the speech of demonstrations
necessarily has 'physical violence as its horizon'.[80] Throughout the nineteenth century and up until today, multiple 'more or less set' intermediary
forms have maintained the link between the spontaneous crowd, the 'rowdy
and disorganised' march and the disciplined procession.

How is coordination carried out? We know it is not reducible to the
momentary coagulation of a 'crowd' around an 'agitator', as the models of
emotional contagion which prevailed from Le Bon to Freud would have it.
Almost all of the authors of this volume insist on the existence of 'solidarities', 'groups' and preexisting 'networks'.[81] 'People rarely arrive at the demonstration individually': the demonstration thus appears as 'the result of
multiple social mobilisations and encouragements linked to the interactions
of everyday life'.[82] A series of local 'micro-mobilisations' precede demonstrations whose visibility depend upon size. Analysing the university and
high school student demonstrations of 1986, M. Dobry[83] thus insists on the
multiplicity and mobilising role of 'microdemonstrations' which precede the
'day' of 27 November. The description of what takes place in these microdemonstrations helps us to understand how coordination is ensured. In
effect they consist essentially in 'giving news of what is happening or should
be happening in other universities where it is thought "things are moving"'
and thereby 'checking that other natural units of the space of mobilisation
equally join in movement'. Members of each of the local demonstrations
are in this way reassured that 'they are not alone' (so that anticipation of the

'chances of success' prevail over evaluations of the 'costs associated with possible modes of action'). Microdemonstrations are in this way 'so many tests of the reciprocal resolution of their actors'.[84]

Speaking about demonstrations at the end of the nineteenth century, M. Offerlé says that those who participate 'to the extent of sacrificing their life, their freedom, their job, or at the very least their time',[85] 'communicate their solidarity' by fulfilling this sacrifice in front of others (to whom they are usually attached by multiple links, of profession or neighbourhood for example, which preexist the moment of demonstrating and continue afterwards) and in this way they make 'visible' for each other 'reciprocal testimonies of belonging' which reactivate prior commitments and create new ones.[86]

10.7 Humanitarian action and social movement

This detour through the demonstration of an effective speech enables us to clarify the point of application of criticism of the use of the media for the ends of humanitarian action, at least when this criticism does not adopt the themes of strength and weakness and target the very act of being concerned about the suffering of others, as is clearly the case when criticism comes from within the humanitarian movement. Criticism can be based on two features of the political situation with which the humanitarian movement must come to terms.

The first is the absence of practical mediations between, on the one hand, actors of the humanitarian movement in France who move around directing action in France, Europe and also, in many cases, in the Third World and, on the other hand, ordinary people whose relationship to this action is basically through the media. Compared with Amnesty International, for example, which according to the organisation's 1992 report has today 6,000 local groups with one million members in seventy countries,[87] the humanitarian movement, and especially the French humanitarian movement, despite its rapid growth[88] has not been in a position until now to call upon the support of organisations or movements or to establish a register of collective action enabling it to avoid the alternative of either on the spot involvement (which we know is particularly demanding in this case) or distant spectacle. Without the relay of practical mediations supporting accusatory speech (as in the case of denunciation) or demonstration of concern (in that of sentiment), and if we rule out aestheticisation (always accessible in an affirmation of oneself as an artist, but more difficult to mobilise on a large scale the more suffering appears real and intense), then the form of concern which appears to the spectator is can he avoid the register of 'shame', 'bad conscience' or 'guilt'.[89]

The second feature is the difference between the social properties of those who dispense aid and those who receive it. There is often a radical difference when action takes place far away (as in the case of famines in the Third World for example). It is this in particular which separates the formation of the humanitarian movement today from that of the trade union movement at the end of the nineteenth century and with which nevertheless it would be tempting to compare it.[90] In the trade union model of action, those who suffer take responsibility for their own destiny by basing their claims on a logic of justice which legitimises denunciation. This is precisely what distinguishes the trade union movement from the philanthropic movement in which assistance is brought to unfortunates from outside by benefactors foreign to their condition and suffering, although many recent works of social history have tended to reduce this difference by bringing to light, especially in Great Britain, numerous intersections between the workers' movement and philanthropy which converged in the birth of the Welfare State.[91] But this convergence was made possible by the fact that the framework of philanthropy and the trade union movement (despite the often internationalist professions of faith of the latter) was essentially a national space and that both were devoted in different ways to putting pressure on the leaders of the nation State for legislative change or the creation of new rights. These combined efforts resulted in the formation of a right to work and also, particularly in France, in a slow and progressive transformation of the mode of representation which, without abolishing the representation of the citizen without special status arising from the French Revolution, doubled it with a complex system of the representation of interests and of citizens as workers in particular.[92] Politics of pity and politics of justice are thus inseparably based on the demand for social justice which sought to bring together the two republican principles of *equality* – founding the rights of the citizen – and *fraternity* – which refers to human rights.

In the case of the humanitarian movement, however, the mutual otherness of those who offer their aid and those who receive it is accentuated by their membership of different States: donors in rich democracies and recipients in poor countries often with authoritarian regimes. The reduction of this otherness therefore appears in the forefront of the pressures on the formation of a range of commitments mid-way between on the spot intervention and distant emotion. It is not extrinsic to the question of the success or failure of collective action.

Take, for example, the question of the action of street demonstrations, this time in the sense of an efficient cause. Summing up on this controversial problem, around which there is an important literature, the authors of the work already cited conclude that, with the exception of situations in which there is a major crisis with considerable 'political fluidity', 'the demonstration very rarely succeeds in changing the course of governmental decisions'. It comes up against the 'tendency to structural insensibility' of 'governmental and administrative sectors . . . *vis-à-vis* an extremely wide class of demonstrations and demonstrators'.[93] Even in the case of significant crises, it is not a particular 'moment of demonstration', whatever its scale, but 'the whole of the crisis', including a succession of actions (strikes, occupations, petitions, delegations, etc.), 'which produces change'.[94] But equally most of the authors suggest that the answer to the question of effectiveness can be seen in a different light if it is posed from a less strictly instrumental perspective. The main action of demonstrations in fact is found in their contribution to the constitution, affirmation or confirmation of a group formed around a cause. There is a relationship of interdependence between this effect of internal construction and the 'effects of external recognition'[95] that the demonstration succeeds in securing: 'Recognition by the authorities of the group in conflict constitutes a success in itself'.[96] This is especially true for those demonstrations that Pierre Favre, in his typological essay, calls 'initiating demonstrations', in which demonstrators who 'tend to represent a potential group' and who only have embryonic organisations at their disposal, attempt to enter the political space. In this case effective speech is both directed towards a definite external aim and is 'foundational for the group' whose speech it is.[97]

The humanitarian claim for more or less distant causes can avoid the alternative of abstract universalism – easily accused of being fired up for distant suffering the better to avert its eyes from those close at hand – or of communitarian withdrawal into itself – which only attends to misfortune when it affects those nearest – by being rooted in groups and thereby linked to preexisting solidarities and local interests.[98] If human beings are able to recognise that they have something essential in common, join together in groups and constitute particular interests by adopting the cause of beings of a different species that they have never even been close to – whales or bears for example – is it utopian to think them capable of forming, interpreting and demonstrating their interests or, possibly, their own suffering, by taking up the cause of human beings far away who they are aware of only through the media? But as the internal critics of the humanitarian movement have often remarked, this would require the media to bring them a representation of these unfortunates not only in the passivity of suffering, but also in the action they take to confront and escape it.

10.8 The politics of the present

To take the internal critics of the humanitarian movement seriously thus leads in the direction of a political insertion of the movement. Moreover, we have seen that this is one of the characteristics of the model of humanitarian action which has developed in France in recent years with, in particular, the desire to put pressure on international law to recognise a right (or duty) of humanitarian intervention, legalising interventions to defend a people against its own leaders and thereby limiting the autonomy of States. Unlike the right to freedom of thought (Declaration of 1789) and social right (Declaration of 1848) which, as François Ewald points out, were 'aimed at States', articulated 'on the principle of and respect for the sovereignty of States', by recognising 'within the framework of a definite State', 'rights that subjects can enforce against the State, or the obligations of the State towards its subjects', the right of humanitarian intervention is opposed to States when, in the 'name of sovereignty', 'entire populations are seized hold of by governments which displace them, starve them and hold them hostage'. In contrast with social rights, which helped establish a connection between human rights and the rights of the citizen, the declaration of a right to humanitarian aid separates them by asserting the need to separate the status of being human from the the status of citizenship. A new, universalisable principle is contained in this, Ewald goes on to say, one which as such may 'open a new age with respect to the philosophy of the international order', international law previously having been always 'a law of States, a law which only recognises man through States'.[99]

But why, then, does criticism of the humanitarian movement insist so much on a final point that we have not yet mentioned, which is the necessity of separating the humanitarian and the political?[100] To find an answer to this final question we must return briefly to the problem of *accusation* and to the related problem of the selection of the unfortunates who matter. Critics of 'humanitarianism', and among them R. Braumann in particular, frequently return to the necessity of choosing between unfortunates and to the necessarily political character of this choice that 'humanitarianism' would like to gloss over.[101] But what do they mean by *political?* Our interpretation is the following. Those choices are seen to be political which connect interests with accusations in a way which calls to mind the communitarian logic. Accusation only allows one to rank unfortunates, to choose those who are worth the effort required to help them and those who are not. To evaluate this argument we must go back to the logic of accusation and specifically to its temporal dimension.

We have seen that according to F. Tricaud the main characteristic of accusation is that of being entirely orientated towards the past, and towards a past which, as many recent examples have shown, has no natural limits. Clearly this orientation is not of an historical kind, in search of the intelligibility of the past, but is of a kind on which one can base on past actions, in the case of peoples on past actions performed by the dead, the conviction of the radical otherness of living beings who have the same name.[102] Perhaps it is not possible to conceive of politics, especially politics between States, without accusation; we leave this complicated problem there. But the humanitarian movement, if it demands recognition for its political dimension, does not claim to occupy the whole of the political space. It seems to us that the logic of its mode of justification can be summed up in the following way: alongside political forms orientated towards the past which, leaning on the memory of suffering, misfortunes and sacrifices of *past victims*, legitimise appeals to the identity of peoples, classes and States, and alongside political forms orientated towards the future which, on the basis of misfortunes to come and the suffering of *future victims*, argue for measures which will not benefit the living (as we see in the case of ecology, for example), there is room also for a *politics of the present* which, without seeking support from an accusation turned towards the past or from a justification of the future consequences of its actions, would be orientated entirely towards present suffering and *present victims*. Is it not true that there is often confusion between these three *political orders* which have supported criticisms arising from the use of the argument from pity in politics, with, in particular, a denunciation of those in power who exploit past victims in order to take possession of the future while ignoring present suffering? On the other hand, without leaving the framework of a politics of pity which has been unsurpassable for two centuries, by focusing on the present the humanitarian movement can even so stay closest to compassion, one of whose principal features is, as we saw at the start of this book, the *presence* of that which arouses it. To be concerned with the present is no small matter. For over the past, ever gone by, and over the future, still nonexistent, the present has an overwhelming privilege: that of being real.

Notes

1 The politics of pity

1. H. Arendt, *On Revolution*, Harmondsworth: Penguin Books, 1990, pp. 59–114.
2. M. Scheler, *Nature et formes de la sympathie. Contribution à l'étude des lois de la vie affective*, Paris: Payot, 1967, p. 23.
3. Arendt, *On Revolution*, p. 73: 'To avert one's eyes from the misery and unhappiness of the mass of mankind was no more possible in eighteenth-century Paris, or in nineteenth-century London, where Marx and Engels were to ponder the lessons of the French Revolution, than it is today in some European, most Latin American, and nearly all Asian and African countries.'
4. Ibid., p. 75: 'The words *le peuple* are the key words for every understanding of the French Revolution, and their connotations were determined by those who were exposed to the spectacle of the people's sufferings, which they themselves did not share.'
5. Ibid., p. 72: 'In order to avoid misunderstandings: the social question with which we are concerned here because of its role in revolution must not be equated with the lack of equality of opportunity or the problem of social status which in the last few decades has become a major topic of the social sciences.'
6. L. Boltanski and L. Thévenot, *De la justification. Les Économies de la grandeur*, Paris: Gallimard, 1991.
7. For this notion, cf. ibid., pp. 271–4.
8. L. Boltanski, *L'amour et la justice comme compétences*, Paris: Métailié, 1990.
9. E. Mersch, 'Communion des saints', *Dictionnaire de spiritualité*, Paris: Beauchesne, 1953, vol. 2, t. II, cols. 1291–4.
10. E. Mersche, 'Corps mystique', ibid., cols. 2378–97.
11. Mersche, 'Communion des saints'.
12. M. Agulhon, *Pénitents et francs-maçons*, Paris: Fayard, 1968.
13. In the collective view of 'works' established at the end of the seventeenth century, within the framework of works of charity it would be artificial to contrast the intercessors we referred to in the previous chapter, and for

which eighteenth century Provençals urged prayers, to the poor who now concern us. For the poor themselves are privileged intercessors; in the emerging traditional view works have an essential place in the dialectic of salvation, and even more than that abstract reality of 'works', the poor in their physical and symbolic reality. By distributing charity, the Provençal notables have the idea, and sometimes say so, of getting more than they give. (M. Vovelle, *Piété baroque et déchristianisation en Provence au XVIIIᵉ siecle*, Paris, Plon, 1973, p. 231)

14. J. Ratcliffe, ed., *The Good Samaritan and the Law*, New York: Anchor Book, Doubleday and Company Inc, 1966.
15. Cf. L. Mazamisa, *Beatific Comradeship. An Exegetical-Hermeneutical Study on Luke 10: 25–37*, Kampen (Holland): Uitgeversmaatschappij J. H. Hok, 1987, p. 85.
16. P. Ricoeur, *Histoire et vérité*, Paris: Seuil, 1955, pp. 99–111.
17. X. Léon-Dufour, *Dictionnaire du Nouveau Testament*, Paris, Seuil, 1978, p. 372.
18. K. Monro, 'John Donne's People: explaining differences between rational actors and altruists through cognitive frameworks', *Journal of Politics*, vol. 53, no. 2, (1991), pp. 392–433.
19. Cf. also the analyses of Todorov who, in the difficult marriage of an orientation towards the particular with an internalisation of general principles, sees the rare quality which defines the specificity of rescuers:

> However, we catch sight of the reasons for the rarity of rescuers: this practice requires qualities which are, to a certain extent, at odds with each other. Rescuers are not as a rule conformists, that is to say people whose conduct is governed by the opinions of their neighbours or even by the law. Rather, they are people who are seen as marginal and resistant to obedience. Nevertheless, they are far from rejecting all law; to the contrary they have within them the means for distinguishing good and evil and possess a lively conscience which they follow in their actions. At the same time, they are not those lovers of principles who happily cherish abstractions. They are beings who are driven both to universalisation, since they are ready to help others unknown to them, thus immediately according them membership of the common human species, and to individualisation, insofar as they do not defend ideals but concrete persons.
> (T. Todorov, *Face à l'extrême*, Paris: Seuil, 1991, p. 280)

20. In his interpretation of the parable, J. Zumstein employs the model developed by P. Ricoeur in *La métaphor vive*, Paris: Seuil, 1975, and in 'Biblical Hermeneutics', *Semeia*, vol. 4 (1975), pp. 27–148, in which there is a metaphorical tension in the parable which 'arises from the shock produced between two conceptions of reality': 'there is a tension between an initial conception arising from the ordinary and everyday life and an extraordinary conception' which 'provokes a crisis in the listener's image of the world'. Cf. J. Zumstein, 'Jésus et les paraboles', in *Les Paraboles évangéliques*, Paris: Cerf, 1989, pp. 89–108.

21. Ricoeur, *Histoire et vérité*, p. 100.
22. Mazamisa, *Beatific Comradeship,* p. 151.
23. Cf. S. Legasse, *Et qui est mon prochain? Etude sur l'objet de l'agapé dans le Nouveau Testament*, Paris: Cerf, 1989.
24. '*Secondary characters* are only characterised insofar as it is necessary. In Luke 10, 30–35, both the traveller who has fallen among thieves and the innkeeper lack any characterisation.' R. Bultmann, *L'histoire de la tradition synoptique*, Paris: Seuil, 1973, p. 238.
25. M. Walzer.
26. Cf., for example, R. Verdier, ed., *La vengeance dans les sociétés extra-occiden-tales*, Paris: Cujas, 1980.
27. Cf., for example, R. Jamous, *Honneur et baraka*, Paris: Editions de la Maison des sciences de l'homme, 1977.
28. 'Two kinds of reaction follow from the respective positions of offenders: one, *outside*, the reaction of vengeance, expresses the *solidarisation* of the offended person and his group faced with an external aggression, and the other, *within*, the reaction of penal sanction, in which the group, attacked by one of its members, is *desolidarised.*' R. Verdier, 'Le Système vindicatoire', in Verdier, ed., *La vengeance*, p. 15.
29. V. A. Sen, *Poverty and Famines. An Essay on Entitlement and deprivation*, Oxford: Clarendon Press, 1981, chapters. 1 and 2. One could also take the example of Charles Booth, the theorist of what he called the 'arithmetic of unhappiness, constructing a taxonomy of indigents for both a philanthropic and statistical use, comprising three classes: the very poor, the poor, and the less poor' (Cf., A. Desrosières, *La Politique des statistiques*, Paris: La Découverte, 1993).
30. C. Orwin, 'Compassion', *American Scholar* (Summer 1980), pp. 309–33.
31. Arendt, *On Revolution*, p. 114.
32. J. Harris, 'The marxist conception of violence', *Philosophy and Public Affairs*, vol. 3, no. 2, (1974), pp. 192–220.
33. P. Singer, 'Famine, affluence and morality', *Philosophy and Public Affairs*, vol. 1, no. 3 (1972), pp. 229–43.
34. S. James, 'The duty to relieve suffering', *Ethics*, vol. 93 (1982), pp. 4–21.
35. A. Honoré, 'Law, morals and rescue', in Ratcliffe, ed., *The Good Samaritan and the Law'*, pp. 225–42.
36. Cf. A. Tunc, 'The volunteer and the Good Samaritan' and A. Rudzinski, 'The duty to rescue: a comparative analysis', both in Ratcliffe, ed., *The Good Samaritan and the Law.*
37. G. Elfstrom, 'On dilemmas of Intervention', *Ethics*, vol. 93 (July 1983), pp. 709–25.
38. Cf. C. Beitz, *Political Theory and International Relations*, Princeton; Princeton University Press, 1979, pp. 71–83.
39. P. Singer, *Practical Ethics*, Cambridge; Cambridge University Press, 1979, pp. 162–71.
40. Cf. I. Hont and M. Ignatieff, eds., *Wealth and Virtue. The Shaping of Political*

Economy in the Scottish Enlightenment, Cambridge; Cambridge University Press, 1983, pp. 26–31.

41. Singer, *Practical Ethics*, p. 165.

2 Taking sides

1. A. Hirschman, *Exit, Voice and Loyalty*, Cambridge, MA: Harvard University Press, 1970.
2. J. Barish, *The Antitheatrical Prejudice*, Berkeley: University of California Press, 1981.
3. Aristotle, 'Rhetoric' and 'Politics' in *The Complete Works of Aristotle*, The Revised Oxford Translation, ed. Jonathan Barnes, Princeton: Princeton University Press, 1984.
4. Cf. T. Brunius, 'Catharsis', *Dictionary of the History of Ideas*, New York: Scribner, 1973, vol. 1, pp. 264–70.
5. Saint Augustine, *Confessions*, trans. with intro. R.S. Pine-Coffin, Harmondsworth: Penguin, 1961, pp. 55–7.
6. Ibid., p. 56.
7. Ibid., pp. 120–3.
8. Tertullien, *Les spectacles*, trans. and intro. M. Turcan, Paris: Cerf (Sources chrétiennes), 1986.
9. '"It is good to punish the guilty." Who but the guilty would deny this? Nevertheless, this does not mean that the innocent should take pleasure in the execution of other people.' Ibid., p. 225.
10. Cited in H. Phillips, *The Theatre and its Critics in Seventeenth-Century France*, Oxford: Oxford University Press, 1980, p. 113. [The quotation is given by Phillips in the original French–*trans.*]
11. Cf. S. Pease and T. Love, 'The Copycat Crime Phenomenon', in R. Surette, ed., *Justice and the Media*, Springfield IL: Charles C. Thomas Publisher, 1984, pp. 199–211.
12. See, for example, R. Surette, ed., *The Media and Criminal Justice Policy. Recent Research and Social Effect*, Springfield IL: Charles C. Thomas Publisher, 1990.
13. Cf. L. Dalston, 'Objectivity and the Escape from Perspective', *Social Studies of Science*, vol. 22 (1992), pp. 597–618. The conception of observation without perspective is linked to the possibility of communication at a distance and through this to the opposition of speech and writing. It is thus connected, in Condorcet for example, with printing which 'made possible a publicity without proximity, a community without visible presence'. R. Chartier, *Les Origines culturelles de la Révolution française*, Paris: Seuil, 1990, pp. 46–7.
14. The study of the uses of the metaphor of the theatre in the eighteenth century, particularly in moral and political reflection, is central in David Marshall, 'Adam Smith and the Theatricality of Moral Sentiments', *Critical Inquiry*, vol. 10 (1984) pp. 592–613; D. Marshall, *The Figure of Theatre: Shaftesbury, Defoe, Adam Smith, and George Eliot*, New York: Columbia University Press,

1986; and D. Marshall, *The Surprising Effects of Sympathy, Marivaux, Diderot, Rousseau and Mary Shelley*, Chicago: The University of Chicago Press, 1988.

15. On the history of the metaphor of the *theatrum mundi*, cf. L. Christian, *Theatrum Mundi, The History of an Idea*, New York, Garland Publishing Inc., 1987.

16. Boltanski and Thévenot, *De la justification*, pp. 126–36.

17. Barish, *The Antitheatrical Prejudice*, pp. 256–94.

18. M. Ketcham, *Transparent Designs. Reading, Performance and Form in the Spectator Papers*, Athens, OH: The University of Georgia Press 1985, p. 44.

19.   It is one of my greatest Delights to sit unobserved and unknown in the Gallery, and entertain my self either with what is personated on the stage, or observe what Appearances present themselves in the Audience. If there were no other good Consequence in a Playhouse, than that so many Persons of different Ranks and Conditions are placed there in their most pleasing Aspects, that Prospect only would be very far from being below the Pleasures of a wise Man.

20. Cf. Brunius, *'Catharsis'*.

21. M. Fried, *Absorption and Theatricality, Painting and Beholder in the Age of Diderot*, Berkeley and London: University of California Press, 1980.

22. See the analysis of Holbein's *Les ambassadeurs* which, for Bruno Latour, marks the transition from involving re-presentation to a Cartesian, quasicartographical kind of representation. B. Latour, 'Quand les anges deviennent de bien mauvais messagers', *Terrain*, ed. 14, (March 1990), pp. 76–91.

23. S. Edgerton, *Pictures and Punishment. Art and Criminal Prosecution during the Florentine Renaissance*, Ithaca: Cornell University Press, 1985.

24. Ibid., pp. 54–5.

25. Ibid., pp. 54–5.

26. Latour, 'Quand les anges'.

27. Edgerton, *Pictures and Punishment*, p. 57.

28. Cf. J. Habermas, *The Structural Transformation of the Public Sphere, an Inquiry into a Category of Bourgeois Society*, trans. Thomas Burger with the assistance of Frederick Lawrence, Cambridge, Polity, 1989. For a genuine ethnography of the way in which popular public opinion is formed, diffused and transformed through its circulation in public places, see A. Farge, *Dire et mal dire. L'opinion publique au XVIIIᵉ siècle*, Paris: Seuil, 1992.

29.   There is no place of general Resort, wherein I do not often make my Appearance; sometimes I am seen thrusting my Head into a Round of Politicians at Will's, and listening with great Attention to the narratives that are made in those little Circular Audiences. Sometimes I smoke a Pipe at Child's; and whilst I seem attentive to nothing but the Post-Man, over-hear the Conversation of every table in the Room . . . I have been taken for a Merchant upon the Exchange for above these ten years, and sometimes pass for a Jew in the Assembly of Stock-Jobbers at Jonathan's.

In short, where-ever I see a Cluster of People I always mix with them,
tho' I never open my Lips but in my own Club.
Quoted in J. C. Agnew, *World Apart: The Market and the Theater
in Anglo-American Thought, 1550–1750*, Cambridge: Cambridge
University Press, 1986, p. 173.

30. Cf. G. Good, *The Observing Self. Rediscovering the Essay*, London, Routledge, 1988, pp. 56–7.
31. In the sense in which we employ this word in *De la justification*.
32. B. Latour, *Science in Action. How to Follow Scientists and Engineers through Society*, Milton Keynes: Open University Press, 1987.
33. As Alpers notes for Dutch painting in the seventeenth century, in S. Alpers, *The Art of Describing. Dutch Art in the Seventeenth Century*, Chicago: The University of Chicago Press, 1983.
34. M. Foucault, *Discipline and Punish: The Birth of the Prison*, Harmondsworth: Penguin, 1977.
35. P. Spierenburg, *The Spectacle of Suffering. Executions and the Evolution of Repression: from a Preindustrial Metropolis to the European Experience*, Cambridge: Cambridge University Press, 1984.
36. Ibid., p. 92.
37. Ibid., p. 85.
38. Edgerton, *Pictures and Punishment*, p. 35.
39. J.-M. Lochman, 'The Lord's Prayer in Our Time: Praying and Drumming', *The Princeton Seminary Bulletin*, supplementary issue no. 2 (1992), pp. 5–19.
40. Edgerton, *Pictures and Punishment*, p. 135.
41. Spierenburg, *The Spectacle of Suffering*, p. 102. See also, Foucault, *Discipline and Punish*, pp. 57–65.
42. Cf. C. Lemieux, 'La Révolution française et l'excellence journalistique au sens civique', *Politix*, no. 19 (1992), pp. 31–6.
43. A detailed analysis of the way in which a crowd gathers around a rumour taking up the issue of shocking suffering can be found in A. Farge and J. Revel, *Logiques de la foule. L'affaire des enlèvements d'enfants. Paris 1750*, Paris: Hachette, 1988.
44. R. Solomon, Review of B. Boruah, *Fiction and Emotion*, in *Review of Metaphysics*, vol. 43 (March 1990), pp. 620–1.
45. Cf., for example, R. Roberts, 'What is Wrong with Wicked Feelings?' *American Philosophical Quarterly*, vol. 28, no. 1 (January 1991), pp. 13–24.
46. E. Claverie, 'Pour une histoire de la constitution de la défence judiciaire: Voltaire et la mise en oeuvre de la notion de cause publique dans l'affaire Calas', communication to the *Journées françaises de Sociologie*, Bordeaux, mimeo., 1987, and E. Claverie, 'Sainte indignation contre-indignation éclairée. L'affaire du chevalier de La Barre', *Ethnologie française*, vol. 22, no. 3, (1993), pp. 271–90.
47. See W. Ong's analyses of the more general properties of orality in W. Ong, *The Presence of the Word*, New Haven: Yale University Press, 1967.
48. E. Tassin, 'Espace commun ou espace public? L'antagonisme de la communauté et de la publicité', *Hermès*, vol. 10 (1991), pp. 23–7.

49. P. Adam, 'Les campagnes de témoignages de l'Agence française de lutte contre le sida', communication to the seminar *Le spectacle de la souffrance*, Paris, EHESS, 1992.

3 The moral spectator

1. D. Raphaël, 'The impartial spectator', in A. Skinner and T. Wilson, eds., *Essays on Adam Smith*, Oxford: The Clarendon Press, 1995, pp. 83–99.
2. Ibid., p. 84.
3. A. Smith, *The Theory of Moral Sentiments*, ed. D. D. Raphael and A. L. Macfie, Indianapolis: LibertyPress/Oxford: The Clarendon Press, 1982 (1976).
4. Cited in T. Campbell, *Adam Smith's Science of Morals*, London: Allen & Unwin, 1971, pp. 43–4.
5. Ibid., p. 134.
6. Ibid., p. 136.
7. Cf. N. Waszek, *Man's Social Nature. A Topic of the Scottish Enlightenment in its Historical Setting*, Frankfurt-on-Main *Adam Smith's Science of Morals,* Verlag Peter Lang, 1986.
8. Campbell, p. 95.
9. 'As we have no immediate experience of what other men feel, we can form no idea of the manner in which they are affected, but by conceiving what we ourselves should feel in the like situation' (*The Theory of Moral Sentiments*, p. 9); 'Every faculty in one man is the measure by which he judges of the like faculty in another. I judge of your sight by my sight, of your ear by my ear, of your reason by my reason, of your resentment by my resentment, of your love by my love. I neither have, nor can have, any other way of judging them' (ibid., p. 19).
10. Agnew, *World Apart*, pp. 178–9.

11.   A man may sympathize with a woman in child-bed; though it is impossible that he should conceive himself as suffering her pains in his own proper person and character. That whole account of human nature, however, which deduces all sentiments and affections from self-love, which has made so much noise in the world, but which, so far as I know, has never yet been fully and distinctly explained, seems to me to have arisen from some confused misapprehension of the system of sympathy.
      (*The Theory of Moral Sentiments*, p. 317)

12. C. Haroche, 'La compassion comme amour social et politique de l'autre au XVIIIᵉ siecle', in CURAPP, *La solidarité*, Paris: PUF, 1991, pp. 11–25.

13.   In order to produce this concord, as nature teaches the spectators to assume the circumstances of the person principally concerned, so she teaches this last in some measure to assume those of the spectators. As they are continually placing themselves in his situation, and then conceiving emotions similar to what he feels; so he is as constantly placing himself in theirs, and thence conceiving some degree of that coolness

about his own fortune, with which he his sensible that they will view it. As they are constantly considering what they themselves would feel, if they actually were the sufferers, so he is as constantly led to imagine in what manner he would be affected if he was only one of the spectators of his own situation. As their sympathy makes them look at it, in some measure, with his eyes, so his sympathy makes him look at it, in some measure, with theirs, especially when in their presence and acting under their observation: and as the reflected passion, which he thus conceives, is much weaker than the original one, it necessarily abates the violence of what he felt before he came into their presence, before he began to recollect in what manner they would be affected by it, and to view his situation in this candid and impartial light.

(The Theory of Moral Sentiments, p. 22)

14. J. Badner, 'The Art of Sympathy in Eighteenth-century British Moral Thought', *Studies in Eighteenth-Century Culture*, vol. 9, ed. R. Runte, Madison WI: University of Wisconsin Press, 1979, pp. 189–210.
15. Raphaël, 'The Impartial Spectator', p. 87.
16. T. Campbell, 'Scientific Explanation and Ethical Justification in the *Moral Sentiments*', in A. Skinner, T. Wilson, p. 72.

17. When I endeavour to examine my own conduct, when I endeavour to pass sentence upon it, and either to approve or condemn it, it is evident that, in all such cases, I divide myself, as it were, into two persons; and that I, the examiner and judge, represent a different character from that other I, the person whose conduct is examined into and judged of. The first is the spectator, whose sentiments with regard to my own conduct I endeavour to enter into, by placing myself in his situation, and by considering how it would appear to me, when seen from that particular point of view. The second is the agent . . .

(The Theory of Moral Sentiments, p. 113)

18. But though man has, in this manner, been rendered the immediate judge of mankind, he has been rendered so only in the first instance; and an appeal lies from his sentence to a much higher tribunal, to the tribunal of their own consciences, to that of the supposed impartial and well-informed spectator, to that man within the breast, the great judge and arbiter of their conduct.   (*The Theory of Moral Sentiments*, p. 130)

19. A. Smith, 'Considerations Concerning the First Formation of Languages' in A. Smith, *Lectures on Rhetoric and Belles Lettres*, ed. .J. C. Bryce, Oxford: The Clarendon Press, 1983, pp. 203–26.
20. 'Could we suppose any person living on the banks of the Thames so ignorant, as not to know the general word *river*, but to be acquainted only with the particular word *Thames*, if he was brought to any other river, would he not readily call it *a Thames?*' Smith, 'Considerations . . .', p. 204.

21. Ibid., p. 219.
22. V. T. Todorov, ed., 'L'énonciation', *Langages*, no. 17 (1970).
23. O. Ducrot, 1980, *Les mots du discours*, Paris: Minuit, pp. 57–92.
24. L. Quéré, 'L'opinion: l'économie du vraisemblable. Introduction à une approche praxéologique de l'opinion publique', *Réseaux*, no.43, (1990), pp. 33–58.
25. O. Ducrot and T. Todorov, *Encyclopedic Dictionary of the Sciences of Language*, trans. Catherine Porter, Baltimore and London: Johns Hopkins University Press, 1994, p. 303.
26. Ibid., p. 324.
27. G. Levine, *The Realistic Imagination. English Fiction from Frankenstein to Lady Chatterley*, Chicago: University of Chicago Press, 1981.
28. G. Good, *The Observing Self. Rediscovering the Essay*, London, Routledge, 1988, p. 13.
29. M. Golden, *The Self Observed. Swift, Johnson, Wordsworth*, Baltimore: The Johns Hopkins University Press, 1972, p. 5.
30. J. Olney, ed., *Autobiography. Essays Theoretical and Critical*, Princeton: Princeton University Press, 1980, pp. 118–19.
31. A. Piper, 'Impartiality, Compassion, and Modal Imagination', *Ethics*, vol. 101 (July 1991), pp. 726–57.

32. As we cannot indeed enter thoroughly into the gratitude of the person who receives the benefit, unless we beforehand approve of the motives of the benefactor, so, upon this account, the sense of merit seems to be a compounded sentiment, and to be made up of two distinct emotions; a direct sympathy with the sentiments of the agent, and an indirect sympathy with the gratitude of those who receive the benefit of his actions.
        (*The Theory of Moral Sentiments*, p. 74)

33. From the start Smith indicates that if sympathy was first of all employed as a synonym for pity, nonetheless it can 'be made use of to denote our fellow-feeling with any passion whatever' (*The Theory of Moral Sentiments*, p. 10.)

34. The principle by which we naturally either approve or disapprove of our own conduct, seems to be altogether the same with that by which we exercise the like judgements concerning the conduct of other people. We either approve or disapprove of the conduct of another man according as we feel that, when we bring his case home to ourselves, we either can or cannot entirely sympathize with the sentiments and motives which directed it. And, in the same manner, we either approve or disapprove of our own conduct, according as we feel that, when we place ourselves in the situation of another man, and view it, as it were, with his eyes and from his station, we either can or cannot entirely enter into and sympathize with the sentiments and motives which influenced it. We can never survey our own sentiments and motives, we can never form any

judgement concerning them; unless we remove ourselves, as it were, from our own natural station, and endeavour to view them as at a certain distance from us. But we can do this in no other way than by endeavouring to view them with the eyes of other people, or as other people are likely to view them. (*The Theory of Moral Sentiments*, pp. 109–10)

35.   Let us suppose that the great empire of China, with all its myriads of inhabitants, was suddenly swallowed up by an earthquake, and let us consider how a man of humanity in Europe, who had no sort of connexion with that part of the world, would be affected upon receiving intelligence of this dreadful calamity.

   (*The Theory of Moral Sentiments*, p. 136)

36. Judgements established from the position of the impartial spectator are thus distinguished from judgements formed by taking account of the opinion of others:

   The jurisdictions of these two tribunals are founded upon principles which, though in some respects resembling and akin, are, however, in reality different and distinct. The jurisdiction of the man without, is founded altogether in the desire of actual praise, and in the aversion to actual blame. The jurisdiction of the man within, is founded altogether in the desire of praise-worthiness, and in the aversion to blame-worthiness. (*The Theory of Moral Sentiments*, pp. 130–1)

Smith later illustrates this distinction through the example of wars, partisan struggles and civil wars. In these conflicts, the actor's 'whole ambition is to obtain the approbation of his own fellow-citizens' and 'all are animated by the same hostile passions which animate himself'. If someone can be found who is opposed to the spirit of faction, he will be 'a solitary individual, without any influence, excluded, by his own candour, from the confidence of either party' (*The Theory of Moral Sentiments*, pp. 154–5). How can we not see in this portrait the figure, which will be illustrated for the first time by Voltaire before becoming an eminent character of the political scene – from Zola defending Dreyfus to Sartre embracing the cause of Henri Martin – of the literary man committed in an *affaire* in which he denounces the partisan accusation of an innocent person (cf. the next chapter).

37.   Even of the passions derived from the imagination, those which take their origin from a peculiar turn or habit it has acquired, though they may be acknowledged to be perfectly natural, are, however, but little sympathized with. The imaginations of mankind, not having acquired that particular turn, cannot enter into them; and such passions, though they may be allowed to be almost unavoidable in some part of life, are always, in some measure, ridiculous. This is the case with strong attachment which naturally grows up between two persons of different sexes, who have long fixed their thoughts upon one another. Our imagination not

having run in the same channel with that of the lover, we cannot enter
into the eagerness of his emotions.

(*The Theory of Moral Sentiments*, p. 31)

38. Ibid., pp. 31–2.
39. 'Mankind, at the same time, have a very strong sense of the injuries that are
done to another. The villain, in a tragedy or romance, is as much the object of
our indignation, as the hero is that of our sympathy and affection' (*The Theory
of Moral Sentiments*, p. 34). Cf. also, for example, p. 160.
40. Piper, 'Impartiality, Compassion and Modal Imagination'.
41. In particular, we find in this article a convincing description of the kind of
extremely limited psychological and social world into which persons would be
plunged if they did not possess this ability. They would have limited access to
their own interiority but could not ascribe their own states to others; they could
not attribute to others, and so generalise, their own experiences which, by the
same token, would become incomprehensible to them in terms of general categories (like love or fear) and would be lived in the way in which we live changes
in the weather for which we do not possess any particular words.
42. Who only indicates genres like the novel, poetry or stories in the first person.
43. Here, and in the following paragraphs, we follow the analyses of Thomas Pavel.
Pavel calls this process of setting at a distance, *mythification*. Cf. T. G. Pavel,
Fictional Worlds, Cambridge MA, London: Harvard University Press, 1986,
pp. 77–80.
44. Cf. Ibid., pp. 46–7, who relies here on the semantics of possible worlds. In fact
we can draw a parallel between the modal imagination, in A. Piper's sense, and
truth according to possibility (following the Aristotelian opposition between
what is possible according to possibility and what is possible according to
necessity) which, according to Pavel, defines 'realist literature' so long as we do
not give this term the narrow sense of the 'stylistic and narrative conventions'
of the nineteenth century novel. Literary propositions are 'possible according
to necessity' when they are 'true in every alternative of the real world'; they are
true according to possibility when they are 'true at least in one alternative of
the actual world'. Now there 'are many real historical and social settings in
which writers and their public accept the assumption that a literary work
speaks of something that is genuinely possible relative to the real world'. It is a
matter of 'a fundamental attitude toward the relationship between the actual
world and the truth of literary texts. In a realist perspective, the criterion of the
truth and falsity of a literary text and of its details is based upon the notion of
possibility (and not only *logical* possibility) with respect to the actual world'.
Thus, if the character of Shakespeare's tragedy *Julius Ceasar* really lived, 'is it
not natural to think that if, owing to an unpleasant accident of history,
Sherlock Holmes does not happen to have existed, he would have existed in
another state of affairs?'
45. Cf. Pavel, *Fictional Worlds*, pp. 50–3.
46. Ibid., pp.123–9.

47. Pavel takes the example of the narrative pre-conventions which guide the reader of English novels:

> A contemporary well-trained reader, as well as her nineteenth-century counterpart, knows quite well that large-sized novels published in England in the first half of that century most often deal with matrimonial questions, especially when the author is a woman and the tone is serious. In such novels, marriage will be actively sought as the optimal state of affairs for the protagonists, under certain social and sentimental constraints. A good reader knows that this regularity is part of the novel's background and that the right expectations makes the game possible. One understands what *Pride and Prejudice* and later *Jane Eyre* are about only when one expects, or realizes, that matrimony and the condition of women are central topics and that an intimate relationship links them to the novel as a literary form.

But, Pavel adds,

> such a regularity does not qualify as a proper convention, since uniform conformity to it does not obtain: not only do many nineteenth century novels have nonmatrimonial topics, but those dealing with matrimony handle the subject in very diverse ways. The situation resembles coordination games, in which the strategies for cooperation are not yet ossified into conventions: each particular instance of the game, while sharing some of its features with other games, asks for specific skills and idiosyncratic solutions.   (Pavel, *Fictional Worlds*, pp. 125–6)

48. Cf., R. De Souza, *The Rationality of Emotion*, Cambridge MA: The MIT Press 1987, p. 182.
49. B. Rimé, 'Le partage social des émotions', in B. Rimé and K. Scherer, *Les émotions*, Neuchâtel: Delachaux & Niestlé, 1989, pp. 271–300.
50. A. Greimas and J. Fontanille, *Sémiotique des passions. Des états de choses aux états d'âme*, Paris: Seuil, 1991, pp. 154–5 and p. 171. See also P. Livet and L. Thévenot, 'Modes d'action collective et construction éthique. Les émotions dans l'évaluation', Contribution to the conference *Limitation de la rationalité et constitution du collectif*, Clerisy, 5–12 June 1993: the emotions employ the 'abilities of reelaboration and self-questioning of the passions in order to spawn the "habitus" which joins cognition and affect'. 'Before arriving at an ethical judgement which must appeal to arguments with as much generality as possible' 'we begin to live ethical evaluation' in 'orders of judgement' which 'are determined by the kind of activation of the emotions of evaluation, even before a value judgement has really been made'.
51. The main problem then becomes that of the articulation between an apparently structural approach which includes an historical orientation, based above all on the study of texts and, on the other hand, an approach of a pragmatic inspiration. It seems to us that by developing the notion of *competence*, already

employed in our earlier works, the topics of suffering could be integrated in a *pragmatics of the spectator.* The idea of a pragmatics of the spectator might appear paradoxical since the first question the spectator must confront is the one that is posed to him by his inaction. But the reflexive relationship to inaction also requires a competence the functioning of which in real situations or in experimental arrangements can be studied by empirical science.

4 The topic of denunciation

1. Jean-Paul Sartre, *Sketch for a Theory of the Emotions*, trans. Philip Mairet, London: Methuen, 1962.
2. V. Goldberg, *The Power of Photography. How Photographs Change our Lives*, New York: Abbeville Press, 1991.
3. L. Blum, *Souvenirs sur l'Affaire*, Paris: Gallimard, 1935.
4. In the words of Elisabeth Claverie in 'Sainte indignation contre indignation éclairée. L'affaire du chevalier de La Barre', *Ethnologie française.*
5. S. Ranulf, *Moral Indignation and Middle Class Psychology. A Sociological Study*, Copenhagen: Levin & Munskgaard, 1938. By emphasising how communities found or restore their unity by accusing and persecuting a victim chosen from foreigners or the marginal, Ranulf presents themes which are taken up in the work of René Girard.
6. S. Ranulf, *The Jealousy of the Gods and Criminal Law at Athens. A Contribution to the Sociology of Moral Indignation*, Copenhagen: Williams and Norgate Ltd., Levin & Munksgaard, 1933.
7. M. Scheler, *L'homme du ressentiment*, Paris: Idées/Gallimard, 1970.
8. Claverie, 'Sainte indignation' . . .
9. On the general characteristics of the *affair form*, cf. Boltanski, *L'amour et la justice comme compétences*, and, for a probing analysis of contemporary affairs, F. Chateauraynaud, *La faute professionelle*, Paris: Métailié, 1991.
10. Again, in the same letter of 25 August 1766: 'The chevalier de La Barre has suffered torments and death without weakness or ostentation. The only time he seemed moved was when he saw Belleval in the crowd of spectators. The people would have torn Belleval to pieces, if there was not a helping hand . . .' Cited in Claverie, 'Sainte indignation'.
11. Pierre Bourdieu, *Distinction. A Social Critique of the Judgement of Taste*, trans. Richard Nice, London and New York: Routledge and Kegan Paul, 1986.
12. Pierre Bourdieu uses this distinction to criticise the Sartrean alienation of the 'body for others' which transforms the effect of the class related 'social gaze' into 'generic alienation':

> The mere fact that the most sought-after bodily properties (slimness, beauty etc.) are not randomly distributed among the classes (for example, the proportion whose waist measurement is greater than the model waist rises sharply as one moves down the social heirarchy) is sufficient to exclude the possibility of treating the relationship which

agents have with the social representation of their own body as a generic alienation, constitutive of the 'body for others'. The 'alienated body' described by Sartre is a generic body, as is the 'alienation' which befalls each body when it is perceived and named, and therefore objectified by the gaze and the discourse of others.   (*Distinction*, p. 207)

13. M. Angenot, *La parole pamphlétaire. Typologie des discours modernes*, Paris: Payot, 1982.
14. Ibid., pp. 74–7.
15. Ibid., p. 25.
16. Ibid., pp. 34–45, 59.
17. Ibid., pp. 34–5.
18. Ibid., p. 51.
19. On the problematic of the trail, cf. Carlo Ginzburg, 'Signes, traces, pistes. Racines d'un paradigme de l'indice', *Le débat*, vol. 7, (1980), pp. 3–44. Cf., also, Carlo Ginzburg, 'Morelli, Freud and Sherlock Holmes: Clues and Scientific Method', *History Workshop*, vol. 9 (Spring 1980), pp. 5–36.
20. Boltanski, 'La dénonciation publique,' in *L'amour et la justice.*
21. On the regime of justice, see Boltanksi and Thévenot, *op. cit.*
22. Jean-Jacques Rousseau, *The Social Contract and The Discourses*, trans. G. D. H. Cole. Revised and augmented by J. H. Brumfitt and John C. Hall, London: Everyman, 1993.
23. That we take, in *De la justification*, from the political writings of Bossuet.
24. R. Dérathé, *Jean-Jacques Rousseau et la science politique de son temps*, Paris: Vrin, 1970, pp. 222–6.
25. Rouseau, *The Social Contract*, p. 210.
26. R. Wuthnow, *Acts of Compassion. Caring for Others and Helping Ourselves*, Princeton: Princeton University Press, 1991.
27. There are a number of examples in J. Godechot, *Le contre-révolution*, Paris: PUF, 1961. We find this in Burke in 1790:

Wickedness is a little more inventive. Whilst you are discussing fashion, the fashion is gone by. The very same vice assumes a new body . . . It walks abroad; it continues its ravages; whilst you are gibbeting the carcass, or demolishing the tomb. You are terrifying yourself with ghosts and apparitions, whilst your house is the haunt of robbers. It is thus with all those, who, attending only to the shell and husk of history, think they are waging war with intolerance, pride, and cruelty, whilst, under colour of abhorring the ill principles of antiquated parties, they are authorizing and feeding the same odious vices in different factions, and perhaps in worse.
(Edmund Burke, *Reflections on the Revolution in France*, ed. with introduction L. G. Mitchell, Oxford/New York: Oxford University Press, 1993)

28. Arendt, p. 75. [Words in French in Arendt – *trans.*]
29. François Furet and Mona Ozouf, *A Critical Dictionary of the French Revolution*,

trans. Arthur Goldhammer, Cambridge MA., London: The Belknap Press of Harvard University Press, 1989. The article 'Terror' by François Furet, p. 148.
30. Ibid., p. 145 and p. 146.
31. Cf., R. Nisbet, *The Sociological Tradition*, London: Heinemann, 1967.
32. Arendt, pp. 51–8.
33. Paul Ricoeur, *Lectures 1. Autour du politique*, Paris: Seuil, 1991, pp. 143–54.

5 The topic of sentiment

1. Goldberg, *The Power of Photography*.
2. Cf. R. Lewinsohn, *Histoire entière du coeur*, Paris: Plon, 1959, which constructs a history of the localisation of sentiments within the heart as an organ.
3. Cf. T. Campbell, 'Scientific Explanation and Ethical Justification in the *Moral Sentiments*', in Skinner and Wilson, eds., *Essays on Adam Smith*.
4. In the sense of the visions studied by E. Claverie in, 'Voir apparaître. Les apparitions de la Vierge à Medjugorje', *Raisons pratiques*, vol. 2, (1991), pp. 157–76.
5. See, for example, S. Shott, 'Emotion and Social Life: A Symbolic Interactionist Analysis', *American Journal of Sociology*, vol. 6, no. 6 (1979), pp. 1317–34, and L. Lofland, 'The Social Shaping of Emotion: The Case of Grief', *Symbolic Interaction*, vol. 8, no. 2 (1985), pp. 171–90. A good, essentially American presentation of the sociology of emotions can be found in P. A. Thoits, 'The Sociology of Emotions', *Annual Review of Sociology*, vol. 15 (1989), pp. 317–42, and a similar work for the history of emotions in P. N. Stearns and C. Z. Stearns, 'Emotionology: Clarifying the History of Emotions and Emotional Standards', *The American Historical Review*, vol. 90, no. 4 (October 1985). Finally, for a wider discussion touching on psychology and philosophy, cf. R. Harré, ed., *The Social Construction of Emotions*, Oxford: Basil Blackwell, 1986.
6. On the distinction between primary and secondary emotions, cf. T. Kemper, 'How Many Emotions are There? Wedding the Social and the Autonomic Components', *American Journal of Sociology*, vol. 93, no. 2 (1987), pp. 263–89.
7. G. Wallbott and K. Scherer, 'How Universal and Specific is Emotional Experience? Evidence from 27 countries on Five Continents', *Information sur les sciences sociales*, vol. 25, no.4 (1986), pp. 763–96.
8. A. Hoschild, 'Emotional Work, Feeling Rules and Social Structure', *American Journal of Sociology*, vol. 85, no.3 (1979), pp. 551–75; A. Hoschild, *The Managed Heart. Commercialization of Human Feeling*, Los Angeles: University of California Press, 1983.
9. R. Frank, *Passions within Reason. The Strategic Role of the Emotions*, New York: Norton, 1990.
10. D. Cohn, *Transparent Minds. Narrative Modes for Presenting Consciousness in Fiction*, Princeton: Princeton University Press, 1978.
11. E. Benveniste, *Problems in General Linguistics*, trans. Mary Elizabeth Meek, Coral Gables: University of Miami Press, 1971. p. 209.
12. Laurence Sterne, *The Life and Opinions of Tristram Shandy, Gentleman*, ed.

Graham Petrie with Intro. Christopher Ricks, Harmondsworth: Penguin Books, 1967, p. 96.

13. Cohn, *Transparent Minds,* p. 104.
14. Ibid., pp. 21–2, 58.
15. Good, *The Observing Self.*
16. Cf. in particular, P. M. Spacks, *Imagining a Self. Autobiography and Novel in Eighteenth-Century England,* Cambridge MA: Harvard University Press, 1976, and J. O. Lyons, *The Invention of the Self. The Hinge of Consciousness in the Eighteenth Century,* Carbondale and Edwardsville: Southern Illinois University Press, 1978.
17. Cohn, *Transparent Minds,* p. 145.
18. J. Starobinski, *La relation critique,* Paris: Gallimard, 1970.
19. Sterne, *Tristram Shandy,* pp. 106–7.
20. Golden, *The Self Observed.*
21. Cf. S. D. Cox, *'The Stranger within Thee.' Concepts of the Self in Late-Eighteenth-Century Literature,* Pittsburg: University of Pittsburg Press, 1980.
22. Laurence Sterne, *A Sentimental Journey and Other Writings,* London: Everyman, 1994, pp. 4–7.
23. Ibid., pp. 29–31.
24. M. Gilot and J. Sgard, *Le vocabulaire du sentiment dans l'oeuvre de J.-J. Rousseau,* Geneva/Paris: Slatkine, 1980.
25. R. F. Brissenden, *Virtue in Distress. Studies in the Novel of Sentiment from Richardson to Sade,* London: Macmillan, 1974.
26. According to V. Mylne, *The Eighteenth-Century French Novel. Techniques of Illusion,* Cambridge: Cambridge University Press, 1981, p. 148.
27. Mylne, Ibid., p. 149.
28. Samuel Richardson, *Pamela; or Virtue Rewarded,* Harmondsworth: Penguin, 1980, letter XXXII, p. 130.
29. Mylne, *The Eighteenth-Century French Novel,* p. 6.
30. D. Diderot, *Oeuvres esthétiques,* Paris: Garnier, 1959, p. 29.

6 The critique of sentimentalism

1. A. Vincent-Buffault, *Histoire des larmes,* Paris: Rivages, 1986. pp. 203–6.
2. Cf. F. Kaplan, *Sacred Tears. Sentimentality in Victorian Literature,* Princeton: Princeton University Press, 1987, pp. 52 ff.
3. An analysis of these contrasting judgements can be found in the chapter dedicated to Dickens in G. Himmelfarb, *The Idea of Poverty. England in the Industrial Age,* London: Faber & Faber, 1984, pp. 453–88.
4. M. Ruff, *L'esprit du mal et l'esthétique baudelairienne,* Paris: A. Colin, 1955. pp. 27 and 385.
5. S. McMillen Conger, *Sensibility in Transformation. Creative Resistance to Sentiment from the Augustans to the Romantics. Essays in Honour of Jean H. Hagstrum,* Rutherford: Fairleigh Dickinson University Press, 1990, p. 13.

6. See the history of arguments based upon the selfish sentiment of one's own vulnerability, Orwin, 'Compassion'.

7. Bernard Mandeville, *The Fable of the Bees: or, Private Vices, Publick Benefits*, volume I, Indianapolis: LibertyClassics, 1988. p. 56.

8.   The principal danger of Novels, as forming a mistaken and pernicious system of morality, seems to me to arise from that contrast between one virtue and another, that war of duties which is to be found in many of them, particularly in that species called the Sentimental . . . In the enthusiasm of sentiment there is much the same danger as in the enthusiasm of religion, of substituting certain impulses and feelings of what may be called the visionary kind, in the place of real practical duties, which in morals, as in theology, we might not improperly denominate good works.

   Quoted in L. I. Bredvold, *The Natural History of Sensibility*, Detroit, Wayne State University Press, 1962, pp. 84–5.

9.   As Mr. *Hobbes* explains all Sensations of *Pity* by our Fear of the like Evils, when by Imagination we place ourselves in the Case of the Sufferers; so others explain all Approbation and Condemnation of Actions in distant Ages or Nations, by a like Effort of Imagination: We place ourselves in the Case of others, and then discern an *imaginary* private Advantage or Disadvantage in these Actions. But as his Account of Pity will never explain how the Sensation increases, according to the apprehended *Worth* of the Sufferer, or according to the *Affection* we formerly had to him; since the Sufferings of any Stranger may suggest the same Possibility of our suffering the like: So this Explication will never account for our high Approbation of brave unsuccessful Attempts, which we see prove detrimental both to the Agent, and to those for whose Service they were intended; here there is no private Advantage to be imagined.
                    (Francis Hutcheson, *An Inquiry into the Original of our Ideas of
                    Beauty and Virtue; In Two Treatises*, reprint of 4th edn, corrected,
                    Farnborough: Gregg International, 1969, Additions and
                    Corrections, etc., insert for p. 117)

10. Cf. N. Waszek, *Man's Social Nature*.

11. Cf. Jacque Derrida's interpretation of Rousseau's ideas on language in J. Derrida, *Of Grammatology*, trans. Gayatri Chakravorty Spivak, Baltimore and London: Johns Hopkins University Press, 1976.

12. R. B. Yeazell, *Fictions of Modesty. Women and Courtship in the English Novel*, Chicago: University of Chicago Press, 1991.

13. Mandeville, *The Fable of the Bees*, pp. 64–70.

14. R. Solomon, 'In Defence of Sentimentality', *Philosophy and Literature*, vol. 14 (1990), pp. 304–23.

15. Cf. P. Séjourné, *Aspects généraux du roman féminin en Angleterre de 1740 à*

1800, Aix-en-Provence: Publication des Annales de la Faculté des Lettres, 1966, pp. 83–6.

16. Quoted in Brissenden, *Virtue in Distress*, p. 10.

17. Ibid., p. 83.

18. Cox, *'The Stranger within Thee'*.

19. F. Baasner, 'The Changing Meaning of "Sensibilité",' in O. Brack, Jnr., ed., *Studies in Eighteenth-century Culture*, vol., 15, Madison WI: University of Wisconsin Press, 1986, pp. 77–96.

20. It is *disinterestedness* which creates the link between the natural sense of beauty and the natural sense of virtue. Cf A.-D. Balmès, avant-propos to Francis Hutcheson, *Recherche sur l'origine de nos idées de beauté et de la vertu*, transl. and ed. by A.-D. Balmès, Paris: Vrin, 1991, p. 14.

21. J. Hagstrum, *Sex and Sensibility. Ideal and Erotic Love from Milton to Mozart*, Chicago: University of Chicago Press, 1979.

22. Brissenden, *Virtue in Distress*, p. 78.

23. E. Auerbach, *Mimesis. The Representation of reality in Western Literature*, transl. Willard R. Trask, Princeton: Princeton University Press, 1953, pp. 400–1.

24. For example, Ruff, *L'esprit du mal*, pp. 20–46, or again, F. Bradbrook, 'Samuel Richardson', in Boris Ford, ed., *The New Pelican Guide to English Literature. Volume Four, From Dryden to Johnson*, London: Penguin, 1957, pp. 286–304, who speaks of the 'repellent characteristics' of Richardson and of the 'coarse-grained vulgarity' of his heroine.

25. K. Straub, 'Reconstructing the Gaze: Voyeurism in Richardson's *Pamela*', in L. Brown and J. Yolton, eds., *Studies in Eighteenth-Century Culture*, vol. 18, East Lansing (MI:), ASECS, 1988.

26. Solomon, 'In Defence of Sentimentality'.

27. M. Tanner, 'Sentimentality', *Proceedings of the Aristotelian Society*, New series, vol. 77 (1976–7), pp. 127–48.

28. M. Midgley, 'Brutality and Sentimentality', *Philosophy*, vol. 54 (1979), pp. 385–9.

29. M. Jefferson, 'What is Wrong with Sentimentality?' *Mind*, vol. 92 (1983), pp. 519–29.

30. Quoted in C. Howells, *Love, Mystery, and Misery. Feeling in Gothic Fiction*, London: The Athlone Press, 1978, p. 153.

31. Quoted in Séjourné, *Aspects généraux*, p. 77.

32.   In the first Treatise . . . all he [the Author] is sollicitous about is to shew, 'That there is some *Sense of Beauty natural* to Men.' And we find to the full as great an Agreement of Men in their Relishes of *Forms*, as in their external Senses, which all agree to be *natural*; and that Pleasure, or Pain, Delight, or Aversion are *naturally* join'd to their Perceptions. If the Reader be convinc'd of such Determinations of the Mind to be pleas'd with *Forms, Proportions, Resemblances, Theorems*, it will be no difficult matter to apprehend another *superior Sense natural* to Men, determining

them to be pleas'd with *Actions, Characters, Affections.* This is the *moral Sense* which makes the Subject of the Second Treatise.
(Hutcheson, Preface to *An Inquiry into the Original of our Ideas of Beauty and Virtue*, pp.xv–xvi)

33. Cf. M. Milner, *Le diable dans la littérature française de Cazotte à Baudelaire, 1772–1861*, in two volumes, Paris: Corti, 1960, pp. 169–82.

34. Cf. Brissenden, *Virtue in Distress*, p. 274.

35. According to R. F. Brissenden, 'La philosophie dans le boudoir; or a Young Lady's Entrance Into the World', in H. E. Pagliaro, ed., *Irrationalism in the Eighteenth Century, Eighteenth Century Culture*, vol. 3, Cleveland: The Press of the Western University, 1972.

36. Cf. G. Cerruti, 1972, 'Le paradoxe sur le comédien et le paradoxe sur le libertin, Diderot et Sade', *Revue des sciences humaines*, vol. 37, no. 146, (April–June 1972), pp. 236–51.

37. Quoted in J. Domenech, *L'Ethique des Lumières, les fondements de la morale dans la philosophie française du XVIIIe siècle*, Paris: Vrin, 1989, pp. 197–8.

38. Cf. the history of criticism of the search for fame since Antiquity by L. Braudy, *The Frenzy of Renown. Fame and its History*, Oxford: Oxford University Press, 1986.

39. Boltanski and L. Thévenot. pp. 126–36.

40. S. Ranulf.

41.   'Without question the silliest thing in the world, my dear Thérèse,' Clément said to me, 'is to wish to dispute a man's tastes, to wish to contradict, thwart, discredit, condemn, or punish them if they do not conform either with the laws of the country he inhabits or with the prejudices of social convention . . . I ask with what right one man will dare require another either to curb or get rid of his tastes or model them upon those of the social order? If then in this world there exist persons whose tastes conflict with accepted prejudices, not only must one not be surprised by the fact, not only must one not scold these dissenters or punish them, but one must aid them, procure them contentment, remove obstacles which impede them, and afford them, if you wish to be just, all the means to satisfy themselves without risk . . . Curiously enough, so long as it is merely a question of trifles, we are never in the least astonished by the differences existing among tastes; but let the subject take on an erotic tincture, and listen to the word spread about!
(Marquis de Sade, *Justine, Philosophy in the Bedroom and Other Writings*, ed. by Richard Seaver and Austryn Wainhouse, with essays by Jean Paulhan and Maurice Blanchot, London: Arrow Books, 1991, pp. 598–602)

42. P. Favre, *Sade utopiste. Sexualité, pouvoir et Etat dans le roman 'Aline et Valcour'*, Paris: PUF, 1967.

43.   I beg you, let us establish from the start as the solid bases of any such system', said Verneuil, 'that in the intentions of nature there is necessarily one class of individuals essentially subordinate to the other by weakness and by birth: given this, if the subject sacrificed by the individual who gives himself up to his passions belongs to this weak and deficient class, then the sacrificer has no more done anything evil than the owner of a farm who kills his pig.

(D. A. F. de Sade, *Système de l'agression*, selected philosophical texts ed. N. Châtelet, Paris: Aubier Montaigne, 1972, p. 119)

44.   How can you want that someone who has received the most extreme inclination for crime from nature, either because of the superiority of his strength, of the refinement of his organs, or due to an education required by his birth or wealth, how I say can you want this individual to be judged by the same law as that of someone which everything directs towards virtue or moderation? Would a law which punishes these two men the same by more just? Is it natural that one which everthing induces to do evil be treated as one which everthing leads to conduct himself prudently?

(Ibid., pp. 120–1)

45. Cf. F. Manuel and F. Manuel, *Utopian Thought in the Western World*, Cambridge, MA: Harvard University Press, 1979, p. 545.

46. Quoted in Favre, p. 86.

47. Marquis de Sade, 'Yet another effort, Frenchmen, if you would become Republicans', in *Philosophy in the Bedroom*, in Marquis de Sade, *Justine, etc.*, pp. 296–339.

48. Manuel and Manuel, *Utopian Thought*, pp. 543–8. The same argument is employed by Roland Barthes, not to bring Sade back within the framework of egalitarianism, but to give the properties of a formal grammar to his constructions: In accordance with 'Sadian grammar',

> In the scene, all functions can be interchanged, everyone can and must be in turn agent and patient, whipper and whipped, coprophagist and coprophagee, etc. This is a cardinal rule, first because it assimilates Sadian eroticism into a truly formal language, where there are only classes of actions, not groups of individuals, which enormously simplifies its grammar: the subject of the action (in the grammatical sense) can just as readily be a libertine, an assistant, a victim, a wife; second, because it keeps us from basing the grouping of Sadian society on the particularity of sexual practices.

Barthes recognises, however, that aside from torture, there is no trait reserved for the libertines alone. But how can 'Sadian scenes' be described by means of this grammar if one excludes tortures from them? See Roland Barthes, *Sade, Fourier, Loyola*, transl. Richard Miller, London: Jonathan Cape, 1977, pp. 30–1.

49. Marquis de Sade, 'Yet another effort, Frenchmen', p. 321.

50. On the impossibility of a eugenic political system, cf., L. Thévenot, 'La politique des statistiques. L'origine social des enquêtes de mobilité sociale', *Annales ESC*, no. (6 November 1990), pp. 1275–300.

7 The aesthetic topic

1. References are made in the text to the following works of Baudelaire: *The Painter of Modern Life and Other Essays*, transl. and ed. Jonathan Mayne, London: Phaidon Press, 1995; *Paris Spleen*, transl. Louise Varèse, New York: New Direction, 1990; and to *Œuvres complètes*, 2 volumes, Paris: Gallimard, Bibliotheque de la Plèiade, 1975 (References to the *Œuvres complètes* are given in the text by volume and page numbers, e.g., I, p. 233).
2. C. Grana, *Bohemian versus Bourgeois. French Society and the French Man of Letters in the Nineteenth Century*, New York: Basis Books, 1964, pp. 139–55.
3. Pierre Bourdieu, *The Rules of Art*, transl. Susan Emanuel, Cambridge: Polity Press, 1996.
4. Arendt, p. 114.
5. On the comparison between Baudelaire and Hugo, cf., Walter Benjamin, *Charles Baudelaire: A Lyric Poet in the Era of High Capitalism*, transl. Harry Zohn: London, NLB, 1973.
6. Meyer Schapiro links this attitude to the experience of the Republic and to the frequent disillusion of writers and artists of the generation of 1848 which distanced them from politics. But it is only in Baudelaire that the renunciation of politics is integrated within the formation of a new aesthetic position based on 'disgust for society, from the bourgeoisie to the people'. M. Schapiro, 'Courbet et l'imagerie populaire', in *Style, artiste et société*, Paris: 1982, Gallimard, pp. 275–328.
7. P. Pachet, *Le premier venu. Essai sur la politique baudelairienne*, Paris: Denoël, 1976, pp. 136–7.
8. Cf., F Coblence, *Le dandysme, obligation d'incertitude*, Paris: PUF, 1988.
9. Coblence, pp. 125–7.
10. On the theme of reflexivity in Baudelaire, see Jean-Paul Sartre, *Baudelaire*, Paris: Gallimard, 1947, pp. 23–4.
11. In recent years the theme of the brothel in French literature and painting of the second half of the nineteenth century has been the subject of several studies published in the United States, partly under the influence of feminist literary criticism. See, for example, C. Bernheimer, *Figures of Ill Repute. Representing Prostitution in Nineteenth-Century France*, Cambridge MA: Harvard University Press, 1989.
12. On the many metaphorical uses of syphilis in French literature of the second half of the nineteenth century, cf., P. Lasowski, *Syphilis. Essai sur la littérature française du XIXe siècle*, Paris: Gallimard, 1982.
13. Cf. J. Seigel, *Bohemian Paris. Culture, Politics and the Boundaries of Bourgeois Life, 1830–1930*, New York: Penguin Books, 1986, pp. 100–1.

14. L. Ferry, *Homo Aestheticus. L'invention du goût à l'âge démocratique*, Paris: Grasset, 1990.

15. We can, like J.-M. Schaeffer, connect this opposition to a distinction between pleasures provoked 'by a representational activity exercised on an object' and pleasure (like sexual or culinary pleasures) in which 'representational activity is only ever anticipation of a transition to (bodily) action'. 'In aesthetic pleasure, it is representational activity as such (as an autonomous activity) which is the source of pleasure, so that we are led to maintain ourselves in that state rather than to transcend it towards a different action.' But, Schaeffer adds, in order to oppose the essentialisation of this distinction: 'A bodily activity can in turn become a self-sufficient representational activity exercised on itself. Thus the fact of eating or erotic activity can become the source of a second, aesthetic pleasure if they induce a pleasing representational activity exercised on the occasion of a bodily action (and no longer leading to that action).' J.-M. Schaeffer, *L'art de l'âge moderne. L'esthétique et la philosophie de l'art du XVIIIe siècle à nos jours*, Paris: Gallimard, 1992, p. 379.

16. S. Guerlac, *The Impersonal Sublime. Hugo, Baudelaire, Lautréamont*, Stanford: Stanford University Press, 1990, p. 9.

17. Cf. S. Monk, *The Sublime: A Study of Critical Theories in Eighteenth Century England*, New York, Modern Language Association of America, 1935.

18. Edmund Burke, *A Philosophical Enquiry into the Origin of our Ideas of the Sublime and Beautiful*, ed. James T. Boutton, Oxford: Basil Blackwell, 1987, pp. 39–40.

19. K. Lokke, 'The Role of Sublimity in the Development of Modern Aesthetics', *Journal of Aesthetics and Criticism*, vol. 40, no. 4 (1982), pp. 421–30.

20. Burke, *Philosophical Enquiry*, pp. 38–41.

21. Cf. C. Hussey, *The Picturesque. Studies in a Point of View*, London: Frank Cass & Co., 1983, p. 61. Published in 1927, the seminal work of Hussey constitutes an excellent introduction to the history of the category of the 'picturesque'.

22. Joshua Reynolds, *Discourses on Art*, ed. Robert R. Wark, New Haven and London: Yale University Press, 1975, p. 99.

23. Hussey, *The Picturesque*, p. 64.

24. Ibid., pp. 65–75.

25. Cf. I. Ousby, *The Englishman's England. Taste, Travel and the Rise of Tourism*, Cambridge: Cambridge University Press, 1990.

26. On the aesthetics of the ugly and the grotesque in Goya, cf. M. Gagnebin, *Fascination de la laideur*, Lausanne: L'Age d'homme, 1978.

27. Cf. Derathé, ibid.

28. Cf. Dalston, ibid.

29. On the many debates on the identification of subjects of taste, cf., in particular, D. Cottom, 'Taste and the Civilized Imagination', *Journal of Aesthetics and Criticism*, vol. 39, (Summer 1981), pp. 367–80.

30. Romantic aesthetics takes sides against Kantian aesthetics in order to construct

'a *doctrine* of art, that is to say a definition of its essence based upon an evaluation'; this results in a 'sacralisation of the arts' and 'the construction of a speculative doctrine supposed to legitimise this sacralisation'. Cf. J.-M. Schaeffer, op. cit., pp. 80–4. On the diffusion amongst painters of a conception of their activity centred on the idea of originality, see the works of Nathalie Heinich and, in particular, 'De l'apparition de l'artiste à l'apparition des Beaux-Arts', *Revue d'histoire moderne et contemporaine*, vol. 37 (January 1990).

31. G. Lebrun, *Kant et la fin de la métaphysique*, Paris: Armand Colin, 1970, pp. 355–87.

32. Schaeffer, ibid., p. 32.

33. Cf. G. Shapiro, 'From the Sublime to the Political: Some Historical Notes', *New Literary History*, vol. 16, no. 2 (1985), pp. 213–35.

34. Cf. J. Seigel, ibid., p. 99.

35. Cf. Cottom, 'Taste and the Civilised Imagination'.

36. M. Walzer, 'La justice dans les institutions', *Esprit*, March 1992, pp. 106–22.

37. Bruno Latour, *Nous n'avons jamais été modernes*, Paris: La Découverte, 1991.

38. Reinhart Koselleck, *Critique and Crisis: Enlightenment and the Pathogenesis of Modern Society*, Oxford: Berg, 1988.

39. G. Froidevaux, *Représentation et modernité*, Paris: Corti, 1989, p. 121.

40. F. Leakey, *Baudelaire and Nature*, Manchester: Manchester University Press, 1969, p. 139.

41. F. Leakey, *Baudelaire. Collected Essays, 1953–1988*, ed. E. Jacobs, Cambridge: Cambridge University Press, 1989, pp. 161–73.

42. Froidevaux, *Représentation*, p. 122.

43. Benjamin, ibid., pp. 35–67.

44. Cf, J. Seigel, 'La mort du sujet: origines d'un thème', *Le Débat*, no. 58 (1990), pp. 160–9.

45. J.-P. Sartre, ibid., pp. 141–2 and 74.

46. Cf. A. Toumayan, *La littérature et le mal. Lectures de Barbey d'Aurevilly, Huysmans et Baudelaire*, Lexington, Kentucky: French Forum Publishers, 1987.

47. Benjamin, ibid., pp. 19 and 34.

48. Cf. P. Emmanuel, *Baudelaire*, Paris: Desclée de Brouwer, 1967.

8 Heroes and the accursed

1. Nietzsche read Baudelaire late. He became aware of him on the occasion of two stays in Paris and through reading Paul Bourget, first in 1883–1884 and then in 1888. If, on the first reading, he interpreted Baudelaire in the spirit of Bourget as a 'master of decadence', that is to say as a shameful Christian obsessed by original sin, in his second reading (which was based upon Baudelaire's posthumous works published in 1887) he saw 'the superman loom up in Baudelaire' in the early form of the dandy with his 'modern heroism', 'his hatred for democracy' and his 'social sadism'. He then discovers in Baudelaire an 'alter ego', a

'double of his own personality', a brother. Cf. G. LeRider, 'Nietzsche et Baudelaire', *Littérature*, no. 86, (1982), pp. 85–101.

2. F. Nietzsche, *Daybreak, Thoughts on the Prejudices of Morality*, transl. R. J. Hollingdale, with an introduction by Michael Tanner, Cambridge: Cambridge University Press, 1982.

3. F. Nietzsche, *La volonté de puissance* (1901), 2 vols., transl. G. Bianquis, Paris: Gallimard, 1948, p. 121, fragment of 1881–1882. [This fragment is not included in the English translation of *The Will to Power* – *translator*].

4. Gilles Deleuze, *Nietzsche and Philosophy*, transl. Hugh Tomlinson, London: The Athlone Press, 1983, pp. 78–9.

5. That at bottom we are thinking very strongly of ourselves can be divined from the decision we arrive at in every case in which we *can* avoid the sight of the person suffering, perishing or complaining: we decide *not* to do so if we can present ourselves as the more powerful and as a helper, if we are certain of applause, if we want to feel how fortunate we are in contrast, or hope that the sight will relieve our boredom.'

(Nietzsche, *Daybreak*, p. 84)

6. In itself [pity] has as little a good character as any other drives: only where it is demanded and commended – and this happens where one fails to grasp that it is harmful but discovers a *source of pleasure* in it – does a good conscience adhere to it, only then does one gladly succumb to it and not hesitate to demonstrate it. He who for a period of time made the experiment of intentionally pursuing occasions for pity in his everyday life and set before his soul all the misery available to him in his surroundings would inevitably grow sick and melancholic.

(Nietzsche, *Daybreak*, pp. 85–6)

7. F. Nietzsche, *On the Genealogy of Morality*, transl. Carol Diethe, ed. Keith Ansell-Pearson, Cambridge: Cambridge University Press, 1994.

8. G. Deleuze, *Nietzsche and Philosophy*, pp. 22–3.

9. Ibid., pp. 114 and 116.

10. Nietzsche, *On the Genealogy of Morality*, p. 21.

11. F. Nietzsche, *The Anti-Christ in Twilight of the Idols and The Anti-Christ*, transl. R. J. Hollingdale, with an introduction by Michael Tanner, London: Penguin, 1991, pp. 154 and 145.

12. Deleuze, *Nietzsche and Philosophy*, p. 132.

13. F. Nietzsche, *The Will to Power*, transl. Walter Kaufmann and R. J. Hollingdale, ed. Walter Kaufmann, New York: Vintage Books, 1968, p. 59. [The translation has been very slightly modified to bring the English more in line with the French translation of Nietzsche used by the author – *translator*].

14. Ibid., p. 407.

15. Deleuze, *Nietzsche and Philosophy*, p. 26.

16. Nietzsche, *On the Genealogy of Morality*, pp. 161–2.

17. Nietzsche, *The Will to Power*, pp. 467–8.

18. Nietzsche, *On the Genealogy of Morality*, p. 157.
19. G. Deleuze, *Nietzsche and Philosophy*, p.58.
20. Ibid., p. 59.
21. Ibid., p. 7.
22. Nietzsche, *La volonté de puissance*, p. 121.

23.   Nietzsche devotes a whole book to the analysis of the figures of reactive triumph in the human world – *ressentiment*, bad conscience and the ascetic ideal. In each case he shows that reactive forces do not triumph by forming a superior force but by 'separating' active force (cf. the three essays of *On the Genealogy of Morality*). In each case this separation rests on a fiction, on a mystification or a falsification.

                        (Deleuze, *Nietzsche and Philosophy*, p. 57)

24. Nietzsche, *Daybreak*, p. 85.
25. Nietzsche, *On the Genealogy of Morality*, p. 25.
26. There is an excellent anthology in the article by André Comte-Sponville in *Pourquoi nous ne sommes pas nietzschéens*, Paris: Grasset, pp. 37–98.
27. Deleuze, *Nietzsche and Philosophy*, p. 18.
28. Ibid., p. 13.
29. Ibid., p. 21.
30. Ibid., pp. 22–5.
31. Ibid., p. 17.
32. Ibid., p. 16.
33. Ibid., p. 17.
34. [Ibid., p. 17. Boltanski misquotes Deleuze who is quoting Nietzsche. Where Boltanski has '*spectateur artiste*' Deleuze, quoting the French translation of Nietzsche, has '*auditeur artiste*' which is translated correctly by Tomlinson as 'artistic listener' – *translator*] The Deleuzian hero is distinguished from a different figure which is of interest to us because it leaves open the possibility of an alliance with the topic of sentiment. Outlined between the two world wars by Karl Jaspers (in *Nietzsche*, Paris: Gallimard, 1980, with a letter-preface by Jean Wahl) and Max Scheler (in *L'homme du ressentiment*, Paris: Idées/Gallimard, 1970), then taken up by Gabriel Marcel and Christian existentialists of the 1950s who linked it with Kierkegaard, this version of Nietzscheanism presents a solitary hero opposed to the sheep-like crowd, a person who faces up to the *anguish* of the human condition. This hero is a higher man because he has the courage to take on the 'being-self of the individual' (Jaspers, *Nietzsche*, p. 287). To be sure, he is not sentimental, but he encounters the topic of sentiment from the angle of *interiority*. He calls upon the most inward force and the autonomy of essence. Interiority is synonymous here with autonomy and so with freedom, in the sense of the German tradition born from the pietism whose history is studied by Leonard Krieger in his *The German Idea of Freedom*, Chicago: University of Chicago Press, 1957.
35. Ibid., p. 17.

36. Ibid., p. 23.
37. J.-M. Schaeffer, *op. cit.*, p. 294.
38. Published in *Pourquoi nous ne sommes pas nietzschéens*.
39. Cf. E. Weber, *L'action française*, Paris, Fayard, 1985, p. 93.

40.   I owe my liberation to Nietzsche. At a time when we were floundering in the democratic and humanitarian quagmire, where we had submerged our good masters of the little science . . . in this period we received a whiplash from Nietzsche which brought us round to consider the true realities sincerely. With a certain brutality, Nietzsche interrupted our bleatings, stripped us of our miserable humanitarian cast-offs, and forced us to examine ourselves pitilessly: it was through him that we saw for the first time what this love of humanity is that we had been taught : in reality, a false love – a ruse invented by the powerless to *disarm* rivals, to remove all desire of elevation, and weaken the competition.
       (G. Valois, *L'homme qui vient. Philosophie de l'autorité*, 3rd edn Paris: Nouvelle Librairie nationale, 1923, p. 33. Quoted in P. A. Taguieff,
                                                                                      p. 279)

41. A contemporary version of the kind of reading of Nietzsche which was current in Action française can be found in a little work by Alain de Benoist published by GRECE in 1973. Alain de Benoist uses Nietzsche in a political synthesis directed against 'the Christian, bourgeois, liberal and socialist idea', and towards a 'consequent anti-egalitarianism' including many references to the authors of the Conservative Revolution or of Italian fascism (particularly Julius Evola).
42. Georges Bataille, *Eroticism*, transl. Mary Dalwood, London: Marion Boyars, 1987, p. 165.
43. Cf. Jean-Paul Sartre's criticism of the interpretation of Nietzsche by Bataille, characterised here as a 'shameful Christian'. J.-P. Sartre, 'Un nouveau mystique', *Situations I*, Paris: Gallimard, 1947, p. 166.
44. E. Chanover, *De Sade: A Bibliography*, Metuchen, NJ: The Scarecrow Press, 1973.
45. Cf., the issue of the review *Obliques* devoted to Sade, nos. 12–13 (1977).
46. Citing only the famous texts which seek to bring out not only the literary but even more the philosophical value of Sade, the following works appeared successively between the years 1946 and 1951. From Maurice Blanchot, 'Quelques remarques sur Sade', *Critique*, nos. 3–4, pp. 230–49 appeared in 1946, in 1947, 'A la rencontre de Sade', *Les Temps Modernes*, and in 1949, *Lautréamont et Sade*, Paris: Editions de Minuit (the essay 'Sade' translated and published in Marquis de Sade, *Justine, Philosophy in the Bedroom, and Other Writings*, is taken from this collection); from Georges Bataille there was 'Le secret de Sade', *Critique*, nos. 15–16 in 1947, which is reprinted in 1957 in *La littérature et le mal*, Paris, Gallimard (1973, *Literature and Evil*, transl. Alastair Hamilton, London: Calder and Boyars), the same year as *L'érotisme*, Paris: Editions de

Minuit was published (*Eroticism*), and which has several chapters on Sade; from Pierre Klossowski there was *Sade mon prochain*, Paris: Editions du Seuil in 1947 (the English translation of which, 1991, *Sade My Neighbour*, translated by Alphonso Lingis, Evanston, Illinois, Northwestern University Press, differs in important respects from the French edition cited by the author); in 1947 Maurice Nadeau also published selections from Sade's writing preceded by an Introduction; in 1951 Simone de Beauvoir published 'Faut-il brûler Sade?' *Les Temps Moderne*, and Albert Camus devoted a chapter to Sade in his *L'homme révolté* with Gallimard, then under the literary direction of Jean Paulham who will himself publish many studies of Sade. The literature on Sade continued to be enriched, especially at the end of the 1960s. Besides other works by the authors already cited, particularly noteworthy are Gilles Deleuze's book on Sacher-Masoch which appeared in 1967 (1971, *Sacher-Masoch: An Interpretation*, transl. Jean McNeil, London: Faber & Faber) and which frequently refers to Sade and, in 1971 (1977 in English) Roland Barthes, *Sade, Fourier, Loyola* (transl. Richard Miller, London: Jonathan Cape).

47. J.-P. Sartre, 'Un nouveau mystique', *Situations I*, pp. 133–74.

48. 'Sade, Lautréamont, Hegel, Baudelaire, Rimbaud, Nietzsche are the names of some of those existences which authenticate themselves inasmuch as they converge on the formation of that order whose mission is to make the sacred world of the totality of being surge up within the profane world of functional servility'. (Pierre Klossowski, *Sade mon prochain*, Paris: Seuil, 1947, p. 168).

49. This study was first published in September 1947 in Critique. It was republished in a modified form in 1957 in *La littérature et la mal*, Paris: Gallimard (1973, *Literature and Evil*, transl. Alastair Hamilton, London: Calder and Boyers).

50. Georges Bataille, *Eroticism*, transl. Mary Dalwood, London: Marion Boyars.

51. Klossowski, *Sade mon prochain*, (a second, considerably modified edition, appeared from the same publisher in 1967).

52. Maurice Blanchot, *Lautréamont et Sade*, Paris: Minuit, 1963. See also the essay taken from this collection, 'Sade', published in Marquis de Sade, *Justine, Philosophy in the Bedroom*.

53. References with page number marked *L* in the text refer to *Literature and Evil*, those with *E* to *Eroticism*.

54. Cf., the pages in Sartre's 'Un nouveau mystique' on the definition of writing, shared by Bataille with the surrealists, as 'commitment' and 'risk' and on the techniques intended to give writing 'all the gravity of a genuine action' (pp. 133–6).

55.   The individual of today possesses a certain amount of strength; most of the time he wastes his strength by using it for the benefit of such simulacra as other people, God or ideals. He does wrong to disperse his energy in this way for he exhausts his potentialities by wasting them, but he does worse in basing his behaviour on weakness, for if he puts himself out for the sake of other people the fact is that he feels he needs to lean on them. This weakness is fatal. He grows feeble by spending his strength in vain

and he spends his strength because he thinks he is feeble. But the true
man knows himself to be alone and accepts the fact; he denies every
element in his own nature, inherited from seventeen centuries of cowardice, that is concerned with others than himself; pity, gratitude and love,
for example, are emotions that he will destroy; through their destruction
he regains all the strength he would have had to bestow on these debili-
tating impulses, and more important he acquires from this labour of
destruction the beginnings of true energy.

> (Blanchot, *Lautréamont et Sade*, quoted by Bataille, *E*, p. 172)

56. Cf. the article by J. Seigel referred to above.
57. Blanchot, 'Sade', p. 50.
58. Ibid., p. 49. The theme is taken up again by Deleuze in 1967 in his *Sacher-
    Masoch: An Interpretation* with regard to the relationship between Sade and
    Masoch which challenges the idea of the unity of sado-masochism. For if the
    pain the libertine suffers is 'an ultimate pleasure' this is 'not because it satisfies
    a need to expiate or a feeling of guilt, but because it confirms him in his inali-
    enable power and gives him a supreme certitude. Through insults and humilia-
    tion, in the throes of pain, the libertine is not expiating, but in Sade's words,
    "he rejoices in his inner heart that he has gone far enough to deserve such treat-
    ment"' (Gilles Deleuze, *Sacher-Masoch: An Interpretation*, transl. Jean
    McNeil, London: Faber & Faber, 1971, p. 35.
59. Blanchot, 'Sade', p. 56 [translation modified].
60. Ibid., p. 42.
61. Ibid., pp. 43 and 43–4.
62. In 1947, in *Sade mon prochain*, Pierre Klossowski draws up an initial balance
    sheet of the work undertaken over the previous ten years by Georges Bataille
    and the group around him: 'Arising from the very heart of Nietzsche's experi-
    ence, this cry (the death of God) found a singular resonance in the hearts of a
    group of young people of the Parisian inter-war years. Ever since the great
    Revolution, there has existed a Parisian messianism which has especially mili-
    tated on the spiritual plane for a *future religion of humanity*' (Klossowski, *Sade
    mon prochain*, p. 157). These young people, Klossowski says, came from surreal-
    ism but rejected it. None-the-less, it is to the surrealist revolution that he attrib-
    utes, without question correctly, the principal coupling of the tradition of the
    sublime and the form taken by the topic of denunciation in Marxism. He is
    concerned however to maintain a clear boundary between Marxism or
    Freudianism – which are on the side of production and reason and so of order
    – and the aesthetic position, on the side of origins, chaos and myth: surrealism

    > principally consisted in a kind of apocalyptic bringing to heel in view of
    > the *imminent world revolution* . . . In the eyes of Marxist rationalism, our
    > present world appears absurd; now, along with Marx, surrealism empha-
    > sised this absurdity and, referring to Freud, exalted it, not with the aim
    > of moral and economic improvement which is in fact the aim of Marx

and Freud, but through love of the mythical conceived of not as a world opposed to reality, but quite to the contrary as expressing the very heart of reality. (Ibid., pp. 159–60)

63. We find indications of this in a recent work of Sabine Chalvon-Demarsay and Dominique Pasquier on the analysis of 1,200 synopses of television dramas, each of twenty pages. These synopses were received in the Autumn of 1991 by Antenne 2 and FR 3 as the result of a competition for award of production of ten first works. Written by young (6 out of 10 were less than 35-years-old), mainly Parisian authors engaged for the most part in professions on the fringes of the audio-visual world (photographers, graphic artists, comedians, television, advertising and cinema technicians, comic strip authors, etc.), the synopses are interesting in not seeking, as is often the case for first novels, recognition by an elite in the field of avant-garde literature, but aiming rather to seduce judges whose main concern is to capture and keep hold of the widest possible public. The first observation of the authors of the report: the scarcity of denunciations which could be linked to established political positions (political parties, unions, associations of social movements, etc.). This does not mean that the social world is seen to be just but, rather, as 'basically perverted', without this view involving an accusation or even an imputation of responsibility. In fact, the bastards are everywhere and each of us would act like a bastard if we found ourselves in the same circumstances. For we all pursue our own interest and everything is manipulation. Second observation: the liquidation of sentiment which does not appear in these synopses, either in the form of amorous passion, or in the form of familial tenderness, much less in the form of altruistic sentiments which only appear in order to be immediately revealed as hypocritical good sentiments intended to disguise power. In many of the cases analysed by the authors, the movement of the synopsis consists in starting from an example of a classical figure of popular literature, calling for tender-heartedness, so as to introduce a paradoxical outcome and make it absurd or horrible. In several of these scenarios, for example, a son goes in search of a father he never knew. But it is only to discover that he is an arms trafficker or even the boss of a prostitute ring: 'The rediscoveries are harrowing'. The candidate for the role of benefactor is, in fact, only a persecutor. Who are the positive characters? The artists. They do not have any power. They live in the urban jungle. Money comes to them by chance. Their vocation is constantly thwarted. They are alone. They are accursed.

9 What reality has misfortune?

1. The excellent issue of the review *Hermès*, published by Daniel Dayan, on the sociology of reception, gives an overview of the extremely lively debate which, particularly in Great Britain, sets a manipulative conception of the media as imposing ideological choices on a passive public against research which particularly emphasises the active character of reception and the critical and more

generally interpretive capabilities of the public (cf., *Hermès*, 'A la recherche du public', nos. 11–12 (993)). A review of mainly American literature on interpretative skills put to work by the television public, and on the 'construction' of different 'realities' by the publics of the same programme, can be found in W. Gamson, D. Croteau, W. Hoynes, and T. Sasson, 1992, 'Media Images and the Social Construction of Reality', *Annual Review of Sociology*, vol. 18 (1992), pp. 373–93.

2. The study by T. Liebes and E. Katz was carried out on six different communities (Americans, Japanese and, in Israel, members of a kibbutz, Jews recently emigrated from Russia, Moroccan Jews and Arabs). Ten or twelve groups were formed in each of the communities by asking one couple to invite two other couples of close friends to watch a single broadcast and to lead a discussion lasting one hour after the broadcast. The highest proportion of statements concerning the hidden intentions of producers, film-makers and scriptwriters were found in the American public and members of the kibbutz. More Maroccan Jews and Arabs made comments, especially moral comments, concerning daily life and did not separate the televisual spectacle from reality.

3. Cf. P. Livet, 'Medias et limitations de la communication', *Hermès*, no. 4 (1989), pp. 67–76. The limitations of communication, on which P. Livet has writtern various articles (cf., in particular, 'Les limitations de la communication', *Les études philosophiques*, nos. 2–3 (1987), pp. 255–75) are four in number: (1) 'we cannot know what meaning is given by the other person to the rule he follows' (Wittgenstein–Kripke); (2) 'the intention to communicate appears reflexive since we not only want to inform, but to inform that we want to inform of this intention to inform' (Grice–Recanati); 'none-the-less, it is impossible really to assure ourselves that the communication is "open", and that this reflexivity is not halted at some stage'; (3) the third limitation of communication concerns speech acts: 'to make a promise is not to guarantee to the other person that one really will fulfill the promised act because one has the intention to keep the promise'; (4) '[in individual communication] we issue demands for truth, authenticity and appropriateness'. 'But the simple expression of these demands is not enough to obtain their recognition by the other person.'

4. Media communication is not a 'normal' communication between individuals. It is not even, contrary to appearances, a 'radiating' communication, that is to say one in which an orator addresses himself to a group or crowd. Because in the task of interpreting what is communicated to him the listener-spectator, does not have available to him all the indicators which make for an effective presence. This is even more noticeable in the case of a 'face to face' discussion or a debate, because the spectator never sees all the actors present at the same time (if he sees the opponents he does not see the studio, etc.). Moreover, quite evidently, the speakers cannot modify their discourse in the light of the reactions of those they address since the majority of these are absent. They address themselves essentially therefore to the reactions they suppose listeners-spectators

have, and this obliges them to imagine what this or that type of public
expects of them'.   (Livet, 'Medias')

5. Cf. D. Good, 'Individuals, Interpersonal Relations and Trust', in D. Gambetta, ed., *Trust. Making and Breaking Cooperative Relations*, Oxford: Basil Blackwell, 1988, pp. 31–48.
6. B. Boruah, *Fiction and Freedom. A Study in Aesthetics and the Philosophy of Mind*, Oxford: The Clarendon Press, 1988.
7. To illustrate the notion of *eliciting situation* containing eliciting conditions for a particular emotion, we can take the example of the coordination of fictional emotions between readers and spectators whose indignation or tears are aroused by the same scenes (the jealousy scene in *Othello* for example) at different times and places. Cf. A. Ortony, G. Clore and A. Collins, *The Cognitive Structure of Emotions*, Cambridge: Cambridge University Press, 1988.
8. A commentary on Walton's theories which contrast sharply with Boruah's opinion can be found in T. Pavel, pp. 109–11.
9. There is, as we know, fierce competition between different subjects for the allocation of media space.
10. There are many examples in R. Moore, *La persécution. Sa formation en Europe, X^e – XIIIe siècle*, Paris: Les Belles Lettres, 1991.
11. M. Calvez, 'Les accusations de contagion comme argument d'exclusion. L'exemple des caqueux en Bretagne', *Ethnologie française*, vol. 22, no. 1 (1992), pp. 55–9.
12. Analysis of a corpus of 275 letters received in 1979, 1980 and 1981 by the newspaper *Le Monde* from individuals or representatives of associations and containing the denunciation of an injustice showed that prior to any examination of whether or not the complaint was well-founded, the denunciation was subject to a judgement which sought to sift out protests coming from deranged individuals, 'paranoiacs' with a 'persecution mania', etc., from normal claims. The same study also showed that denunciations of injustice had greater chance of being considered if they came from a collectivity – an association, political movement or trade union – than if they came from a solitary individual and a fortiori from the victim himself. These results once again emphasised the very close links formed in the course of the political struggles of the nineteenth and early twentieth centuries between the topic of denunciation and social movements, especially the workers' movement. The progressive weakening of trade unionism since the 1980s seems to have deprived denunciation of much of the means it had been given by two centuries of pamphlets, scandals, conflicts and theoretical writings. Cf. L. Boltanski, 'La dénonciation publique', in *L'amour et la justice comme compétences*, pp. 255–366. Furthermore, it would be interesting to connect the development of modern forms of denunciation, which must concentrate on setting out proofs, and the establishment at the end of the last century of a symptomatology of paranoia centred on 'interpretation mania' which brings the suspicion of abnormality on those who seek to 'disentangle the truth and secret relations of things', as P. Serieux and J. Capgras,

the two psychiatric doctors among the first to describe this new nosological entity, write. P. Serieux and J. Capgras, 'Délire d'interprétation, délire de revandication', in *Classiques de la paranoïa*, Paris: Analytics, Navrin/Seuil, 1982, p. 105.

13. This criticism has been pursued more vigorously and supported more proofs the more its effects have extended into ordinary language with, in particular, the contemporary ban on the word *charity*, now cut off from its theological meanings so that it only ever refers to the hypocritical sentimentality of a rapacious bourgeoisie.

14. A summary of the interpretation of humanitarianism in terms of social control can be found in T. Haskell, 'Capitalism and the Origins of the Humanitarian Sensibility', *The American Historical Review*, vol. 90, no. 2 (April 1985), part I, pp. 339–61.

15. Giovanna Procacci, *Gouverner la misère. La question sociale en France, 1789–1848*, Paris: Seuil, 1993, p. 175.

16. A good example of this can be found in F. Lurçat, 'Médias, langage, ontologie', *Les Temps modernes*, vol. 45, no. 527 (1990), pp. 91–103.

17. Maurice Merleau-Ponty, *Humanisme et Terreur*, 1947; Paris: Gallimard, 1980. Quoted here in the *édition de poche* of 1980 which contains an important Introduction by C. Lefort.

18. Maurice Merleau-Ponty, *Les aventures de la dialectique*, Paris: Gallimard, 1955.

19. There is no question of going into details here, which would require a book to itself.

20. Jean-Paul Sartre, 'Merleau-Ponty', *Situations, IV*, Paris: Gallimard, 1964, pp. 189–290.

21. Raymond Aron, *L'opium des intellectuels*, Paris: Calman Lévy, 1955, pp. 189–290.

22. See, for example, A. Cohen-Solal, *Sartre*, Paris: Gallimard, 1985, pp. 428–67.

23. Aron, *L'opium*, pp. 54–8.

24.   They arise from similar values. Both of them are humanitarians, they want to reduce suffering and liberate the oppressed; they struggle against colonialism, fascism and capitalism. Whether it is a question of Spain, Algeria or Vietnam, Camus has committed no crime of lèse-progressivism. When Spain was admitted to UNESCO he wrote an admirable letter of protest. The entry of the Soviet Union or of sovietized Czechoslovakia found him silent. In essentials, he himself also belongs to the correct-thinking left.   (Aron, *L'opium*, p. 63)

25. C. Lefort, Introduction to *Humanisme et Terreur*, p. 12.

26. 'Like everyone else we know that our fate depends upon world politics. We are neither above it nor on the sidelines. But we are in France and we cannot confuse our future with that of the USSR or with that of the American empire.' Maurice Merleau-Ponty, *Humanisme et Terreur*, *op. cit.*, p. 58.

27. Lefort, Introduction to *Humanisme et Terreur*, pp. 16 and 35.

28.   We find ourselves in an inextricable situation therefore. The Marxist critique of capitalism remains valid and it is clear that anti-sovietism today brings together the brutality, pride, vertigo and anxiety which were already expressed in fascism. On the other hand, the revolution has been immobilised on a position closed in upon itself: it maintains and aggravates the dictatorial apparatus while giving up on the revolutionary freedom of the proletariat within its Soviets and within its Party and on the human appropriation of the State. We cannot be anticommunist, we cannot be communist.   (Merleau-Ponty, *Humanisme et Terreur*, p. 49)

29.   Any criticism of communism or of the USSR which makes use of isolated facts without putting them in their context and in relation to the problems of the USSR, every apology for the democratic regimes which passes over their violent intervention in the rest of the world in silence, or fiddling the books debits it to a special account, any politics which does not seek to 'understand' the rival societies in their totality can only serve to mask the problems of capitalism, aims in reality at the very existence of the USSR and should be regarded as an act of war.
                      (Merleau-Ponty, *Humanisme et Terreur*, p. 299)

30. Lefort, Introduction to *Humanisme et Terreur*, p. 14.

31.   Marxism was first of all that idea that there are two poles in history, on one side boldness, the primacy of the future, the will to create humanity, and on the other prudence, the predominance of the past, the spirit of conservation and respect for the 'eternal laws' of society, and that these two tendencies almost infallibly discern and grab hold of whatever can be of use to them. This is confirmed every day on the local scale. But Marxism is also the idea that these two attitudes are borne by two classes in history. Now if the spirit of capitalist circles in the old countries is indeed roughly what it must be according to the Marxist schema, it happens that American capitalism benefits from natural resources and an historical situation which enables it to represent boldness and the spirit of enterprise, at least for a time, and that inasmuch as the world proletariat is enframed by communist parties its orientation is one of tactical wisdom, and to the extent that it eludes its grasp is too exhausted or divided by the diversion of world wars to exercise its function of radical critique.   (Merleau-Ponty, *Humanisme et Terreur*, pp. 298–9)

32. Merleau-Ponty, *Humanisme et Terreur*, pp. 68–75.
33. Merleau-Ponty, 'L'URSS et les camps', republished in, *Signes*, Paris: Gallimard, 1960, pp. 330–43,

34.   We mean that to the extent that we are geographically and politically distant from the USSR, we find communists who are always men more like ourselves and a healthy communist movement . . . when one of us

speaks to a Martiniquese communist about Martinique affairs, he always finds himself in agreement with him.

('L'URSS et les camps', pp. 337–8)

35.   A reader of *Le Monde* recently wrote to the paper that all the declarations about the Soviet labour camps could well be true but that after all he was a worker without resources and without home and that he always found more support from the communists than from the others.

(Ibid., p. 338)

36. J.-P. Sartre, 'Merleau-Ponty', *Situations*, *IV*, Paris: Gallimard, 1964, pp. 189–290.

37. Ibid., p. 237.

38.   In the beginning he wanted to keep together what he thought was of value in the two systems; to the better of the two he wanted to make a present of what the other had acquired. Deceived, he then resolved to denounce exploitation everywhere. After a new deception he decided, in the calm, not to denounce anything anywhere until a bomb, from the East or from the West, put an end to our short histories.

(J.-P. Sartre, 'Merleau-Ponty', pp. 237–38)

39. Ibid., p. 238.

40. The result of this conversion is found in 'Les communistes et la paix', published in *Les Temps modernes* in three instalments from 1952 to 1954. J.-P. Sartre, 'Les communistes et la paix', *Situations*, *VI*, Paris: Gallimard, 1964, pp. 80–384. Merleau-Ponty responds in 1955 in *Les aventures de la dialectique*, Paris: Gallimard, chapter 5, 'Sartre et l'ultra-bolchèvisme', pp. 131–272.

41. J.-P. Sartre, *L'affaire Henri Martin*, Paris: Gallimard, 1953.

42. When the book appeared Henri Martin had been released for good conduct. The publication, prepared when he was still in prison, was justified by the fact that the government had accepted neither a trial review nor pardon on the grounds of 'not giving in to communist blackmail'. The book therefore sought to clear Henri Martin (see pp. 7–8 and 205–6).

43.   Actually, nothing less than a miracle was needed to transform our 'police operation' into a crusade, and our very Christian ministers prayed for it every day. It took place in Korea: as soon as the Americans were prepared to massacre Asians on their own account, their press substituted praises for insults and our war magically ceased being a colonial one: France took its place as advance war party in the fore-crusade of freedom; gold, arms and a good conscience will be given to her; a common aggressor draws nearer: the aggressor, of course, was the USSR; to account for this we need only some simple assimilations: who is Hô Chi Minh? an auxiliary of China. And China? A henchman of the USSR. Therefore Hô Chi Minh is a Soviet agent. It is not the Indochinese who have rebelled against French domination: it is the Soviets who have attacked Western

democracy through native intermediaries: the outcome of the Third
World War is decided in the paddyfields of Tonkin.

(J.-P. Sartre, *L'affaire Henri Martin*, p. 193)

44. Sartre will later adopt an explanation of the Korean war which gives the role of
persecutor to Imperialism: 'Yes, I no longer doubt it: in this wretched affair,
those fomenting war are the feudal landowners of the South and the imperial-
ists of the USA.' Sartre, 'M. Merleau-Ponty', p. 239.

45. A. Glucksmann, *La cuisinière et le mangeur d'hommes. Essai sur l'ètat, le marxisme, les camps de concentration*, Paris: Seui, 1975.

46.   When we speak as scholars about the Soviet Union – that State which
probably owes the crown of having already massacred a number of
internees many times that of the dead in the Nazi camps not to any
genius but more innocently to the time at its disposal and the space it
covers – when we call its space *socialist* and its history *revolutionary*, what
is it that makes us deaf to the open laughter of future generations considering our theoretical debates? What is it that has made us so blind to
the tears and blood with which our present runs?

(Glucksmann, *La cuisinière et le mangeur d'hommes*, p. 33)

Let us note however that the identification of the Nazi and Soviet camps comes
up against objections which are not overcome solely by reference to the
numbers of victims, but which take into consideration the existence of a will to
a massive and systematic extermination in the case of the Nazi camps. See, in
particular, Primo Levi, 'Afterword' to *If This is a Man*, transl. Stuart Woolf,
London: Abacus, 1987, pp. 391–2.

47. A. Glucksmann, *Stratégie de la révolution*, Paris: Christian Bourgois, 1968.

48. On the conception of the proletariat as 'pure action', see J.-P. Sartre, 'Les communistes et la paix', *Situations*, *VI*, pp. 80–384, and Merleau-Ponty's criticism
of this conception in *Les aventures de la dialectique*. In the chapter entitled
'Sartre et l'ultra bolchèvisme', Merleau-Ponty shows how the conception of the
Party and the militant as 'pure actions' leads to the suffering on which revolt is
based being left out of account: 'The militant is not a worker who militates, a
certain past of suffering which becomes political action. Suffering belongs to
the producer, to the "concrete man"' (quoting Sartre) 'and the active proletar-
ian appears beyond the concrete man. His suffering would reduce him to acceptance if a pure refusal did not make him militant'; 'the Party, like the militant
is pure action. If everything comes from freedom, if the workers are nothing,
not even proletarians, before they have created the Party, they do not rest on
anything given and not even on their common history.' (Merleau-Ponty, *Les
aventures de la dialectique*, pp. 144 and 147)

49. Cf. André Glucksmann, *The Master Thinkers*, transl. Brian Pearce, Brighton:
The Harvester Press, 1980, and in particular the long note on p. 307 which takes
up a text by Michel Foucault: 'There is doubtless no sociological reality corresponding to "the *plebs*". But there certainly always *is* something in the body of

society, in classes, groups, and individuals, which in a certain way eludes relations of power'; '"The *plebs*" is non-existent, no doubt: but there is "something plebeian"'. [Michel Foucault quoted by Glucksmann – translation slightly modified.]

50. Glucksmann, *La cuisinière et le mangeur d'hommes*, p. 17.
51. Ibid., p. 11.
52. J. A. Amato, *Victims and Values*, New York: Praeger, 1990, pp. 175–201.
53. An example of uncertainty about the ranking of victims can be found in a recent number of *Le débat stratégique*: 'The role of the United Nations in those affairs covered most extensively by the media hides what is happening in other regions where comparable carnage is being perpetuated. Human dignity in Somalia or in Bosnia seems a much more important cause than in Angola where civil war has resumed with unprecedented violence.'
54. Amato, *Victims and Values*, p. 200.
55. Many examples of this instability could be given and we limit ourselves to two extracts from newspaper articles concerning intervention in Somalia on humanitarian grounds.

> The pseudo-United Nations humanitarian epic which is currently unfolding in Somalia, just like the previous one in Bosnia, serves as an alibi and mask for ulterior motives and interests very far from the noble sentiments evoked by officials and the media to explain and proclaim these forceful interventions 'in the name of the right to intervene'. If one seeks to shed light on the other side of this Technicolour show one appears as a killjoy, an awkward customer or, worse, a child starver.
>
> (L. Wiznitzer, *La Croix*, 15 December 1992)

The second example concerns the transformation of unfortunates into persecutors:

> After pity, disgust? After the terrible but moving images of the starving in Somalia come those of the 'gangsters', the 'ungrateful' and the 'heartless': through their spectacular violence the rioters of Mogadiscu have cast doubt on the justification of the humanitarian operation and the need for a foreign presence. How can one save people who do not want you to save them? And who 'thank' you with rock throwing and rifle shots?   (*Le Monde*, 27 February 1993.)

The second part of this editorial, however, emphasises the limited and 'not very spontaneous' character of this violence.

10 How realistic is action?

1. This theme turns up almost every week in the television sections of the major daily and weekly papers and particularly in *Le Monde*, *Libération* and *Télérama*, which want to promote reflection on the professional ethics of the media. It also

appears in Anglo-Saxon texts on the ethics of journalism, often in connection with the question of the defence of privacy (cf., for example, C. Fink, *Media Ethics*, New York: McGraw Hill, 1988, pp. 31–7 and C. Christians, K. Rotzoll and M. Fackler, *Media Ethics. Cases and Moral Reasoning*, New York: Longman, 1987, pp. 110–30; both of these text-books give a series of interesting case-studies concerning, for example, how a press photographer should behave when faced with the corpses of children etc.). Finally, for an analysis more specifically devoted to the representation of suffering on television and the accusation of 'voyeurism', see M. Ignatieff, 'Is Nothing sacred? The Ethics of Television', *Daedalus*, vol. 114, no. 4 (Autumn 1985), pp. 57–78.

2. A. Fouillé quoted by T. Ferenczi, *L'invention du journalisme en France. Naissance de la presse moderne à la fin du XIXe siècle*, Paris: Plon, 1993, p. 215. An interesting feature of this work is that it brings together criticism which accompanied the formation of professional journalism at the end of the nineteenth century and contemporary criticism of the media.

3. In the vast literature on philanthropy as a soft form of domination which is often inspired by Foucault or Deleuze we restrict ourselves to the studies of the CERFI published in the review *Recherches* and, especially, L. Murard and P. Zylberman, 'Le petit travailleur infatigable', *Recherches*, no. 25 (November 1976); I. Joseph and P. Fritsch, 'Disciplines à domicile', *Recherches*, no. 28 (November 1977); and L. Murard and P. Zylberman, 'L'haleine des faubourgs', *Recherches*, no. 29 (December 1977).

4. A late but typical example of this theme can be found in J. Verdès-Leroux, *Le travail social*, Paris: Minuit, 1978. We read there, for example, in a chapter entitled 'Power and Assistance': 'Repressed, supervised, corrected and raised with the fear of sin, the exaltation of suffering and sacrifice, and the condemnation of pleasure, the young bourgeois cannot and do not have any idea of how to do anything other than repress, supervise, etc. They speak of the workers' "childishness" and characterise their tiredness as "childish irritation"' (p. 31).

5. *Champ social*, selected texts, Paris: Maspero, 1976, p. 126.

6. Ibid., pp. 179–84. Innumerable examples could be given of these commonplaces. Cf., for example:

> All those of the social profession who work to 'help humanity' are, beneath the surface of their activity, very ambivalent. Before those who are close to him and before his own conscience, the social worker feels obliged to consider the main motive of his activity as being the desire to help. But then in the darkness of the soul there figures at the same time not just the desire to help but the opposite, pleasure and the drive to dominate and reduce the client to impotence.
>
> (A. Guggenbühl-Craig, *Pouvoir et relation d'aide*, Brussels: Mardaga, 1977, p. 29)

7. *Le militantisme, stade suprême de l'aliénation*, supplement to issue no. 4 of the review *Quatre millions de jeunes travailleurs*, Paris, 1972.

8. This theme is developed in psychoanalytic terms in B. Chouvier, *Militance et inconscient*, Lyons: Presses universitaires de Lyon, 1982.

9. F. Fourquet, 'L'idéal historique', *Recherches*, no. 14 (January 1974) (second volume of 'Genealogy of Capital').

10. The venom of resentment has seized hold of the workers' movement; a new race of priests, the militants, has been formed; the communists are its most perfected species. To justify their existence and establish their power these new priests have provided the proletariat with capitalism as the universal culprit, responsible for all its unhappiness. The bourgeoisie is no longer simply a dominant force; it is responsible for the bitter suffering which eats away at the proletariat from inside.

11. One symptom never deceives: denunciation. To denounce is always to adopt the point of view of a betrayed truth, a violated justice: the point of view of the will to truth and resentment itself . . . There is also critique – that polite and well brought up, sometimes scientific denunciation which always wants to be radical. There are also those shrill protests which scorch our ears: 'This is rubbish! This is disgusting! This is not correct!' What is this about then? This virtue so quick to become indignant, to what does it succomb? To forces, always forces and relations of forces, those great enemies of truth, desire and revolution.

12. It is no longer a case of 'consciousness raising' etc., but of *releasing* a different libidinal regime, the active regime of desire, but then to speak of the avant-garde no longer has any meaning, nor of the militant, nor of the 'working class', because to be militant then becomes itself to desire, to 'act' in the sense of active force, for itself and not for 'the' proletariat which doesn't give a damn, unless this touches it somewhere from an angle about which no-one can have the least idea.

13. For a synthetic presentation see, for example, J.-M. Cotteret and C. Emeri, 'De la communication élective à la communication cathodique', in L. Sfez, ed., *Dictionnaire de la communication*, Paris: PUF, 1993. vol. 2, pp. 1335–48.

14. P. Champagne, *Faire l'opinion. Le nouveau jeu politique*, Paris: Minuit, 1990.

15. We will try to show that what exists in reality is not 'public opinion', nor yet 'opinion as measured by opinion polls', but actually a new social space dominated by a set of agents – pollsters, political pundits, communication and political marketing advisers, journalists and so on – who use modern technologies like poll investigations, minitel, computers, radio and television, etc., and thereby give an autonomous political existence to a 'public opinion' that they themselves have fabricated simply by pursuing their profession of analysing and manipulating it, in the process profoundly transforming political activity as it is presented on television and as it may be seen by political men themselves.

(Champagne, *Faire L'opinion*, p. 30)

16. 'The "public opinion" of opinion poll institutes exists because the latter have succeeded . . . in creating belief in the "scientific" value of their investigations and in thus transforming into social reality what to a large extent was originally a simple technical artefact' (ibid., p. 121).
17. 'What to us seems "natural" today in the way in which politicians intervene on television for example, is actually a "naturalness" manufactured by and for the political game as it is expressed in modern means of communication.'(ibid., p. 31).
18. P. Yonnet gives an extreme form of this argument when he seeks to show that the desecration of the Jewish cemetry at Carpentras in the Spring of 1990 was an event constructed by 'politico-media personnel and structures'. P. Yonnet, 'La machine Carpentras. Histoire et sociologie d'un syndrome d'épuration', *Le Débat*, no. 61 (September–October 1990), pp. 18–34.
19. 'It would be interesting to analyse in this perspective a movement like "SOS Racisme" which is unarguably based upon a reality (racist attacks) but the size of which has been, in part, encouraged by a set of agents who have a common interest in making the movement exist.' (Champagne, *Faire L'opinion*, p. 262).
20. Jean Baudrillard, *Simulacra and Simulation*, transl. Sheila Faria Glaser, Ann Arbor: University of Michigan Press, 1994.
21. Jean Baudrillard, *La guerre du Golfe n'a pas eu lieu*, Paris: Galilée, 1991.
22. Jean Baudrillard, *The Illusion of the End*, transl. Chris Turner, Cambridge: Polity Press, 1994.
23. 'Of the same order as the impossibility of rediscovering an absolute level of the real is the impossibility of staging illusion. Illusion is no longer possible because the real is no longer possible' (Baudrillard, *Simulacra and Simulation*, p. 36).
24. Even if we strive to stay within the author's terms, the question still arises of how this circularity can be grasped and described if it is absolute.
25. J. Baudillard, *The Illusion of the End.*
26. To the question asked by SOFRES: 'Do you think that things did *not* take place in the way television showed them?', 24% of the people questioned answered in the affirmative in 1975, 32% in 1989, and 48% in 1991. This skepticism, more widespread among executives and intellectual professions (57%) than workers (42%), among those with higher educational qualifications (58%) than those without (43%), and most of all among the young, is none the less increasing considerably in all the categories analysed. J.-L. Missika, 'Les médias contestés' in SOFRES, *L'état de l'opinion*, Paris: Seuil, 1992. The immunity from which radio benefited during the same period, its high credibility being only very slightly reduced, suggests we could link these results to upset caused by the meaningful character of visual representations of suffering.
27. Many studies in social psychology show that , on the one hand, the sight of a spectacle of suffering (like an execution, for example) can affect self-esteem when it takes place in passivity and, on the other hand, that the maintenance of self-esteem plays a very important role in the mastery of anxiety. Cf., in particular, J. Greenberg *et al.*, 'Why do people need self-esteem? Converging

evidence that self-esteem serves anxiety-buffering function', *Journal of Personality and Social Psychology*, vol. 63, no. 6 (1992), pp. 913–22.

28. As T. Liebes and E. Katz note with regard to critical abilities developed by television viewers, 'each of these forms of opposition is therefore a different form of "defence" against the message of the programme, but also involves a different form of vulnerability'. Thus, the opposition that they call 'ludic' and which consists in transferring all attention to the medium by suspending judgement on what they transmit 'may end up breaking all links with reality' (pp. 140–1).

29. A. and M. Mattelard, 'Crises et communication', in L. Sfez, ed., *Dictionnaire de la communication*, vol. 2, pp. 1011–5.

30. On this point, J. C. Rufin, *Le piège humanitaire*, Paris: Hachette-Pluriel, 1993, is useful and contains in particular elements of the history of Anglo-Saxon and French humanitarian organisations since the Second World War.

31. Cf. ibid., pp. 42–65.

32. Cf. M. Bettati and B. Kouchner, *Le devoir d'ingérence. Peut-on les laisser mourir?* Paris: Denoël, 1987.

33. 'Le mouvement humanitaire. Questions à Bernard Kouchner', *Le Débat*, no. 67 (November–December 1991), pp. 30–40.

34. 'In the Kurdish affair, which in certain respects was a model of disinformation, how aid to populations could also be aid to very dubious "national liberation movements" who were in fact holding these populations hostage was carefully hidden from us.'

35. Let us note straightaway that the second and third objections are hard to reconcile with each other: either images which provoke emotion are effective and succeed in mobilising public opinion, or they are turned around in the direction of egoist desires and arouse apathy.

36. 'It doesn't keep me awake. It is perhaps a homeopathy of brute horror. The shock image is immediately annulled by another . . . And then, this little visual traumatism is immediately compensated for by the noble gesture. The *french doctor* [English in the original] and the American GI are me . . . we have made up at the end, the little disagreement we had at the beginning' ('Un entretien avec Régis Debray', *Le Monde*, 19 January 1993). Debray develops criticism of 'the humanitarian State' in a long interview with Marc Fumaroli published in *Le Débat*, no. 74 (March–April 1993), pp. 3–21, in which he expresses the idea that media publicity given to humanitarian action will be 'an elegant way for us to recolonise', of allowing a 'moral rearmament of the West which once again considers itself as the field of the good' by joining together 'Rambo in his F 16 and charity workers on the ground'.

37. G. Lipovetsky, *Le crépuscule du devoir. L'éthique indolore des nouveaux temps démocratiques*, Paris: Gallimard, 1992, pp. 138–45.

38. A.-G. Slama, *L'angélisme exterminateur. Essai sur l'ordre moral contemporain*, Paris: Grasset, 1993, p. 15.

39. G. Sebbag, 'De la purification éthique', *Le Débat*, no. 75 (May–August 1993), pp. 24–35.

40. In terms which recall the work in which Paul Yonnet sets about 'the immigration-
    ist utopia', the 'culture of human rights', the neo-racialism of SOS Racisme, the
    'destruction of the national romance' by the clear demonstration of Vichy anti-
    semitism, and also the "moral generation" of SOS Racisme, the student-high
    school movement of November–December 1986 and the charity food distribu-
    tion centres' (P. Yonnet, *Voyage au centre du malaise française*, Paris, 1992, p. 169).
41. M. Gauchet, 'Les droits de l'homme ne sont pas une politique', *Le Débat*
    (July–August 1980), pp. 3–21.
42.   It is then that in order to appreciate the whirlwinds of the present in a
       hypermoral and media explosion we raised on high the bloody flag of the
       crime against humanity . . . genocide – the flight of the boat people, abor-
       tion, mixed marriages; genocide – the Timisoara massacre, the crushing
       of Saddam Hussein's army, the disappearance of the peasant; genocide
       – the bombed towns and hamlets, the skeletal Somalian or Ethiopian
       children, sometimes abandoned by healthy parents.

    Humour about genocide is also one of the main themes of a little pamphlet
    against humanitarian action recently published by two journalists: M. Floquet
    and B. Coq, *Les tribulations de Bernard K. en Yougoslavie*, Paris: Albin Michel,
    1993, particularly pp. 34–48.
43. Consider, for example, this extract:
       . . . man has every human right. But behind this tautology, humanitarian
       modernity hides a poor wretch, a perpetual victim, a suffering body,
       someone lacking responsibility from birth . . . Every right rains on this
       big or small fine fellow, if he is sickly the right to health, to transplants,
       to artificial and belated procreation, if he is motor handicapped the right
       to ski down Olympic pistes, if he fails at school the right to pursue
       lengthy studies, if he comes from a so-called disadvantaged environment
       the right to museums, philosophy and poetry, if he is ugly the right to
       beauty, if he is seropositive the right not to know it, if he is fat the right
       to be obese, if he is frustrated the right to sexual favours, if he gets the
       urge to write the right to graffiti, if he is of no fixed abode the right to be
       accomodated at the Sorbonne when the temperature falls below zero, if
       he is a foreigner the right to a white wedding in order to become French,
       if he has a child the right to give him an original first name, if he is polyg-
       amous and camps out with his large family the right to be housed in
       Paris, if he is tough the right to win a prize on the radio and spend a day
       at the telly, if he is a crook the right to be praised on his death, if he has
       struggled for the independence of his country the right to find refuge in
       France, if he sports the most incredible outfits the right to move around
       without being commented upon, if he does nothing or has nothing to say
       the right to communicate, if he is a politician or journalist the right to be
       unaware of the name of André Breton and to use the word 'surrealist'.'
                                          (Sebbag, 'De la purification éthique')

44. While the media periodically kindle hearts, they exonerate consciences and work possibly subterraneously to turn individuals away from obligations of mutual aid and charity. The altruism of post-duty delights in distance: we have become more sensitive to misery shown on the little screen than to immediately tangible misery, there is more commiseration with the distant other than for our everyday neighbour.

(Lipovetsky, *le crépuscule*, p. 143)

45. Who are we? Communitarian societies answer this metaphysical question ostensibly by appealing to their status, their identity. How many individuals are we? Even when it cultivates an historical memory, modern democracy is defined instead by its relative number. It counts on the citizens it counts. But unlike in the heroic epoch, it is not a self-enclosed isolated entity – city, principality, island, canton. Nevertheless, it is not open to the four winds. On one side it gives up the spirit of parochialism, on the other it does not surrender to the cosmopolitan temptation. If it brings dozens of millions of inhabitants together on its territory, it is obliged to intensify local, regional and national democratic procedures. The political authorities and media have, without too much success, administered two moral medications, ethical cleansing within democracies in turmoil and humanitarian health on the ground for States in distress.

(Sebbag, 'De la purification éthique')

46. 'The worst is found in those who sell the misfortunes of others, the intellectuals of difference, the folklore guides to guaranteed dyed in the wool human perversions. Like poverty, more beautiful in the sun.' (B. Kouchner, 'Le mouvement humanitaire', *Le Débat*, no. 67 (1991), pp. 30–40.

47. Particularly in, *L'île de lumière*, Paris: Ramsay, 1980, the story of the operation 'Un bateau pour le Vietnam', at the end of the 1970s which led to the break with Médecins sans frontières which Kouchner left to then create Médecins du monde. The existence of these two competing organisations has since fed the debate within the French humanitarian movement.

48. B. Kouchner, *Charité Business*, Paris: Le Pré aux Clercs, 1986, pp. 21–3.

49. Abbé Pierre and B. Kouchner, *Dieu et les hommes*, Paris: Robert Laffont, 1993, p. 112.

50. Cf., in particular, B. Kouchner, *Le malheur des autres*, Paris: Odile Jacob, 1991, in which there are many autobiographical elements.

51. 'Criteria of intervention are not a problem for those who, whether doctor, first-aid worker or rescuer, go to the bedside of someone in distress. It is the protection of life . . . For everything resides in the imminence of danger' (Kouchner, 'Le mouvement humanitaire').

52. 'The humanitarian spirit', J.-C. Rufin says, 'is born of a turning back on to the present'(*Le piège humanitaire*, p. 334).

53. F. Tricaud, *L'accusation. Recherche sur les figures de l'aggression éthique*, Paris: Dalloz, 1997, p. 24.

54. Rufin, *Le piège humanitaire*, p. 334.
55. Kouchner, *Charité Business*, p. 13. This is what Kouchner sometimes calls 'the law of minimal oppression': 'What does this law prescribe? To prefer to find oneself alongside those being bombed and not those sending the bombs. A single rule therefore, but ferocious: to stay at the bedside of the minorities and the oppressed. Without illusions however, since these minorities may themselves become oppressive. It is truly a very sad rule' (Kouchner, 'La loi d'oppression minimale', in Bettati and B. Kouchner, *Le devoir d'ingérence*, p. 21).
56. Kouchner, 'Le mouvement humanitaire'.
57. Cf. Pierre and B. Kouchner, *Dieu et les hommes*, pp. 31 and 51.
58. Kouchner, *Le malheur des autres*, p. 303.
59. Ibid., p. 78.
60. Ibid.
61. Take, for example, the account of the first meeting which followed the appeal on the boat people in November 1978. 'Bernard-Henri Levy continued by proposing to attack the Vietnamese embassy in Paris. One more demonstration, some clashes with French policemen, this did not seem very convincing to us. I have tried to assail many embassies, with or without success. I recalled the first attack on the American embassy at la place de La Concorde in 1965. Despite the comic side of the situation, I hardly saw myself playing the clown again in front of a closed door. We have had too many marches, petitions, meetings and historical analyses' (Kouchner, *L'île de lumière*, pp. 28–9).
62. To the question asked by the review *Le Débat* on the Kurdish problem, Bernard Kouchner answers: 'Are you a specialist in the Kurdish problem? Are you on the spot? To speak from Paris one says no matter what, the humanitarian also learns this' ('Le mouvement humanitaire').
63. Cf., in particular, X. Emmanueli, *Les prédateurs de l'action humanitaire*, Paris: Albin Michel, 1991, who explains the break away of Médecins du monde on the occasion of the 'Ile de lumière' operation by the refusal of mediatisation; J.-C. Guillebaud, president of Reporters sans frontières who denounces 'the outburst' and 'false participation' of 'live TV coverage' in 'Les médias contre le démocratie?', *Esprit*, March–April 1993, pp. 86–101; and above all, R. Brauman, president of Médecins sans frontières, who, in an article entitled 'Contre l'humanitarisme', *Esprit*, December 1991, pp. 77–85, energetically lays the blame on the 'spectacle of the humanitarian', the 'staging' 'of edifying representations on false live TV'.
64. Kouchner, 'Le mouvement humanitaire'.
65. Kouchner, *Le malheur des autres*, p. 194: 'Without image, no indignation: misfortune strikes only at the unfortunate. The hand of aid and fraternity cannot then be held out to them. The essential enemy of dictators and under-development remains the photograph and the bursts of activity it releases. We accept it without resigning ourselves to it: it is the law of the uproar. We make use of it.'
66. Pierre and Kouchner, *Dieu et les hommes*, p. 85. In this work, which is in the

form of a dialogue, Bernard Kouchner credits the abbé Pierre with being the inventor of humanitarian mediatisation with his appeal on behalf of the homeless on Radiodiffusion française during the winter of 1954.

67. Thus, for example, Rony Brauman, while highly critical of what he calls the 'dictatorship of mediatisation' does not question the importance of mediatisation for the success of humanitarian action. 'Un entretien avec Rony Brauman', *Le Monde*, 24 November 1992.

68. Maurice Merleau-Ponty, *Phenomenology of Perception*, transl. Colin Smith, London: Routledge & Kegan Paul, 1962, p. 178.

69. Ibid., p. 216.

70. Here we follow J.-L. Petit, 'L'action intentionnelle', *Raisons pratiques*, no. 1 (1990), *Les formes de l'action*, published under the direction of P. Pharo and L. Quéré, pp. 71–84.

71. Cf. Charles Taylor, 'Explaining Action', *Inquiry*, no. 13 (1970), pp. 54–89.

72. Charles Taylor, 'Action as Expression', in C. Diamond and J. Teichman, eds., *Intention and Intentionality*, Brighton: The Harvester Press, 1979, pp. 73–90.

73. L. Quéré, 'Agir dans l'espace public. L'intentionalité des actions comme phénomène social', *Raisons pratiques*, pp. 85–112.

74. Ibid., p. 101.

75. C. Tilly, *From Mobilization to Revolution*, Reading, MA: Addison-Wesley, 1978, especially chapter 5.

76. P. Favre, ed., *La manifestation*, Paris: Presses de la Fondation nationale des sciences politiques, 1990.

77. On forms of demonstration arising from rumour and staying close to the spontaneous crowd, see Farge and Revel, *Logiques de la foule*.

78. M. Offerlé, 'Descendere dans la rue: de la "journé" à la "manif"', pp. 90–122.

79. Cardon and Heurtin, '"Tenir les rang". Les services d'encadrement des manifestations ouvrières (1909–1936)', pp. 122–155.

80. Favre, 'Manifester en France aujourd'hui', pp. 11–68.

81. With regard to demonstrations during the Algerian war, for example, Mann, 'Les manifestations', pp. 271–303.

82. Offerlé, 'Descendere dans la rue', p. 109.

83. Dobry, 'Calcul, concurrence et gestion du sens. Quelques réflexions à propos des manifestations de novembre-décembre 1986', pp. 357–86.

84. Ibid., pp. 366–9.

85. Ibid., p. 100.

86. Mann, 'Les manifestations', p. 278.

87. Amnesty International 1992 report. See also, particularly on the action of Amnesty International toward the United Nations, N. Rodley, 'Le rôle d'une ONG comme Amnesty International au sein des organisations intergouvernementales', in M. Bettati and P.-M. Dupuy, *Les ONG et le droit international*, Paris: Economica, 1986, pp. 127–52.

88. The number of non-governmental organisations multiplied by 100 between 1970 and 1986 while intergovernmental organisations increased only ten-fold

over the whole world. M. Bettati, 'Un droit d'ingérence humanitaire', in Bettati and Kouchner, *Le devoir d'ingérence,* p. 23.

89. Such at least is how televisual criticism has frequently given a voice to its public either by publishing readers' letters expressing this sentiment (one from many examples: 'This evening I felt shame, shame for having shed tears on seeing those Somalian children starve' *Télérama,* 30 September 1992), or by expressing it in its name, or even by denouncing the media and particularly television, since, the media, like humanitarianism, is often subject to internal arguments. Thus the critic for *Le Monde,* starting from the observation that 'to speak about television is in the first place to evoke a pile of corpses' (15 October 1992), can describe the 'heartfelt shame' of the spectator who can only 'fall silent, fall silent and weep' (12 September 1992), denounce the 'usual harvest of tattered emotions' (24 November 1992) or deplore the fact that 'the spectacle of horror' is now 'defused and ineffective' (31 October 1992).

90. The connection between the formation of the humanitarian movement today and the building of the workers' movement in the second half of the nineteenth century is suggested in François Ewald's contribution to the volume published by M. Bettati and B. Kouchner on the duty to intervene. In order to show how the Declaration of the Rights of Man, necessarily anterior to any legislation, must take account of the historical circumstances in which this declaration was realised, Ewald compares it with the proclamation of 1789 which emphasised the principle of *freedom of conscience,* the so-called universal Declaration of 1848 which, faced with the exploitation of workers, proclaimed the existence of *social rights,* and finally the duty to assist which affirms an even more primitive principle, that of the *right not to die.* Cf. F. Ewald, 'Droit naturel des victimes', in Bettati and Kouchner, *Le devoir dingérence.,* pp. 209–12.

91. This is the position taken by Gertrude Himmelfarb, for example, in her *Poverty and Compassion. The Moral Indignation of the Late Victorians,* New York: Alfred Knopf, 1991, (particularly the introduction, pp. 3–18). Against the theory of social control and domination she undertakes to show, that: (1) the moral imagination of the philanthropists of the Victorian period was neither sentimental nor utopian but on the contrary characterised by a cold rationalism. 'The titles of some of [the books on the poor and poverty] sound like sentimental novels'. What is remarkable is how few of them . . . were in fact sentimental' (p. 5). They sought to establish a 'science of charity'; (2) that far from moralisation being imposed from on high by the bourgeoisie, it was a demand of the workers' movement itself, and finally; (3) that we pass smoothly and uninterruptedly from charitable action to the Welfare State. The position of François Ewald, in, *L'Etat providence,* Paris: Grasset, 1986, is half-way between the radical theories of domination and social control and the rehabilitation of philanthropy undertaken by Himmelfarb. In his analysis of charity (pp. 122–36), Ewald is actually concerned to bring out the logic of what he calls the personalised and domestic 'regime of patronage ' by contrast with the contractualist logic of 'juridical seizure'.

92. In France the constitution of institutionalised and represented socio-professional groups marked an important moment in this process. Cf. L. Boltanski, *Les Cadres. The Making of a Class, Cadres in French Society*, transl. A. Goldhammer, Cambridge: Cambridge University Press, 1987.
93. M. Dobry, 'Calcul', p. 384: 'Despite the claims (and illusions) of media people, they have in no way broken the autonomy from which both governmental and administrative sectors in the political field benefit in French society and which normally tend to 'deal with' demonstrations and news about demonstrations through the filters, stakes, relations of force, local cultures, institutional routines and so forth peculiar to their specific social logics.' On this point, see also M. Dobry, *Sociologie des crises politiques*, Paris: Presses de la Fondation nationale des sciences politiques, 1986.
94. Favre, 'Manifester en France aujourd'hui', p. 61.
95. Dobry, 'Calcul', pp. 381–2.
96. Mann, 'Les manifestations', p. 275.
97. Favre, 'Manifester en France aujourd'hui', pp. 34–5.
98. Expressing his views on the war in Bosnia, J.-M. Le Pen recently declared that he would consider it right to concern himself with the rapes in Sarajevo only when there were no longer any rapes in the Paris region. Raymond Aron dealt justly with this attitude in *L'opium des intellectuels*:

> This is precisely the reasoning of reactionaries and pacifists in France between 1933 and 1939 when they reproached those on the Left with multiplying manifestoes and public meetings in favour of persecuted Jews. 'Mind your own business', they said, 'and set your own house in order. The best way to help the victims of the Third Reich is to reduce the suffering of victims of the crisis, of colonialism or imperialism'. In fact this is false reasoning. Neither the Third Reich nor the Soviet Union are radically indifferent to the opinion of the world outside. The protests of Jewish organisations in the world have probably contributed to the slowing down of the anti-Zionist and anti-cosmopolitan campaign under cover of which Jews on the other side of the Iron Curtain were being persecuted anew. The propaganda unleashed in Europe and Asia against segregation in the United States helps those who strive to improve the condition of the Blacks and accord them the equality of rights promised by the Constitution.
>
> (Raymond Aron, *L'opium des intellectuels*, Paris: Calman-Lévy, 1955, pp. 64–5)

99. Ewald, 'Droit naturel des victimes', pp. 211–12.
100. Humanitarianism does not replace politics. The political blindness of the humanitarian movement or its call for a global politics *in fact* disguises governmental positions and national political interests. This, very briefly summarised, in the argument of R. Brauman: 'More than ever good sentiments, and most of all their staging, replaces political discourse in a game in which

each of the actors, organisations, humanitarians, media, governments, takes a role which is not really its own, and cashes some profits.' Cf. R. Brauman, 'Contre l'humanitarisme', *Esprit*, no. 172 (December 1991), pp. 77–85.

101. Cf., for example, R. Braumann, 'Morale et politique: le baiser du vampire', *Politique internationale*, no. 50 (1990) pp. 329–37. Why come to the assistance of 'the victims of bloody clashes in Rumania' but not, for example, to the 'Touaregs' massacred by 'the Malian army' etc.

102. 'To be sure, there is an *a priori* form of the perception of moral evil; but this form, which is that of accusation, is not a principle of intelligibility: on the contrary, it is the *a priori* form of human incomprehension. For evil is unintelligible, and any project of *comprehension* is ruled out in principle, whether or not it is aware of the fact, from encountering it if it exists' (p. 194).

Index